Effective
Web
Animation

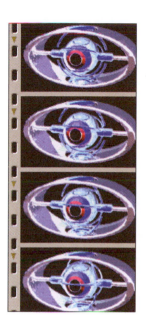

Effective
Web
Animation

Advanced Techniques for the Web

J. Scott Hamlin

ADDISON–WESLEY

An imprint of Addison Wesley Longman, Inc.

Reading, Massachusetts • Harlow, England • Menlo Park, California
Berkeley, California • Don Mills, Ontario • Sydney
Bonn • Amsterdam • Tokyo • Mexico City

The publisher offers discounts on this book when ordered in quantity for special sales.
For more information, please contact:

Corporate, Government, and Special Sales
Addison Wesley Longman, Inc.
One Jacob Way
Reading, Massachusetts 01867
(781) 944-3700

Library of Congress Cataloging-in-Publication Data

Hamlin, J. Scott.
    Effective Web animation: advanced animation techniques for the
  Web / J. Scott Hamlin.
       p.   cm.
   ISBN 0-201-60600-3
   1. Computer animation.   2. Web sites—Design.   I. Title.
  TR897.7.H36 1999
  006.6'96—dc21   99–20537
                                        CIP

Copyright © 1999 by Addison Wesley Longman, Inc.

Web graphics from the WebSpice Collection courtesy DeMorgan Industries.
http://www.webspice.com.

The Animation Stand and *How to Convert Your Studio to an Automated Powerhouse* guides ©Linker Systems Inc.

Extensis PhotoAnimator Demo © Extensis Corp. Extensis PhotoAnimator is one of nine components found in Extensis PhotoTools 3.0. A fully functional thirty-day demo version can be found on the CD-ROM with this book. For more information, visit *http://www.extensis.com.*

Demo animations from Animation Factory courtesy of Eclipse Digital Animation Factory.
http://www.animfactory.com.

Universal Animator and Webvise Totality Demos © Auto F/X Corporation. *http://www.autofx.com.*

HVS Animator Demo courtesy of Digital Frontiers.

GIF Movie Gear trial version courtesy of Gamani Productions.

SWT Pro and SWT Essentials Demos courtesy of SPG, Inc.

ISBN 0-201-60600-3
Text printed on recycled, acid-free paper
1 2 3 4 5 6 7 8 9 10—VH—0302010099
First printing, April 1999

This book is dedicated to the spirit of imagination in all of us.

Contents

Preface

In many ways, animation's importance to Web design could be seen from the moment the `<blink>` tag was introduced on the Web. Early netizens will recall the swift adoption, and abuse, of the `<blink>` tag throughout the Web. Although it was a visual annoyance, its misuse was due to a vast void: The Web lacked movement. To millions of viewers used to seeing motion on a television screen, its absence on the Web has always begged relief. The `<blink>` tag offered some slight relief to the static world on the Web. Even though its use quickly became tantamount to high treason, it was merely symptomatic of a virtual playground dying for a little action.

Fortunately, a then little-known aspect of the GIF format (Graphic Interchange Format)—the ability to contain multiple frames and display them in a user-defined, timed sequential manner—offered a more robust animation solution for the Web. GIF animation subsequently launched an explosion of motion, bringing accessible motion to the Web page. You didn't need special tools, skills, or even very much imagination. If you had some sort of graphic program and a shareware GIF animation utility you were in business. Furthermore, the animation didn't have to generate anything close to the quality of the work of animation legends such as Walt Disney: in the early days of the Web, if it moved, it was very cool.

Over the years, however, Web design has become an increasingly sophisticated profession, and its standards and requirements have become more stringent. During the dawn of Web animation, it was a matter of little consequence if your GIF animation had a large file size or if the colors were distorted, but today, professional Web design requires svelte animation file sizes with a high degree of color integrity. In fact, the animation requirements of many Web designers go beyond what GIF animation, by itself, can provide. Web designers must now support such things as interactivity, audio, and faster delivery over the Internet. These requirements have led to the development of new Web animation technologies.

Web animation has progressed to the point that it would not be feasible for this book to cover each technology to a depth that would make it worthwhile. Instead, this book focuses on the Web animation technologies that are among the more versatile, accessible, and widely used. Specifically, this book deals with professional techniques using GIF, JavaScript, and Macromedia Flash animation. Many of the concepts and techniques covered here apply to a wide range of animation technologies, but in the interest of covering substantial material, this book focuses largely on GIF, JavaScript, and Flash animation.

The main purpose of this book is to provide in-depth Web animation techniques with professional Web design requirements in mind. For example, this book goes to great lengths to detail techniques for minimizing the file sizes of animations to reduce the bandwidth load that your animations add to your Web pages. Also, we look at time-saving techniques to streamline the tedious process of creating individual animation frames, giving you more time to make your animations more ambitious and imaginative.

I wrote this book because I felt that many valuable bread-and-butter Web animation techniques did not seem to be common knowledge. Many Web designers appear to be using very old techniques and utilities for creating Web animations, particularly GIF animations. I hope that techniques such as those featured in this book will lead to more-sophisticated techniques, perpetuating the growth and viability of high-quality animation on the Web.

More than anything, this book attempts to demonstrate that Web animation is no longer the exclusive realm of the Web page hobbyist. There are plenty of techniques that help make even the limited GIF animation a valuable tool on the Web designer's palette, and, with the likes of JavaScript and Flash animation, we are freed from the limitations imposed by the animated GIF. This book covers techniques that you can use to add high-quality motion to the Web without reducing Web access to a crawl.

Acknowledgments

I can't thank anyone before thanking the source. It is only by the grace of God that I came to be capable of writing and illustrating this book. If you find any portion of it worthwhile or inspirational, He should be given the credit and not I.

You also wouldn't be reading a word of this book if it weren't for Mike Hendrickson and Mary O'Brien at Addison Wesley Longman. I thank them both for giving this book a shot and for providing me with the flexibility to give the whole manuscript another solid workover.

I'm also greatly obliged to Scott Balay, Ron Gery, Chris Dickman, Richard Koman, Joel Comm, Genevieve Rajewski, and Elizabeth Spainhour for their help, support, guidance, and motivation. I would also like to thank all the excellent Web design studios, such as Organic Online, Blue Hypermedia, Speared Peanut, Precision Design, and Second Story, for allowing us to feature their excellent work in the book.

I would also like to recognize the amazing talents and dedication to excellence in animation embodied in the work of the great animators such as Walt Disney, Chuck Jones, and Tex Avery. If it weren't for the likes of these animators, animation might still be the stuff of lame carnival sideshows and children's novelties.

Last but by no means least, I need to express my deepest appreciation for Staci, Aidan, and Audrey—my family. I continually receive tremendous stimulus from my children, Aidan and Audrey—from their enchanting play, their delightful moments of discovery, and the telling observations that spring from their fresh perspectives. They are a powerful source of raw inspiration, and I am among the richest of men from having had the opportunity to watch them grow up. Of my wife, Staci, I can only say this: without her, I am not half a man—I am no man. Staci holds me in a debt that leaves me hoping for a long lifetime to repay.

J. Scott Hamlin
January 1999

CHAPTER 1

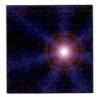

Animation and the Web

Motion has always been innately intriguing to the human eye. If something moves, we are often compelled to notice it. Animation not only grabs our attention but also is an effective way to communicate information. Most people subscribe to a "Don't tell me—show me" attitude. A sophisticated flashing animation can communicate an idea such as "This is important" or "This is neat" faster than words can. Unfortunately, that same flashing animation can also annoy viewers, and if the animation takes too long to download over the Internet, it can also subtract from the overall Web experience. There is a fine line between compelling animation and animation that detracts from the purpose of a Web page. This book helps you put your animations on the compelling side of that line. ❯

How to Use This Book

The Illusion of Motion

Animation Delivery Mechanisms

New Web Animation Technologies

Animation Technologies Compared

With the emergence of Web-friendly animation technologies in the past couple of years, the Web has greatly benefited from the fundamental appeal of animation. Accessible animation has propelled the Web from "print with hyperlinks" to a true multimedia communication medium. Although the art of animation is not new, the unique characteristics of the Web as a delivery mechanism impose a new spin on the various techniques for creating and delivering animation.

Animation itself is a familiar technique to most of us. Simply put, it's the simulation of motion through the sequential display of still images. The key to animation is to present the images at a speed fast enough to trick the brain into believing that it's seeing motion.

On film or paper, as we shall see, that's not terribly hard to do. Displaying 24–30 frames per second (fps) through a projector does the job. Unfortunately, the Internet, where servers must move frames to clients across limited bandwidth, cannot deliver that kind of speed. Multiple images compound file sizes, and the Internet's throughput is limited by high traffic, slow modems, overrun servers, and a host of other problems. Consequently, Web animations operate under a unique set of limitations that makes designing Web animation completely different from creating animation for any other medium. These limitations define the hows and why of Web animation.

Because file size—and thus time—is of the essence, the primary objective for Web animators is to deliver the animation using no more information than is absolutely necessary. Before you jump into the techniques outlined in this book, it is helpful to understand the key concepts of animation, the main methods and tools used to create animations, and the main mechanisms used to deliver Web animations.

This chapter provides some perspective on Web animation as a means to show why the techniques in later chapters go to great lengths to deliver a little motion. If there is one key factor that guides Web animation, it is the need for efficiency and economy. It is easier to arrive at a balance between economy and visually compelling animation when you understand the problems and the benefits and drawbacks of the various solutions.

How to Use This Book

The conventions of this book should be familiar and self-explanatory, but there are a few elements that you should note. First, this is a book on animation and numerous examples show dozens of frames. To fit all these frames on the pages of this book, sometimes we have rearranged the order of the frames.

This introduces a bit of a problem: how do you know what order the frames play in? For example, Figure 1-1 shows a series of animation frames of a little creature called a "Jitter,"

Figure 1-1   Can you determine the frame order of this animation?

from Zania (zania.com). The little fella makes such wild movements that it's impossible to determine the progression of the animation's frames. Does the animation start on the frame at the upper-left and then go down to the frame below and then up to the top frame in the middle and so on? Or does the animation start at the frame in the upper-left, go through to the last frame on the upper-right, move to the frame in the lower-left, and go through to the frame on the lower-right?

To remove confusion I took advantage of a feature inside GIF Movie Gear (gamani.com), my favorite GIF animation utility. Figure 1-2 shows the same animation. Each frame of the animation is framed using GIF Movie Gear's standard mode of displaying multiple frames of a GIF animation. The film reel border graphics along the top of each row help indicate that these are animation frames, and the small olive arrows help indicate the sequence of the animation's frames, which, in this case, is top to bottom, left to right. The animation starts with the frame in the upper-left and ends with the frame in the lower-right.

The red arrows in Figure 1-2 are another convention of this book. Many of the figures in this book have similar red arrows to point out important elements. These arrows should not be taken as part of the actual figure but rather serve as visual aids for pointing out key portions of the figure.

The CD-ROM that comes with the book contains most of the sample animations as well as several working demos of animation programs. I encourage you to open the animations and inspect them for yourself. Often, there is no better way to learn animation techniques

Figure 1-2   The film reel border and olive arrows (pointed out by the red arrows) indicate the sequence of the animation's frames.

than to look through the individual frames of animations, and it will also help substantially to see the animations play at full speed. Furthermore, the CD-ROM contains additional step-by-step tutorials for creating specific animation effects with Photoshop. All the tutorials come with fully customizable layered Photoshop files, so not only will you learn some great animated effects, but also you can quickly generate professional-looking animations that you can use on your Web site.

The Illusion of Motion

Film tricks the brain into seeing motion by displaying 24 slightly different images every second. Figure 1-3 shows some frames of an astronaut on the moon. The shot pans up from the lower left until the astronaut is in view. On the printed page, we see only the static images in sequence, but when these images are displayed quickly, one after another, the illusion of motion is created.

Many computers have a hard time processing just 24 frames of full-motion video at high resolution, so it is common to have much slower frame rates. Web animations typically have frame rates of 5–15 frames per second. Fortunately, this drop in frame rate does not necessarily destroy the illusion of motion. After several generations of television and movie watching, our eyes have been trained to interpret motion. For example, if we see a character holding a ball at

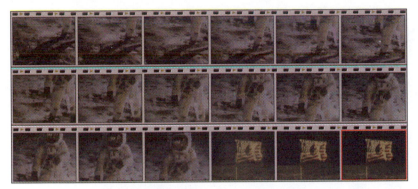

Figure 1-3   A movie's illusion of motion is achieved when slightly different still images are displayed at 24 frames per second (fps).

about eye level in one frame and then see the ball at about knee level in the next frame, our eye (and brain) sees the ball dropping. There may be only three or four frames that create the dropping motion, but that can be enough to create the illusion of downward motion.

In Figure 1-4 you can see that the imagery in individual frames jumps noticeably from frame to frame, but when the animation is played for the viewer at full speed, the images appear to move in fluid motion. How does this work? Basically, the human brain must make sense of the information it receives. When the brain receives partial information, it often fills in the blanks. Have you ever been stymied by a puzzle, only to have the answer suddenly pop into your head? Something like this happens with low-frame-rate animations. The eye does not actually see 24 frames per second. Instead, to interpret the motion the brain effectively adds extra frames to aid perception. Any scrutiny of an animation with a low frame rate reveals its lack of fluidity, but often a few frames is enough to communicate the motion.

In many ways, Web animation thrives on this principle. That is not to imply that reducing the number of frames is a Web designer's only asset for delivering Web animation or even the best technique for keeping the size of Web animations manageable. But the fact that animation can be interpreted even if its frame speed is less than the broadcast standard is in many ways the foundation of Web animation. The fewer frames that an animation uses to portray the motion effectively, the fewer frames that must be created by the animation designer and downloaded over the Internet.

Animation Delivery Mechanisms

The need for efficiency has long been a key factor that has shaped how animations are produced. However, the efficiency of an approach depends on how the animation will be

Figure 1-4   The human eye perceives fluid motion even when there are obvious gaps between individual frames of the animation.

delivered to viewers. Just as the Internet's bandwidth issues and the nature of digital images impose limitations on Web animation, other display mechanisms have certain characteristics that affect the art of animation. To understand the basic concepts of Web animation, it's helpful to look at early animation delivery mechanisms to see how their idiosyncrasies influence current terminology and approaches. For our purposes, the two most noteworthy animation-delivery mechanisms, before the advent of digital imagery, are paper and film.

Flip-Book Animations

One popular delivery mechanism for animation, even today, is flip books. A single cel, or frame, of animation is drawn or printed on each page of a small book. Viewers "play" the animation by flipping the pages very quickly. Many basic animation principles spring from this humble beginning. Professional animators often draw frames on sheets of paper and then quickly flip the pages to get a quick feel for how the animation is working.

The good thing about flip-book animations is that they are inexpensive to create and play back. All you need is a pencil, a stack of paper, and a thumb. However, this form of animation has a substantial drawback: it's highly inefficient. Each frame must be drawn from scratch on a separate piece of paper. For example, if you want to create an animation of a character running, you must draw the character over and over again for each frame. The face on the character may look exactly the same every time, but you must redraw it again and again.

As a result, the term *flip-book* has come to be associated with inefficient Web animation mechanisms such as GIF, JavaScript, and Java animations. To be clear, the term *flip-book* animation can be used to refer to an animation in which each new frame is a new image that replaces the preceding one. As you will see in this book, most Web animations are not necessarily limited to this approach. At this point it is important to understand that for the purposes of creating and displaying Web animations, you typically should make your animations as little like flip-book animations as possible. To begin to understand how to do this, let's look at another popular animation delivery mechanism: cel-based animations.

Cel Animations

Many of the early animation studios, particularly Walt Disney Studios, quickly realized that it was a waste of time to fully illustrate each frame of animation when only small portions of the frame had changed. They devised more-efficient techniques based on painting on sheets of layered celluloid (a transparent acetate material).

To produce cel animation, animators drew the background on one sheet of celluloid and then drew each object they wanted to animate on a separate celluloid sheet. So, for example, to create a scene in which a character skips through a forest an artist might draw the forest on one sheet of celluloid and then draw each of the various states of the character skipping on separate sheets of celluloid, as shown in Figure 1-5. In this way, the artists did not have to redraw the forest background scene for every frame. To create each frame, they switched only the celluloid sheets for the skipping character.

This approach is a far more efficient one than flip-book animation for several reasons. First, with the background drawn separately from the moving elements and characters, the animators need draw the background only once. This makes it easier to ensure that the background looks the same in each frame of the animation. Also, it makes it easier to correct mistakes and make changes. If one frame contains an error, you can edit only the cel that contains the error rather than redraw the entire frame's contents; if you want to

Figure 1-5   To create frames for cel animations, artwork is drawn on layered transparent
celluloid sheets (here labeled A, B, C, and D) and photographed.

change a moving element or character entirely, you need only replace the cels for that
element or character.

To create each frame of a cel animation, animators stack celluloid sheets and then photo-
graph them. These shots are then strung together on film. When the film is played at the
correct speed through a projector or VCR, the result is a moving image. Because each
frame of animation is composed of these celluloid sheets, each frame is known as a *cel*. Al-

though the term *cel* refers to a single frame or shot of animation, it also is used to mean a composite shot of multiple layers of celluloid sheets. It's important to understand that the term *cel* is used in this book as an equivalent to the term *layer*—that is, a cel is a layer of artwork. The term *frame* is used to refer to the composite of all the cels for a given frame of animation. Therefore, a cel is a component of a frame.

Although some animations are created from scanned photography, sketches, or digital video captures, much of the animation on the Web is created directly on the computer. The fundamental concept of layering, combined with the advantages of digital imagery, has fostered many of the robust computer animation techniques used in Web animation, such as

- Object-oriented or sprite-based animation

- Path-based animation

- Animation via tweening

Object-Oriented Animation

Objects, or *sprites*, are images or animations that can be manipulated independently. They are analogous to the individual celluloid layers of cel animations. These objects are treated as discrete units. Not only can they be animated separately from other objects, but they are also efficient because the computer can repeatedly refer to a single object rather than physically reproducing the image or animation (animations themselves can be objects). In other words, you can use an object numerous times over multiple frames without substantially adding to the file size.

Figure 1-6 shows a simple animation in Macromedia Flash 3. The animation of a laughing face is created using four objects (Flash refers to its objects as "symbols"); the object named Smile3 is used over and over again (other objects are also used repeatedly). When the animation plays back, the same image or Smile3 object is displayed. Each Smile3 image that is displayed during the animation is a copy of the original Smile3 object. Although the Smile3 object is displayed five times, the data for only one copy is added to the file size of the Flash animation. The amount of data required to display the Smile3 object is essentially the same whether the object is used one time or 1,000 times. As you will see in later chapters, JavaScript and Macromedia Flash are both capable of object-oriented animation.

Path-based Animations

One of the advantages of using objects is that you can apply automated animation processes to them. One common automated process is to generate animation by applying the objects to a path. You draw a path and specify a number of frames for the animation. The computer

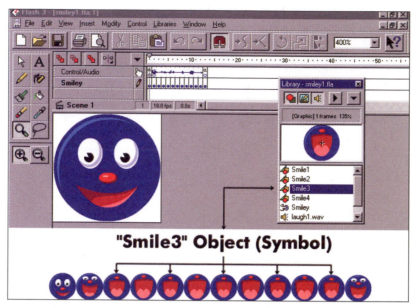

Figure 1-6   The Smile3 object (symbol) is used five times, but the amount of data used by the duplicates of the first Smile3 image doesn't add anything to the animation's overall file size.

then uses this information to generate an animation by moving the object along the path over the specified number of frames. For example, programs that support path-based animation allow you to assign a fly-by path to a jet or a liftoff path for a rocket. The animation program automatically creates the animation by generating frames that show the object moving along the path at a rate you assign. This means that you don't need a copy of the flying image for every frame of the animation; all you need is one image and a path description.

Figure 1-7 shows an example of this path-based animation from Parable's ThingMaker. The example is from a game called Jitter the Space Bug from a Web site called ToyLab (toylab.com). Players must drag a little alien in a space ship around the screen to help him avoid rockets that are being shot at him. Each of the little rockets moves along a path at a specified rate of speed. When the rocket reaches the end of the path, the rocket image is placed back at the beginning of the path and the animation starts over. Each of the rockets starts and ends at a unique position, and all their timings are set slightly off. Parable also allows you to set objects to move back and forth on a path, and you can specify how many times you want the object to move along the path (from one time to infinite, or continuous, movement).

Unfortunately, many types of movement cannot be emulated accurately by using a path-based approach on a single static image object. For example, although characters typically walk along a path, bipedal walking motion is complex. Walking involves what is

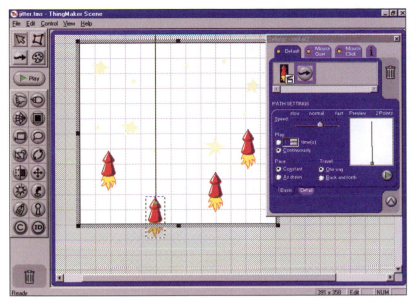

Figure 1-7 Parable's ThingMaker allows you to apply objects to a path to generate animation.

known as *secondary motion*; that is, not only do a character's legs move, but also the arms swing forward and back, the hips sway, and the head bobs. To make a walking animation look realistic, all these secondary motions are required.

To accommodate this kind of complexity, many animation programs allow you to make animations into objects. For a walking character, you could create a series of images of the character in different walking positions and then use those images to create an animation of the character walking in place. Then you make this animation an object and use a path-based animation program to create the effect of the walking character object moving along a path.

Figure 1-8 shows this principle in action. This game, also created in Parable ThingMaker, is from a Web site called Zania (zania.com). Players click on the horn-billed bird, startling it. The bird loses a feather, which floats down and tickles the little yellow character (called a Giggle). The feather animation effect is created with a static animation of a feather (shown at the bottom of Figure 1-8). The animation is static in the sense that it does not move over the area of the game field by itself. The movement over the game field follows a path. ThingMaker moves the animation along the path while the animation plays.

Tweened Animations

Tweening is similar to path-based animation in that the computer is employed to generate the animation of objects. To understand how tweening works, you need to know about key

Figure 1-8   Parable's ThingMaker allows you to apply objects to a path to generate animation.

frames. *Key frames* are the start and end points of a desired motion. You specify the start point key frame and the end point key frame for an object, and the computer calculates the in-between ("tween" for short) frames to generate the animation. For example, you could specify the start point key frame for a car object with its position to the far right and the end point key frame for the car object with its position to the far left. The computer would "tween" the two key frames. As with path-based animations, many static image objects do not look natural when tweened, but, again, you can often remedy this problem by using animated objects.

Figure 1-9 shows an example of tweened animation. This animated interface is from a Web site called InfiniteFish (infinitefish.com). This interface, created in Macromedia Director 6, is used as a basic navigational design for the InfiniteFish Web site. The semitransparent/chrome fish shapes constantly animate behind the buttons and stylized screen. Each of the semitransparent/chrome fishes is animated with tweening. Generating the animation was simple. First, the fish object (called a *sprite* in Director) was placed in a frame on one side of the screen; then a copy of the fish object was placed in another frame on the other side of the screen. All the frames between the two frames were then selected, and Director's tweening feature was applied. Director generated the animation, automatically creating an

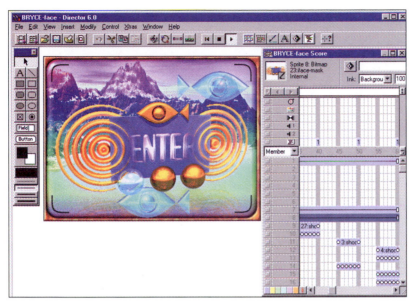

Figure 1-9   Programs such as Macromedia Director make it easy to animate simple movement with tweening, used here to animate the translucent fish shapes in the background (design by Scott Balay).

array of translucent fish copies positioned incrementally between the start and end positions of the original fish objects.

Notice that tweened animations are very similar to path-based animation. The fundamental difference is that path-based animations employ a path to generate the motion. Paths need not be straight; they can be circular, angular, and so on. Tweened animations are typically limited to linear paths, but you can combine tweened paths to generate more-interesting paths. For example, you could tween a shape going to the left and then generate another tween going up. The final effect would be that the object would move left and then up.

Although tweening is not as generous as path animations in terms of the types of motion that can be generated, tweening is better for creating effects. For example, Macromedia Flash allows you to use tweening to perform adjustments over time, such as having a shape change color or transparency or even morph into another shape. If you're paying attention, you might think that shape morphing would mean that you would lose the benefit of object-oriented animation. In the case of Macromedia Flash 3, however, this is not true because Flash performs the morphing operation on-the-fly *after* the animation has been downloaded. On the other hand, you cannot perform a shape tween between two symbols (remember that Flash refers to objects as "symbols").

▦ New Web Animation Technologies

The innovations just discussed help ease the process of animating while keeping file sizes down. However, Web developers wanting to deliver increasingly richer and more-robust animations have found that these technologies, by themselves, are still not enough. Fortunately, several recent innovations have dramatically improved the ability to deliver high-quality animation over the Web. The two most important new Web animation technologies are streaming animation and vector-based animation.

Streaming Animations

Before streaming was developed, animations had to be fully downloaded before they began to play. (GIF animations play frame by frame as they load, but they run smoothly only after they are fully downloaded.) *Streaming* animations can begin playing before the entire animation has downloaded. Before we talk about how streaming works, you need to understand the process referred to as *caching*. Streaming works by caching data. A *cache* is essentially a collection of data that is located on the user's system in a place that is readily accessible.

Figure 1-10 shows a simplified model of how caching works. The example on the top shows how data might typically flow over the Internet. There is a great distance between the data source and the client's central processing unit (CPU), so data takes a long time to arrive. The example on the bottom shows how caching works. The data from the data source is stored in a cache. The cache is much closer to the client's CPU. When enough data is in the cache, the client's computer starts processing the data from the cache. The idea is that not all of the data need be downloaded before the CPU starts working with the data. The CPU works on the data located in the cache while more data is downloaded, or streamed, into the cache. As long as the cache contains enough data, the CPU can work on the data from the cache in a smooth, timely fashion.

Suppose that we want to play an animation that's located on a server on the other side of the world. Let's say that the animation, when played for a viewer at full speed, lasts one minute. Assuming that people have a slow Internet connection, such as a 28.8-Kbps modem, one of two things would likely occur without caching. Either viewers would have to wait until the entire animation downloads before they could see it, or they would see it in a disjointed series of jumps.

With caching, however, the animation can be played smoothly. The data is downloaded to the cache. After enough of the animation is downloaded to the cache, the animation starts to play using the data in the cache. As the animation plays from the front end of the cache, more of the animation is downloaded and added to the back end of the cache. Therefore, the animation can play smoothly as long as the front end of the cache doesn't catch up to the back end.

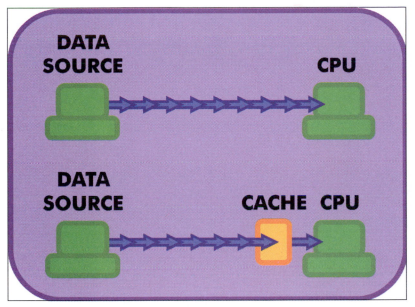

Figure 1-10   Normally data is displayed in a browser as it downloads over the Internet.
Streaming animations provide smoother playback by storing a small
amount of the animation data in a local cache before playback.

Streaming technology is not exclusive to animation. Streaming has been applied to audio, video, and even general multimedia applications (as with Shockwave). The advantage of streaming is that you can work with larger animations because as a developer you're not so concerned with total download time as long as the stream remains uninterrupted.

Vector-based Animations

Macromedia Flash has created a buzz in animation circles because of its revolutionary use of vector images in animation. Vector graphics are not a new concept; most designers are familiar with them through programs such as Adobe Illustrator, CorelDRAW!, and Macromedia FreeHand. In *vector* graphics, mathematical algorithms describe the shapes, shadings, colors, and location of objects. Contrast this with *bitmap* graphics (such as GIF, JPEG, and PNG—the bitmap graphic formats used on the Web), in which the image is physically represented by pixels arrayed on a rectangular grid. With bitmaps, a bigger image necessarily requires more pixels (and thus more data). This is not the case with vector images. Making a vector image larger essentially requires making the numbers in the mathematical algorithms bigger, and that usually adds very little to the overall file size. The economy of vectors makes them potentially very interesting in the limited-bandwidth world of the Web.

Even with the compression offered by GIF and JPEG, bitmap images tend to be larger than current bandwidth constraints can comfortably handle. For example, it's not uncommon for a typical image to run 15K. On the Web, 15K can be a relatively large file size. If each frame of a 10-frame animation were 15K, your animation would be 150K. That file size can be prohibitive for people connected to the Web on 28.8-Kbps modems. As you'll discover later in this book, Web animators have many important tools at their disposal that can help keep Web graphics from getting prohibitively large. With compression, lower bit depths, and other optimization techniques, 10-frame GIF animations one square inch in size can often be held to 5K or less.

That said, vector-based technology can easily achieve far better results than GIF animation. Because vectors are no more than mathematical expressions, vectors offer not only dramatically smaller file sizes but also the flexibility to select, resize, rotate, and otherwise deform images, all while maintaining pristine visual quality.

BITMAP FACTS

A *pixel* is the smallest discrete unit of a bitmap graphic. The term *bitmap* is derived from the fact that pixels are mapped to a grid or map.

Bitmap images are measured in pixels per inch (ppi). The ppi of a bitmap image is called its *resolution*. Web graphics typically have a resolution of 72 or 96 ppi. You can arrive at the total number of pixels in a bitmap image by mutliplying the image's height in pixels by its width in pixels. A one-square-inch image in 72 ppi contains 5,184 pixels. A one-square-inch image in 144 ppi contains 20,736 pixels.

Bitmap graphic formats must keep track of not only the location of each pixel in an image but also the color of each pixel. The total number of colors available to a bitmap image has a substantial bearing on its file size.

The total number of colors available to a bitmap image is referred to as its *bit depth*. Standard Web graphic bit depths are 1-, 2-, 3-, 4-, 5-, 6-, 7-, 8-, and 24-bit.

Essentially, *bit* refers to how many bits of information each pixel contains in order to store its color information. Twenty-four-bit images require 24 bits to describe each color. Therefore, without any compression, an image that contains 5,184 pixels requires 124,416 bits (15.19K) of data for the color information alone. ◗

Figure 1-11 shows a few frames from an online ad created with Macromedia Flash. The ad is 320 pixels wide by 200 pixels high—roughly twice the size of a typical Web banner ad. Although the ad is more than 290 frames long and plays for approximately 30 seconds, the file size is only 16.2K. Saved as a fully optimized GIF animation, the same ad weighs in at 1.18 MB. In other words, the Flash version is more than 74 times smaller than the GIF animation version.

Vector-based imagery is not always smaller than bitmap imagery. Vector technology works well when the imagery is basic. For example, a red circle five inches in diameter would have a substantially smaller file size as a vector-based graphic than as a bitmap image; however, a complex picture with thousands of intricate shadows and highlights would be far smaller as a JPEG. Also, when vector images have many intricate highlights, shadows, blends, and effects, the mathematical algorithms are more complex. This makes it harder for the computer to make the calculations, and it may take a longer time to render the elaborate scene.

For most Web animations, however, vector technology proves to be far more efficient than bitmaps. Photo-realism is rarely a fundamental requirement for Web animation. The solid colors and basic gradients popular in most cartoons (and the fact that cartoons are no longer just for children) have made the Web a natural platform for vector-based animations.

Figure 1-11   This Flash-based ad, created to advertise Xara 2.0 software from I/US Corp., is 74 times smaller than an equivalent GIF animation. Copyright © i/s corp. http://www.i-s.com.

Animation Technologies Compared

Now that we've looked at the basic innovations for Web animation, let's look at some popular Web animation technologies and consider their advantages and disadvantages. Because each Web animation technology has its own set of pluses and minuses, knowing them makes it easy to determine which one best suits your needs and requirements. Because good tools are an essential element of any art's potential, we also briefly discuss the animation tool options for each mechanism.

GIF Animation

Although many of the newer Web animation technologies offer more-robust features, GIF animation remains one of the Web's most versatile means of animation. GIF animations require no special browser plug-in, and they are compatible with most Web browsers. It is easy to create images for GIF animations using graphics tools that most designers have on hand, such as Adobe Photoshop or Jasc's Paintshop Pro. You can assemble GIF animations using numerous shareware or otherwise inexpensive GIF animation utilities. Table 1-1 shows the advantages and disadvantages of this animation workhorse.

Putting a GIF animation on a Web page is exactly like putting a static image on a Web page. Here's a basic image tag for a GIF animation:

```
<IMG SRC=gifanimation.gif HEIGHT=72 WIDTH=72 BORDER=0 ALT=GIF Animation rocks>
```

The SRC tag gives the file name of the GIF animation. The HEIGHT and WIDTH are specified in pixels. Setting the BORDER attribute to 0 ensures that no unsightly border will be displayed if the GIF is hyperlinked, and the ALT attribute tells users what they are missing if their browser does not support graphics display.

Another important advantage of GIF animations is that the GIF format lets you make parts of a GIF animation totally transparent. This fact offers valuable compression options for GIF animations, and it means that GIF animations can be integrated into Web designs in ways that aren't possible with some of the more-robust Web animation technologies.

An easily overlooked advantage is the fact that there are thousands, if not millions, of GIF animations on the Web. It is easy to download any of these animations, open them in a GIF animation utility, and look at the individual frames. This is a great way to learn about GIF animation and animation techniques in general. On the other hand, the easy availability

Table 1-1   Advantages and Disadvantages of GIF Animation

Advantages	Disadvantages
Standard file format	Not object-oriented
Ease of creation	No sound
Large number of inexpensive tools available	No interactivity
	Limit of 256 total colors per frame
Ease of implementation	Animation is easy to steal
No server configurations needed	
Portions of animation can be transparent	
Highly compressible	
Many examples on the Web to learn from	
Easily viewed frame by frame in many GIF animation editors	

of GIF animations presents a problem: it makes them easy to steal. Unfortunately, it is easy for unscrupulous surfers to nab your well-crafted animations and claim them as their own.

There are plenty of downsides to GIF animation. GIF animations are not object-oriented. For example, if the animation shown in Figure 1-6 were a GIF animation, each instance of the laughing face would represent a unique frame, adding to the animation's file size.

Also, the GIF format cannot perform any sort of streaming. As mentioned earlier, each frame in a GIF animation displays as it loads, so typically GIF animations play disjointedly at first. Some crafty Web designers build in long pauses within the first frame of the GIF animation, allowing time for the remaining frames to download. However, that pause shows up every time the animation loops, and that does not work for some animations.

One of the most notorious drawbacks of GIF animations is that they are limited to a maximum of 256 colors per frame. As discussed in Chapter 3, Mastering the Palette, having 256 different colors on each frame is impractical because it usually results in unsightly flashes and color jumps from frame to frame. This means that the limit for GIF animations, in practice, is 256 colors for the entire animation. This is a problem for animations that contain many gradients, such as 3-D animations, or for colorful photograhic animations. Image quality typically suffers with these types of animations. On the other hand, the 256-color limit can be a benefit because fewer colors means smaller files.

As one of the Web's oldest animation options, GIF animation has benefited, especially recently, from a wide range of GIF animation tools. GIF animation tools have become so numerous that they have begun to specialize. Now there are not only tools for basic GIF animation assembly but also tools that specialize in optimization, special effects, and painting. There are even numerous tools for low-level administrative tasks such as removing comment blocks and previewing.

Many of the basic GIF animation tools still treat GIF animation, to some extent, as if it weren't a bona fide animation mechanism. Tools such as GIF Construction Set and GIFBuilder use a basic stacking metaphor. Animations can be previewed but only one frame at time. Critical options such as timing, transparency, and interlacing must be edited by selecting options from pull-down menus. More important, these GIF animation utilities have very limited capabilities for file size optimization.

The lack of depth in these tools explains in part why many GIF animations are of poor quality. This is not to imply that all Web animations need be broadcast quality—after all, you may be creating animation for fun. Nevertheless, many basic tools don't make it easy to create high-quality GIF animations. The result has been a flood of low-quality GIF animations, creating the false impression that GIF itself is strictly a low-level animation option for the Web.

The point is this: It is important to understand that GIF animation utilities such as GIF Construction Set and GIFBuilder do not have the depth of capability required to apply sophisticated adjustments to GIF animations. You should be aware that the GIF animation format is not limited to the capabilities of these utilities. As with most things, better tools provide for better results.

Many of the more-capable GIF animation utilities, such as Ulead GIF Animator and Boxtop Software's GIFmation, still largely follow the basic model established by GIF Construction Set and GIF Builder. These second-tier tools have better file size optimization and even some animated special effects features, but overall they raise the standard only nominally.

Recently, a new generation of GIF animation tools has emerged. Products such as GIF Movie Gear and the GIF animator in SPG Web Tools for Photoshop (both PC-only options) treat GIF animation production in a more sophisticated manner. These tools allow you to see all the frames of your animation at once. This approach lets you work in a more traditional fashion, allowing you to make local decisions about specific frames in an animation by evaluating the animation as a whole. These tools also have more-powerful optimization features. For example, GIF Movie Gear allows you to see "before" and "after" versions of an animation during color reduction optimization.

Another excellent example of a more feature-rich tool for creating GIF animations is Extensis PhotoAnimator. PhotoAnimator employs a layer paradigm similar to that of Adobe Photoshop and Adobe After Effects. With PhotoAnimator, you can apply effects to different cels on different layers. You can edit the animation as much as you like before exporting it to an animation.

Other important features found in some of the more feature-rich GIF animation programs include the ability to import layered Photoshop files, automatically optimize the animation (both for the palette and for transparency), resize an animation, and provide estimated download times for the animation in its current state. These GIF animation tools provide increased capabilities and control, and that translates into more-compelling animations.

For a more comprehensive and updated list of GIF animation utilities along with their features and pricing information, see http://navworks.i-us.com.

JavaScript Animations

Table 1-2 shows the advantages and disadvantages of JavaScript animations.

Although JavaScript is a scripting language and not an animation technology per se, it can be used to implement a wide range of animation effects, such as interactivity and randomness. Figures 1-12 and 1-13 show an example. Figure 1-12 shows a static screen from

Table 1-2 Advantages and Disadvantages of JavaScript Animations

Advantages	*Disadvantages*
Interactivity	Easy to steal
Object-oriented	Supported only by latest browsers (Netscape3 and later, Internet Explorer 4 and later)
Works with JPEG, GIF, and PNG	
Easy to implement	Currently only a few tools
No server configurations	
Transparency with GIF and PNG (PNG only with 5.0 versions of Netscape and Internet Explorer)	
Variable image quality	

infinitefish.com. When the user rolls the mouse over the screen, the images in Figure 1-13 move into view. It's nice that the animation is interactive, but there is an even greater benefit realized by the use of JavaScript. The Web page that contains this animation also contains about a dozen similar animations. They are so similar that many of them share the same frames. For example, when a visitor rolls the mouse over a different screen, the same frames move into view except the final frame, which has a title for the different section of the InfiniteFish Web site. This shows that JavaScript can make a small number of frames work for a large number of different animations, achieving a compelling animation effect without adding excessively to the Web page's overall download requirements.

JavaScript can be used with GIF animations or with static JPEG or PNG images. As you will see in Chapter 8, Keeping Web Animations Fresh with JavaScript, you can reuse individual graphics in animations. This means that JavaScript animations can be, in essence, object-oriented. Dynamic HTML (DHTML) has given JavaScript a boost. Using

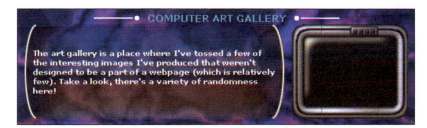

Figure 1-12 This interactive JavaScript animation by Scott Balay (**infinitefish.com**) starts with a blank screen.

Figure 1-13   When the user rolls a mouse over the small blank screen, the JavaScript
animation begins to play.

JavaScript with DHTML gives you many valuable capabilities such as layering and precise positioning.

JavaScript doesn't have any plug-in requirements, but JavaScript's faults include the fact that many of the interesting animation possibilities require JavaScript 1.1. Sadly, JavaScript 1.1 didn't make it into Internet Explorer 3.0, and JavaScript was only up to version 1.0 in Netscape 2.0. In addition, because JavaScript is a scripting language, learning it takes much more time than learning to use an animation tool. For example, you must learn to code things such as browser checks so that people using old browsers don't get nasty error messages when they visit your pages. Animations implemented with JavaScript are limited to bitmap images. However, JavaScript can be used with Shockwave and Flash animations. This is particularly valuable for Flash because it has no internal programming language comparable to Director's (Shockwave) Lingo.

Development environments for JavaScript are very scarce. One of the few exceptions is NetObjects, which is an excellent scripting environment for scripters but offers little in the way of automation. The advent of DHTML, however, has produced a rush for the development of DHTML tools, resulting in such tools as Macromedia Dreamweaver, Astound Dynamite, and MBED Interactor. These tools can help you create animation using JavaScript with little or no programming.

Macromedia Flash

Table 1-3 shows the advantages and disadvantages of Macromedia Flash animations.

Table 1-3   Advantages and Disadvantages of Macromedia Flash Animations

Advantages	*Disadvantages*
Interactivity	Limited interactivity
Object-oriented	Limited scriptability
Works with JPEG, GIF, and PNG	Plug-in required
Streaming	Separate utility exposes Flash files to the possibility of theft
Some protection from theft	
Java alternative for plug-in	
Vector-based compression	
Inexpensive	
No programming required	
Ability to script functionality with JavaScript	

Macromedia Flash is an inexpensive ($299) authoring tool that allows you to implement basic interactivity without programming. The interactive possibilities of Flash have been substantially improved with Flash version 3, but they still fall short of the range of possibilities offered by Director. The key advantage of Macromedia Flash is that it is vector-based. Although there is no internal programming language, Flash supports a basic set of buttons and frame actions and you can control many aspects of a Flash movie with JavaScript, a capability much improved in version 3. Also, the Flash Asset Xtra, which is incorporated into Director 7, allows for Flash movies to be imported into Director, opening the door for the infinite possibilities that Lingo offers.

Flash is object-oriented, and you can animate with tweening or by using a combination of paths and tweening. Flash 3 introduced transparency options and morphing, a new tween-based animation option. Also, buttons can contain animations in Flash 3 without losing their object-oriented status. This opens the door for more interactive animation possibilities. Bitmap and sound capabilities came with Flash 2, making Flash one of the more accessible general-purpose Web multimedia authoring tools. Flash offers streaming delivery for both the overall Flash movie and the audio.

Although Flash supports audio at abnormally small bit depths (appropriate for small sound effects), its internal audio capabilities are less than broadcast quality. However, Macromedia has teamed up with RealNetworks to offer Real Flash. Real Flash offers the advantages of Flash's highly compressible vector-based animations with RealNetworks' Real Audio, which is one of the better broadcast-quality streaming audio mechanisms available for the Web. Part of Flash's early appeal was that its required plug-in is much smaller than Shockwave's plug-in, making it a more acceptable download for the general public. Like Shockwave, Macromedia now offers a Java playback option for Flash. Flash movies are reduced to a crawl on the Java player, but at least the results can be more graceful when surfers view a Flash page without the Flash plug-in.

Although this book focuses on GIF, JavaScript, and Flash for Web animation, this should not be taken to imply that there aren't other excellent Web animation options. We focus on the Web animation mechanisms that have better market penetration, viability, and accessibility. Technologies such as Shockwave, Java, and DHTML offer powerful animation options that are worth looking into, but they also require a significant time and money investment. These technologies also come with prerequisites that discourage their general use on the Web. For example, Shockwave requires a plug-in that is more than five times larger than the Flash player. Java is slow, and a high level of mastery is required to minimize its notorious bugginess. DHTML has multiple strains of existence and only the more recent browsers support it. DHTML is at the bleeding edge of Web animation options even a year after its "release" (at the time of this writing).

Nevertheless, a steady stream of Web animation innovations is being generated at a dizzying pace. For example, MBED Interactor offers the ability to create Web animations with DHTML, Java, or the proprietary, plug-in-based MBED format, offering developers an attractive array of publishing possibilities. Other notable Web animation tools include Macromedia Dreamweaver for DHTML animation and Emblaze Creator for Java-based interactive animation. Also, streaming video with the likes of Real Networks' RealVideo, Microsoft's ActiveMovie, and Emblaze Video offers valuable animation-like effects. These technologies open the door to using powerful animation and video tools such as Adobe AfterEffects, Adobe Premiere, and Ulead MediaStudio because streaming video allows you to convert large AVI and Quicktime movie files for streaming Web delivery. Another up-and-coming technology that can be used for Web animation is Microsoft's ChromeEffects.

▣ Summary

On the Web, the technological status quo is always changing. A great new animation technology may come along tomorrow and upend everything we know about animation on the Web. The reality is that as Web developers we use tools that have widespread support and are likely to stick around for a while. As of this writing, that means GIF animation, JavaScript interactive animations, and Flash. This book focuses on these core technologies, exposing important new techniques for making the most efficient, compelling, and user-friendly animations possible.

PART I

GIF Animation

CHAPTER **2**

GIF Animation: Basics and Beyond

Animation's main requirement—multiple images—is at odds with the Web's key limitation: bandwidth. We are used to seeing real-time movement on TV and in movies, but even the tiniest Web animations can take a while to download from the Web. It is common for television programs and movies to have thousands of frames, but in almost any Web setting, that would be impractical. At 2Kbps over the common 28.8-Kbps modem, Web animations are forced to more humble aspirations. Web designers must carefully craft their animations so that they are as efficient as possible. ❯

The Basics of GIF Animation Construction

Reducing Colors

Frame Cropping Optimization

Using Interframe Transparency Optimization

Removing Frames

Cropping the Animation

Resizing the Animation

Removing Interlacing

Removing Comment Blocks

Timing and Looping Techniques

In Chapters 3 and 4 we take an in-depth look at the finer points of optimizing the file sizes of GIF animations. Subsequent chapters provide sophisticated strategies for creating images in Photoshop, managing color palettes, and disposal methods. In this chapter we look at the basics of creating tiny GIF animations with maximum effect. First, we look at fundamental GIF animation construction. Then we look at a series of examples that demonstrate some of the key techniques you can use for making the most of a little animation.

The Basics of GIF Animation Construction

In the simplest GIF animation scenario, you simply create the images for each frame of the animation and import them into a GIF animation program. As we'll see, it's easy to set the timing for each frame and specify whether the animation will loop. Setting bit depth and frame cropping and transparency options is more complicated, and we cover those topics thoroughly in Chapters 3 and 4. Also, for now we bypass the step of creating the art for the animation. Chapters 3, 4, and 5 cover issues and techniques for generating the individual frames of an animation. In this chapter we establish a basic framework for creating GIF animations and show that even the basics, such as timing and looping, can be valuable tools for creating GIF animations.

To discuss the basics of compiling a GIF animation, we use my favorite general-purpose GIF animation utility: GIF Movie Gear (GMG). With the exception of a few low-end GIF animation utilities, notably GIF Construction Set and GIFBuilder, most GIF animation utilities can perform the same or similar tasks that we demonstrate in GMG.

Figure 2-1 shows six frames for a simple bouncing ball animation. The individual frames were created in Adobe Photoshop and exported from Photoshop as GIF files. I named each frame according to the order of the display: frame 1 is ball1.gif, frame 2 is ball2.gif, and so on.

After each frame was exported as a separate GIF, each GIF image was imported into GIF Movie Gear. To follow this discussion, locate the directory named chapter2 on the CD-ROM that comes with this book. Using your GIF animation utility of choice (the CD-ROM contains several demo GIF animation utilities for your convenience), open the files named ball1.gif, ball2.gif, ball3.gif, ball4.gif, ball5.gif, and ball6.gif.

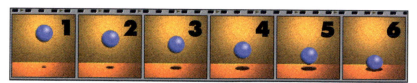

Figure 2-1 Six frames for a bouncing ball animation.

Most GIF animation utilities allow you to open multiple frames at once. To start creating this GIF animation, I opened GMG and used GMG's **Open** command to import all six of the frames at once. Like most GIF animation utilities, GMG imports multiple frames in alphanumeric order (ball1.gif becomes frame 1, ball2.gif becomes frame 2, and so on).

These six frames create the effect of the ball dropping; I needed to generate more frames to complete the loop and make it appear as if the ball were bouncing. To do this, I performed a series of copy and paste operations. I started by copying frame 5 and pasting it behind frame 6. Then I copied frame 4 and pasted it behind the newly created frame 7. I continued this process with frames 3 and 2, pasting each copy behind the newly created frames 8 and 9, respectively.

When I finished this operation, the frames of my animation looked like those shown in Figure 2–2. Now the ball drops in frames 1–6 and bounces back in frames 7–10. With the animation set to loop (start over at frame 1 after displaying frame 10), it looks like a bouncing ball.

At this point, I could have exported the frames as a GIF animation by choosing **Save As** from the File menu. I typically generate a GIF animation right after I import frames so that I have a version of the animation to use as a frame of reference. GIF Movie Gear, like many GIF animation utilities, has several built-in methods for optimizing a GIF animation (we look at them in a moment), so it can be useful to save a version of the animation before you do any optimizing to get a clear idea of how much file size you save.

When I saved this unoptimized version of the bouncing ball animation, its file size was almost 45K (45,781 bytes). A file size of 45K is far too large for this kind of animation. On a 28.8-Kbps modem, this animation would take 12.7 seconds to download. No one's going to grow any gray hairs in that time frame, but in Web time 12.7 seconds is much too long.

It takes only a fraction of a second for a Web page visitor to click on the browser's **Stop**, **Back**, or **Home** button. The longer it takes for your animations to load, the more likely it is that they won't be seen at all. GIF animation utilities make it easy to compile a GIF animation, but they also make it easy to compile GIF animations with oversized files. That's why whenever we deal specifically with GIF animation in this book we explain the finer points of keeping GIF animation file sizes to a minimum.

Figure 2-2 Frames 2–5 were duplicated and arrayed in reverse order to complete the motion of the ball bouncing down and back up.

Fortunately, it isn't hard to trim some bytes from this animation's file size. The following are the eight fundamental ways to reduce the file size of a GIF animation.

1 Reduce the number of colors (palette optimization).

2 Perform frame cropping, or "dirty rectangle," optimization.

3 Use transparency (interframe transparency optimization).

4 Remove frames.

5 Crop portions of the animation, reducing its physical size.

6 Resize the animation to a smaller dimensional size.

7 Remove interlacing.

8 Remove comment blocks.

GIF Movie Gear can perform all these operations. Let's look at each one briefly.

Reducing Colors

You can reduce the number of colors in GMG by clicking on the **Reduce Colors** button on the toolbar or by selecting **Reduce Colors** from the Tools menu. Figure 2-3 shows the Reduce Colors dialog box, which contains two preview windows.

The window on the left shows the original animation, and the window on the right shows the animation after it has been color reduced, allowing you to determine whether the color reduction adversely affects the animation's visual quality. You can also zoom in within the preview windows to scrutinize the differences more closely.

In this example, the animation's palette started with 256 colors. Notice that the preview windows also provide before and after file size information. In Figure 2-3, it indicates that going from a 256-color palette to a 128-color palette will remove 4,269 bytes, a 9.3% savings. Reducing the bouncing ball animation to a 128-color palette reduced the overall animation to 40.5K (41,512 bytes).

Reducing the animation to 128 colors results in a little bit of banding on the ball's gradient, but when the animation is seen at full size at full speed, it's not noticeable. Such trade-offs—trading a little quality loss for a little file size optimization—are common with GIF animations. It's a good trade-off as long as it's not noticeable.

We discuss palettes more thoroughly in Chapter 3. For now, it's important to know that many GIF animation programs have automated palette optimization features that are, by and large, useful and reliable.

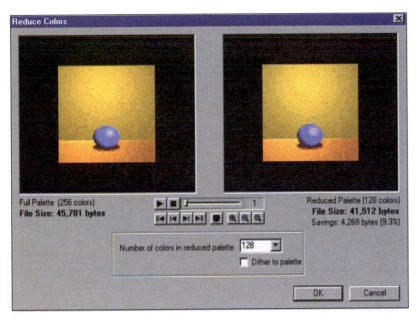

Figure 2-3   GIF Movie Gear's Reduce Colors dialog box.

Frame Cropping Optimization

The GIF format allows for frames to be different sizes. For example, a GIF animation can have a first frame that is 100 pixels square and a second frame that is only 50 pixels square. This aspect of GIF animation can be difficult to grasp (almost as difficult as it is to explain). Let's depart from the bouncing ball example for a moment and look at a very simplified example.

Figure 2-4 shows a basic two-frame animation. I created this animation by exporting a green 100-pixel-square GIF from Adobe Photoshop. Then I used Photoshop to create another GIF file, this one only 50 pixels square and colored burgundy. Then I imported these two files into GMG separately. Notice that the second frame—the 50-pixel-square burgundy frame—appears to be the same size as the first frame. However, the medium gray area essentially indicates transparency. In other words, frame 2 shows through to frame 1 wherever you see gray in frame 2, as shown in the Preview Animation dialog box, which is showing frame 2 in Figure 2-4.

Many GIF animation programs can use this capability to reduce a GIF animation's file size by comparing frames and cropping redundant portions. This technique is known as "dirty rectangle" optimization. That name isn't very descriptive, so we also use the term *frame cropping* in this book to refer to this technique.

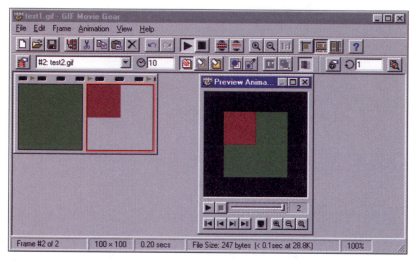

Figure 2-4 The second frame of this animation is one-fourth the size of the first frame. The gray areas in the second frame are essentially transparent.

Now let's look again at the bouncing ball example to further clarify frame cropping optimization. Figure 2-5 shows the animation after it has been optimized using frame cropping. I performed this operation in GMG by selecting the **Optimize Animation** option. The options I used for GMG's Optimize Animations dialog box are shown in Figure 2-6.

Each of the frames in Figure 2-5 after frame 1 has been reduced to the smallest needed rectangle. The unnecessary or redundant portions of the frames have been cropped. In other words, GMG took the GIF images used for frames 2–10 and cropped them to smaller GIF files. So each frame after frame 1 is simply a smaller GIF file. The smaller GIF files are displayed over the first frame using pixel coordinates for their placement. Because

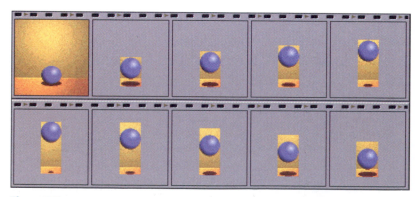

Figure 2-5 The bouncing ball animation optimized with frame cropping.

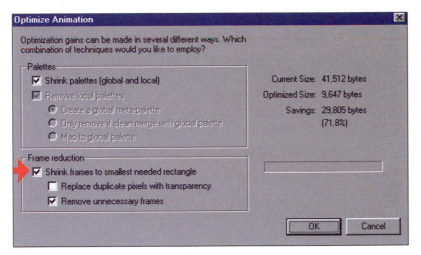

Figure 2-6   GIF Movie Gear's **Shrink frames to smallest needed rectangle** option in the **Optimize Animation** dialog box performs the frame cropping optimization. (Arrow added.)

the smaller GIF images cover the first frame only partially, you can still see parts of the original frame as the animation plays. We look at this frame cropping technique more thoroughly in Chapter 4, Frame Cropping and Interframe Transparency Optimization.

Before frame cropping optimization, the file size of the bouncing ball animation was 40.5K (41,512 bytes). After frame cropping optimization, the animation's file size is only 9.4K (9,647 bytes), a savings of almost 72%. Now the animation takes only

> Many GIF animation utilities that support frame cropping optimization allow you to change the pixel coordinates of the optimized frames. This feature usually isn't very valuable for animations that have gone through automated frame cropping (the GIF animation will position the optimized frames using the proper coordinates), but it means that you can manually position any frames that you import. ▶

2.7 seconds to download. We've talked about only two of the eight methods for optimizing a GIF animation, and already we've taken 10 seconds off the download time!

Using Interframe Transparency Optimization

One of the key advantages of the GIF format is that GIF images can contain *transparency*. In the GIF file format, a single color is defined as transparent. Any pixels in the animation that contain that color are then made transparent. The GIF file format also allows you to remap colors in a GIF image to the same color as the transparent color, increasing the portions of a GIF image that are transparent.

One benefit of this mapping is that it can aid GIF file compression. The GIF format uses LZW (Lempel-Ziv-Welch) compression, which is a run-length encoding compression algorithm. Essentially, *run-length encoding* means that the GIF format compresses best when there are contiguous strings of pixels that have the same color. For example, a GIF file compresses better when there are 10 pixels in a row that are the same color than if each of the 10 pixels were a different color. When you use transparency and then remap more colors to the transparent color, you tend to increase the number of pixels that use the color being used for transparency. As a result, there tend to be more strings of pixels that have the transparent color in the GIF file, and the GIF file compresses better.

Many of the newer GIF animation utilities, including GMG, can take advantage of GIF transparency to optimize GIF animations. This form of optimization makes redundant portions of animation frames transparent, usually resulting in file size savings. The key to this form of optimization is to use the correct disposal method. Disposal methods control how the frames of a GIF animation display over one another.

For the purposes of optimization, we are concerned with only two disposal methods: the disposal method that displays each frame as fully opaque, one frame atop the other, and the disposal method that allows transparent areas of a frame to display as transparent, allowing frames to show through to earlier frames. Don't worry if this doesn't make sense. We cover disposal methods and interframe transparency optimization more thoroughly in Chapter 4.

Animation programs have various names to refer to the key disposal methods. The disposal method that allows for transparency in frames (called "no disposal method" in GIF Movie Gear) is on by default in GMG. GIF Movie Gear allows you to change the disposal method using the **Global Frame Properties** setting (available from the Edit menu).

The correct disposal method is on by default in GMG. To optimize the animation with interframe transparency, you need only click the **Optimize Animation** button or select **Optimize Animation** from the Tools menu. Figure 2-7 shows GIF Movie Gear's Optimize Animation dialog box.

The Frame Reduction section shown in Figure 2-7 has three options: **Shrink frames to smallest needed rectangle**, **Replace duplicate pixels with transparency**, and **Remove unnecessary frames**. The **Shrink frames to smallest needed rectangle** option is used for frame cropping. The **Replace duplicate pixels with transparency** option is used for interframe transparency. When this option is selected, GMG checks between frames for redundancy and then turns any pixels transparent that it can.

The idea is to make as many unnecessarily redundant pixels transparent as possible in the interest of helping the LZW compression scheme compress the overall animation better. Not all redundant pixels between frames are unnecessarily redundant. Sometimes, pixels in a given frame must remain opaque for the overall animation to look right.

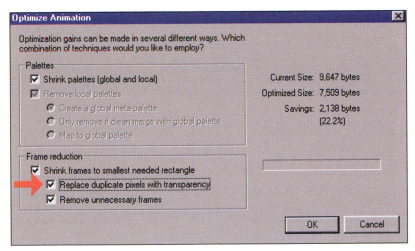

Figure 2-7 GIF Movie Gear's **Replace duplicate pixels with transparency** option
in the Optimize Animation dialog box performs the interframe
transparency optimization. (Arrow added.)

Figure 2-8 shows what the overall interframe transparency process looks like. Because you
can choose any color to be the color of transparency, I made the transparent color for the
bouncing ball animation bright green to make it easy to see which pixels have been made
transparent. All the bright green pixels have been made transparent. Using interframe
transparency optimization has reduced the bouncing ball's file size an additional
2,138 bytes. Now the animation takes only 2.1 seconds to download with a 28.8-Kbps
modem, a modest savings.

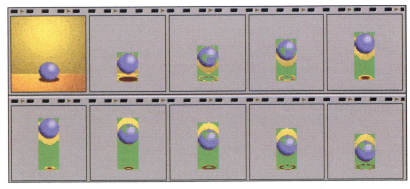

Figure 2-8 The green areas show the portions of each frame that have been
optimized with interframe transparency.

▦ Removing Frames

As discussed in Chapter 1, the human brain has a remarkable ability to interpret a series of images as fluid motion. As long as there is a reasonable pattern in the frames, the viewer can usually interpret the motion correctly. This means that in some cases a few frames can be removed without damaging the effectiveness of the animation very much. The fewer frames there are in an animation, the smaller the file size will be.

No special technique is involved in removing GIF animation frames, although some utilities make it easier to delete frames than others. This happens to be one of the reasons I prefer GIF Movie Gear. It allows you to see all the frames of the animation at once. If the animation contains a lot of frames, you can zoom out to see more thumbnails.

The value of seeing all the frames of your animation at once cannot be overstated. For one thing, it allows you to make intelligent decisions, such as determining whether one of the frames is unnecessary. Also, GMG allows you to see how frames have been optimized with transparency as shown in Figures 2-5 and 2-8. So, for example, you can open an existing animation and see whether it has been optimized with transparency and whether the optimization looks good.

Another key advantage of GIF Movie Gear is that it has multiple levels of undo. You can delete a frame and then preview the animation to see whether it is still acceptable. If it is not, you can undo the deletion and try something else.

After some experimentation with the bouncing ball animation, I found that deleting the second frame and the final frame (shown in Figure 2-9) had no visible effect after I previewed the changes. When I deleted these frames, the animation was reduced to 6,998 bytes. Now the animation took only 1.9 seconds to download over the Internet with a 28.8-Kbps modem.

One final note about removing frames. As we discuss later in this chapter, each frame in a GIF animation can have its own timing. For example, you can set frame 1 to display for one-tenth of a second and then set frame 2 to display for five seconds. However, most GIF animations set imported frames to a default timing scheme, typically to 10 frames per second.

> For the animation to work correctly, you must remove frames before you perform the frame cropping and interframe transparency optimization. (Sometimes it also helps to remove frames before palette optimization.) Therefore, it's best to try to remove frames from an animation before you perform any other optimizations. However, usually the combination of palette optimization, frame cropping, and interframe transparency results in far more file size saving, and that is why we cover those techniques first. ❯

Some people assume that the default timing used by a GIF animation utility is the only timing that can be used. If they wanted to, for example, display a given frame for half a second they would use five copies of the frame (assuming that the GIF animation utility defaults to 10 frames per second). Each copy of the frame would display for one-tenth of a second, adding up to half a second. This approach is very inefficient. Why use

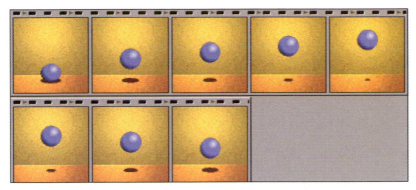

Figure 2-9 No noticeable effect can be seen when the second and final frames of the bouncing ball animation are deleted (animation shown here unoptimized).

five frames when you can use one? Although frame cropping and interframe transparency can deal with this oversight, it's always better to delete fully redundant frames and set the timing of the frame to make it display for the desired duration.

Cropping the Animation

The overall dimensions of a GIF animation can often be reduced. Logically, the smaller the overall dimensions of a GIF animation, the smaller the animation's file size. If there is an area around the perimeter of an animation over which nothing changes or over which no motion occurs, it's possible that the animation can be cropped to reduce the file size.

In Figure 2-2, notice that the bouncing ball motion occurs over a very small portion of the animation—the center. This animation is a prime candidate for cropping. You can perform this operation in GMG using the **Crop** option available from the Animation menu.

Figure 2-10 shows GMG's Crop Animation dialog box. To crop the animation, you simply drag the handles of the marquee in the preview window to the position you wish to crop to and then press **OK**. GIF Movie Gear also allows you crop numerically, and you can preview the results before cropping. Another important feature available in the Crop Animation dialog box is the ability see the previous frame, next frame, or first frame ghosted in the preview. This feature makes it easier to avoid cropping needed portions of the animation.

It's helpful to look at the issue of cropping an animation from another angle. After all the optimizations have been administered to the bouncing ball animation before cropping, recall that the entire animation's file size was 6,998 bytes. When all the frames except the first frame were deleted, the file size was 4,565 bytes. More than 65% of the animation's file size was in the first frame. Therefore, the easiest way to reduce the overall file size was to reduce the file size of the first frame. Because all the other frames had had frame cropping applied to them, only the first frame stood to gain (or lose, depending on how you look at it) from cropping the entire animation. ▶

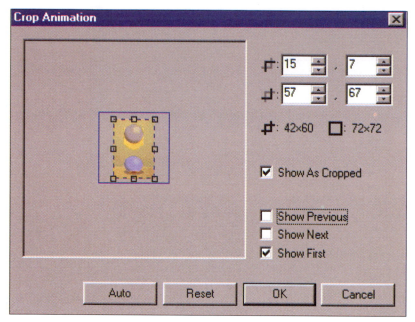

Figure 2-10   In GIF Movie Gear's Crop Animation dialog box, you can crop an image using a marquee or numerically.

The crop shown in Figure 2-9 is fairly conservative (more of the image could have been cropped). Nevertheless, cropping the animation dropped the file size to 4,880 bytes. Now the animation would download in 1.4 seconds with a 28.8-Kbps modem.

Resizing the Animation

Reducing an animation's physical size is an obvious way to reduce its file size. Like many of the newer GIF animation utilities, GIF Movie Gear allows you to resize animation by using the **Resize** option available via the Animation menu. Figure 2-11 shows GMG's Resize dialog box. You can resize animations according to numerical pixel dimensions or by percentages. A **Maintain aspect ratio** option keeps the animation from becoming deformed. Resizing animations can adversely affect the palette and interframe transparency optimization, so usually it is best to resize the animation before performing these optimizations. Reducing the bouncing ball to 80% of its cropped size reduced the file size to 3,573 bytes. At this size, the animation takes exactly one second to download using a 28.8-Kbps modem.

> Resizing animations with GIF animation utilities can produce dubious results. It's always better to try to create your original artwork at 100% of its final size. Therefore, when you are creating the artwork ask yourself whether the animation could be a little smaller and still produce the desired effect. ▶

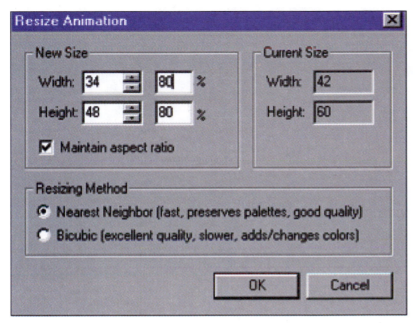

Figure 2-11 GIF Movie Gear's Resize Animation dialog box allows you to resize with percentages as well as pixel dimensions.

Removing Interlacing

Interlacing can be somewhat helpful for static GIF images, but it has no place in GIF animations because GIF animation frames typically display for a short period. Interlacing even slows down GIF animations and adds slightly to file size. GIF Movie Gear has interlacing turned off by default. Turning on interlacing adds 22 bytes to the animation. Most GIF animation utilities have a Global Properties settings dialog box, where you can turn interlacing on and off.

Removing Comment Blocks

The GIF format contains something called *comment blocks,* places where you can add text such as credits or your Web site address. Many GIF animation utilities automatically add a comment block that contains the name of the utility and other information. Comment blocks add slightly to the file size of a GIF animation. GIF Movie Gear has comment blocks turned off by default, but you can add or remove comment blocks using the Edit GIF Comments dialog box shown in Figure 2-12. Adding a comment block to the bouncing ball animation adds 55 bytes to the file size. The more text in the comment block, the more it adds to the file size. A GIF animation can have more than one comment block.

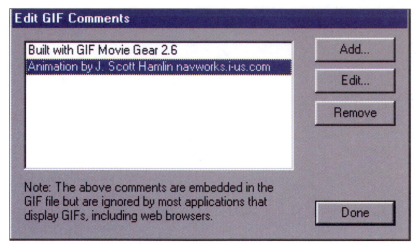

Figure 2-12 Deleting comment blocks can shave a few bytes off your animation.

Timing and Looping

In addition to optimization, GIF animation programs typically allow you to adjust the timing and looping of an animation. Timing is usually measured in hundredths of a second. For example, if you enter **10** for the timing of a specific frame, it will display for 10/100th of a second (1/10th of a second). If you wanted the frame to display for half a second you would enter **50**. If you wanted the frame to display for 5 seconds, you would enter **500**.

GIF Movie Gear allows you to adjust the timing of the animation in several ways. To adjust the timing of a specific frame, you click on the frame and enter the timing setting on the toolbar or in GMG's Properties dialog box (accessed via the Frame menu). You can also adjust the timing for all the frames of the animation at once by using GMG's Global Properties dialog box (also found in the Frame menu).

The looping setting determines how many times the animation replays, from one time to infinite looping. To set an animation to loop infinitely in most GIF animation utilities, including GMG, you enter **0** for the looping setting. Any other number in the loop setting establishes the number of times the animation will loop. For example, if you enter **10** for the loop setting, the animation will play 10 times and then stop. GIF animations display the last frame when they stop looping. GMG allows you to adjust the looping settings via either the toolbar or the Properties dialog box (accessed from the Animation menu).

Timing and looping are powerful features. In the remainder of this chapter we look at techniques for employing timing and looping to maximize the impact of GIF animations.

Looping and Timing Techniques

One of the most popular ways to give a Web animation some staying power is to make it loop. Effective looping can essentially turn a two-frame animation into a million-frame animation. Unfortunately, looping is also somewhat responsible for the bad reputation of GIF animations on the Web. When GIF animation emerged, Web pages quickly began to sport numerous blinking and otherwise annoying animated loops that distracted from, rather than enhanced, a given Web page's content.

Looping animations should almost always loop seamlessly. In other words, when a looping animation plays, it should be a little difficult to tell at what point the animation begins and ends. For example, the bouncing ball animation loops so that the ball appears to bounce forever (in spite of Newton's theories on gravity). In Chapter 5, Advanced Animation Techniques in Photoshop, we look at numerous techniques for generating animations that loop seamlessly. For now, let's look at some timing techniques that can help make looping animations more interesting.

In video, each frame is displayed for a set amount of time, typically 1/24th of a second. In GIF animation (as well as other Web animation technologies such as Shockwave, Flash, Java, and JavaScript), you can define the length of time each frame of an animation displays. Most utilities default to a standard delay for each frame (say, 10/100th of a second). If you like, one frame can display for 1/100th of a second and then the next frame can display for 100 seconds.

Creative timing can add depth to animations. A two-frame flashing light animation can become slightly more interesting when it flashes once every five seconds rather than twice every second. An example should help clarify this point. Figure 2-13 shows an animation that serves as a button to access ToyLab (toylab.com), a kids' online toy and game site. The animation starts with the text "ToyLab" over a blue background that suggests a laboratory. After about five seconds a little robot character peeps out from the upper-right edge of the animation. The character stares at you for about two seconds and then goes away. This animation repeats endlessly.

The timing of this animation works like this. The first frame is set to play for five seconds, the second and last frames play for one-tenth of a second, and the third frame plays for two seconds. If each frame were set to the GIF animation utility's default timing, each frame would play for one-tenth of a second and the animation would loop 2.5 times per second. If the animation played like that, the effect of the character peeping out would get old quickly. As it is, the five-second pause between peeks helps keep the effect fresher and helps prevent it from becoming annoying.

Figure 2-13   The first frame in this animation displays for five seconds, the third frame displays for two seconds, and the other frames display for a fraction of a second.

There are times when you should consider limiting the number of times your animation loops. Banner ads are particularly susceptible to becoming annoying after repeated looping. Figure 2-14 shows a banner ad for XaraXone (xaraxone.i-us.com), a site dedicated to the graphics application Corel Xara. The first frame is shown in the upper-left corner of the first column, and the final frame is at the bottom of the second column. The animation progresses from frame 1 down through column 1, then up to the top of column 2, and then down through column 2.

The 15-frame banner ad's timing works like this: the first frame plays for one second, then the next 13 frames play for one-tenth of a second each, and finally the last frame plays for four seconds, then the animation starts over again. Rather than loop infinitely, the animation stops looping after the fifth repetition. As noted earlier, GIF animations display their final frame when they stop looping. Note that the banner ad's main message—the text

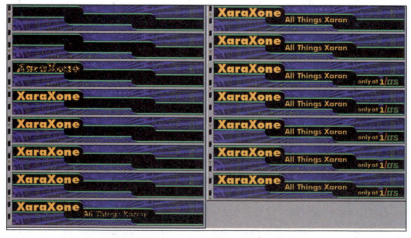

Figure 2-14   To keep the banner ad animation from becoming annoying, this animation loops only five times. The animation stops on the final frame. Copyright © i/us Corp. http://www.i-us.com.

"XaraXone, All Things Xaran, only at i/us"—is on the final frame. This key frame is the one that the animation stops looping on.

Incidentally, the timing in frame 1 of this animation is set to one second to help give time for the next 13 frames to load. All the frames after frame 1 are optimized (not shown in Figure 2-14), so they download much more quickly than frame 1. The extra second built into frame 1 not only helps make the looping more interesting but also provides a little extra time for the following frames to load. This technique allows the animation to play back smoothly on the first run.

These examples help underscore the point that timing can help make looping animations more interesting. So when you are creating your animations, consider trying to vary the timing somehow rather than keep each frame's timing set to the same duration. That said, it's worth noting that not all animations work well with varied timing. For example, Figure 2-15 shows an animation of a little space alien in a spaceship. Each frame in this animation is set to 5/100th of a second. Part of the animated effect is that the alien is bouncing around erratically. To maintain the effect that he is constantly flying in space, all the frames must play at the same rate.

Web animation times are typically set in hundredths of a second (or even thousandths of a second, as with JavaScript animations). However, we are used to seeing video in movies and on TV at 30 frames per second. Although in theory you can set Web animations to display hundreds or even thousands of frames per second, in reality this depends on the computer's ability to play that many frames within that time frame.

For example, if you set a series of GIF animation frames to display every 1/100th of a second, you would expect that it would display 100 frames per second. In fact, even some of the fastest computers will display the frames at a much slower rate. Indeed, you would probably hope it would, because if the frames were really displayed at 100 frames per second,

Figure 2-15 Each frame in this animation plays for the same amount of time.

everything would be a blur (and animations that were even one second long would have tremendous file sizes). Fortunately, even when delays are set to increments of thousandths of a second, most computers do well to display frames even at 30 frames per second and often achieve more like 15–20 frames per second at best.

As a result, it can be a little difficult to make an animation seem to be going fast. The basic solution is to add *motion blur* to the frames. Figure 2-16 shows an animation created by Eclipse Digital Imaging for XOOM Software. The animation depicts an out-of-control clock winding backward. Although the animation is set to display at 10 frames per second, one-third of video's normal speed, the motion blur added to the clock's hands creates the illusion that the animation is moving at a much faster rate. Because we are used to seeing clocks rotate clockwise, the counterclockwise movement coupled with the illusion of extremely fast movement makes the animation far more interesting than it would be if it moved like all the other analog clocks we are used to seeing.

Timing techniques—such as adding creative delays within an animation or adding blurring effects to make parts of the animation seem to go faster—can add interest to an animation, but one of the more effective timing tricks is to combine animations that have varied timings. Figure 2-17 shows a "crazy counter" animation that is really five separate animations combined. Each animation has its own unique timing. For example, the animation on the far right uses motion blurring, and each frame is set to display every 1/100th of a second. The animation second from the right alternates between frames that display for half a second and frames that display for one-tenth of a second. Because each animation plays at a different pace, the overall effect is a richer animation, as it is always slightly different in appearance. See Chapter 6, Seamless Integration, for more techniques that you can use to integrate animations seamlessly.

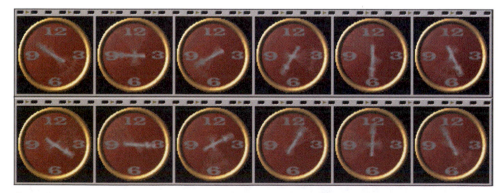

Figure 2-16   Adding motion blur creates the illusion of faster movement. Courtesy of Eclipse Digital Animation Factory. http://www.animfactory.com.

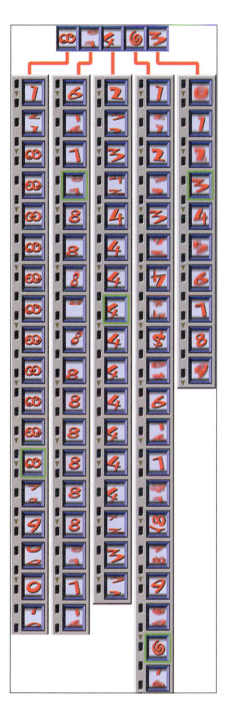

Figure 2-17 This "crazy counter" animation is really five separate animations, each with a unique timing.

▦ Summary

This chapter demonstrates that the basics of GIF animation can be used to generate animations that are anything but basic. Many of the examples show small animations that add substantially to the overall design of a Web page. With a little optimization and irregular timing, you can make a little animation go a long way. However, despite all that has been covered in this chapter, perhaps the most important trick of all is thoughtful implementation. Don't make the mistake of thinking that GIF animations don't require any thought. If you take the time to optimize your animations and use a little creative looping and timing, your GIF animations can become a compelling part of your overall Web designs.

CHAPTER **3**

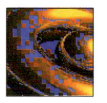

Mastering the Palette

One of the most common ways to reduce the overall file size of a GIF animation is to reduce the number of colors it contains. The fewer the colors, the smaller the file size. The problem is that when you have fewer colors to work with, the overall visual quality of the animation can suffer. The trick is to find the best trade-off between the number of colors and the overall visual quality of the animation. Achieving this balance is easy when you are armed with a little technical information and a few excellent tools. ▶

The key to this chapter is that when it comes to Web animation, visual integrity is not always the prime objective. In the interest of delivering animations more quickly, some amount of quality loss is often acceptable. Furthermore, animations benefit from an important factor: the pictures don't stay still. When images are displayed for short amounts of time, they are subjected to a reduced amount of scrutiny. In addition, our minds are somewhat distracted, at least initially, by the need to interpret the motion.

These factors allow Web animation designers a bit of leeway with which to balance the need to create visually compelling animations and the need to keep an animation's file size as small as possible. Before we discuss palette-related techniques, we need a conceptual framework. We present a basic understanding of the logic behind palettes and the reasons they work the way they do. It serves as a basis for the discussion and helps explain why it is sometimes worth going to great lengths to massage an animation's palette. With this foundational information in place, we then turn to a series of techniques that can be employed to deliver a balance of the best visual quality and the smallest possible file size for a Web animation.

How Color Affects File Size

Typically, the more colors there are in an animation, the larger its file size. Because of the way the GIF format is compressed (using the LZW compression scheme), this generalization is not always true, but it holds true for the majority of GIF animations. It's important to understand that each frame in an animation can have a maximum of 256 colors. These colors must be stored with the GIF file in a *palette*. The more colors in a palette, the larger the file's size.

To make matters worse, each frame in an animation can have a unique palette. Each palette adds three bytes for every color in the palette. So a 256-color palette adds 768 bytes to the animation—just for the palette information. Palette information is not compressible. If you have a 10-frame animation and each frame has its own unique 256-color palette, that's 7,680 bytes (7.5K) of data added to the animation. Once again, that's 7.5K for the palette information alone.

Fortunately, you can use a single color palette for all the frames in an animation. This palette is often referred to as a *global* palette. Because palette information in a GIF animation is not compressed, an excellent way to optimize a GIF animation is to use a global palette for all the frames and to minimize the number of colors in the global palette.

Understanding Bits and Bytes

It helps to understand why the words *bit* and *depth* are used in terms such as *bit depth*. *Bit* refers to the binary numbering system used by computers. A binary number system has only two numbers: 0 and 1. A *byte* is composed of eight bits. Because a bit has two potential values, you can calculate the potential number of values in a byte by multiplying the number 2 eight times (or by calculating 2 to the eighth power). By calculating 2^8 we arrive at 256 potential values in a byte. When we apply this math to digital imagery, it explains why an 8-bit image contains 256 potential colors. Furthermore, it explains why a 24-bit image potentially contains more than 16 million colors (2 to the power of 24 equals 16,777,216). So *depth* essentially refers to the number of bits in a color scheme. The higher the power that the number 2 is multiplied by, the greater the color depth. Put another way, the more potential colors an image has, the more depth it can be said to have.

When it comes to bits and bytes, even a neophyte should be familiar with one basic thing about the digital world. The more bits and bytes there are, the longer it will take the computer to process them and the longer it will take for all of them to travel over the Internet. Let's take the example of a simple one-inch-square image. Let's compare a TIFF image to a GIF image to help demonstrate that a large portion of an image's file size comes from the color information stored with the file.

A one-inch-square image at 72 pixels per inch (ppi) contains 5,184 pixels ($72 \times 72 = 5,184$). If each pixel contains 24 bits of color data, the entire image contains 124,416 bits of color data, which translates into roughly 15.2K just for the color information. As a rough test, open a bitmap editor and crop or create any image to one inch square and save it as an RGB TIFF image without LZW compression. In my tests, the file sizes ranged from 16.6K for a single-color image to 24K for a photographic image.

Taking the example of the single-color square image, if 15.2K of the 16.6K is color information, this means that the color data for the image takes up almost 92% of the overall file size. When this square is saved as a GIF, it is only 111 bytes. To be fair, the GIF format uses LZW compression. When the single-color one-inch-square TIFF image is saved with LZW compression, it is reduced to 3,120 bytes. That is much smaller, but there is still a difference of 3,009 bytes, most of it color data. That's 3,009 bytes of excessive data.

Web designers rarely, if ever, use TIFF images, but this example helps to point out how much data in a graphic image's file size can be composed of color data. Reducing the amount of color data in a GIF image is the driving motivation for taking the time to master palettes. The goal is to ensure that your Web animations (and still images, for that matter) contain no more color information than is absolutely necessary.

Why Use Palettes?

If you were paying attention earlier, you may have noticed that our single-color image contained only one color but when it was 24-bit the computer had to account for 16,777,215 other potential colors per pixel. This accounts for the 3,009 bytes of extra data. It didn't matter that there was only one actual color in the image; the computer color data essentially had to treat it as if it contained millions of colors.

As it turns out, very few bitmap images contain 16,777,216 pixels, and that means they can't possibly contain 16.7 million colors. Our one-inch image contains only 5,184 pixels and thus can display at most 5,184 colors. In most images, the same colors are often used on multiple pixels. In fact, it's extremely rare to find an image with 5,184 pixels that contains 5,184 separate colors. Furthermore, it's remarkably common for a one-inch-square image to contain only few hundred or even a few dozen colors.

It is here that palettes come in. Essentially, palettes can minimize the amount of color data that an image must contain by putting in the image only the data of the actual colors rather than the potential colors. To do this, the color of each pixel in a bitmap image is mapped or indexed to what is known as a color lookup table (CLUT). Another name for the CLUT is a palette or index, hence Photoshop's Indexed Color mode.

When a color image is displayed on a computer monitor, it uses the RGB (red, green, blue) color model. If you look at a color monitor with a magnifying glass, you will see that the screen comprises thousands of tiny red, green, and blue lights grouped together. You can achieve a wide range of colors by varying the amount of color displayed in each group. When bitmap images are in RGB color mode, their color scheme works in the same way: a range of colors is achieved by mixing RGB color values. Each color can have values ranging from 0 to 255. Each pixel in a bitmap image can have a unique RGB color value assigned to it.

Palettes or CLUTs are a collection of specific RGB color values used in a bitmap image. With digital images, you can create a palette from the colors contained within the image or index an image to a preexisting palette. When you create a palette using the colors contained within an image, the palette is known as an *adaptive* palette. When there are more colors in an image than can be mapped in a palette, some colors must be removed; the pixels that contained these colors must be remapped to different colors. Generally, software programs attempt to remap these pixels to colors similar to the removed colors.

As more colors are removed, the visual quality of an image begins to suffer. Many images contain subtle *gradients*, which are in essence smooth transitions of color. It is these areas that typically are most vulnerable to having colors removed. For example, a gradient from green to blue would contain a series of uniquely colored blue-green pixels to achieve a smooth gradient. If there are too many gradients in an image, many of these colors get removed.

You can use a technique called *dithering* to help alleviate the loss of image quality. Dithering attempts to simulate intermediate colors that are not in the palette by arraying subtle patterns of colors that are in the palette. For example, a computer might attempt to simulate a certain shade of orange by dithering two different shades of orange. When an image is remapped to a preexisting palette, dithering is effectively the only tool available for attempting to maintain the image's original visual integrity.

Dithering is something of an enemy to the GIF format, which employs the LZW compression algorithm. One of the main techniques of the LZW compression algorithm is run-length encoding. As described in Chapter 2, run-length encoding compresses an image by describing it as the sum of its same-color pixel horizontal runs. For example, if there are 10 blue pixels followed by 20 green pixels in a given row on a bitmap image, LZW essentially describes the image this way: "Draw 10 blue pixels. Draw 20 green pixels." Without LZW compression, the image would essentially be described as "Draw a blue pixel" 10 times and "Draw a green pixel" 20 times (see Figure 3-1).

The problem is that dithering results in far fewer contiguous strings of solid colors. Often, blocks of apparently solid-colored areas in an image are actually dithered. The problem is that software programs that index the images look at all the colors in the image, and they attempt to arrive at the best collection of colors and the best approach to dithering that will maintain the visual integrity of the image. The calculations and assumptions used to arrive at adaptive palettes can vary widely; usually, no two programs arrive at exactly the same palette for any given image or set of images. Some images will look overly polarized if you use no dithering, but you will almost always get better file size results by avoiding dithering.

Figure 3-1 LZW compression looks at an image line by line and attempts to describe it as groups of colored pixels rather than describe it one color or pixel at a time.

Before we move to the techniques, let's recap. Color data can take up a huge portion of a graphic's file size. Paletted or indexed images remove this problem by limiting the number of colors to 256. If an indexed image contains only a few colors, the palette can be reduced to only a few colors, thereby reducing the file size. When you reduce the number of colors in an image, it is important to be mindful of the resultant dithering, which can adversely effect the LZW compression scheme used by the GIF format. Now let's look at what can be drawn from these basic premises.

Palette Considerations During Production

The way many designers create GIF animations is counterproductive. Often, they generate the frames for the animation and become concerned with the palette only when they get to the point of compiling the frames into a GIF animation. An increasing number of programs take a series of images and conform all of them to a single global palette. Some programs do a better job than others. Notable applications include HVS Animator Pro, GIFmation, and Equilibrium's Debabelizer Pro.

For many animations, this process works just fine. As noted earlier, many images condense easily to 256 colors or fewer without apparent loss of visual integrity. An automated approach to creating a global palette often does not produce the smallest possible file size for a given animation, but in many cases it's not worth the trouble to create your global palette manually in an effort to shave off a few extra bytes. However, there are plenty of important reasons to keep the palette in mind during production (while you are creating or compiling your animation's frames), whether or not you are going to create your global palette manually.

Using the Web Palette

A significant factor that justifies early attention to palettes for many GIF animations is the Web palette. (For background information about the Web palette, see the sidebar, Why Do Browsers Use the Web Palette?) The idea of using any colors you like in your adaptive palette would work great if there weren't any 8-bit video cards out there. Unfortunately, adap-

WHY DO BROWSERS USE THE WEB PALETTE?

All color monitors are powered by some sort of video card. Video cards vary in the number of colors they can display. Although many recent computer systems sell with video cards capable of displaying millions of colors, not long ago the vast majority of systems sold with 8-bit video cards, which are capable of displaying only 256 colors. When a video card can display millions of colors, it doesn't matter how many different types of color images are displayed on the screen at once. With millions of colors to choose from, the images are always displayed in perfect color (or at least as "perfect" as the given monitor is capable of).

An 8-bit video card doesn't have the benefit of millions of colors. It can display only 256 colors at a time. When an 8-bit video card encounters a 24-bit image, it must decide which of those 256 colors to display. In effect, it reduces millions of colors to 256 colors on-the-fly. The more images on the page, the more they will tend to suffer from the color reduction, because the video card must balance its limited set of colors between all of them. These on-the-fly conversions are not insubstantial, but video cards typically feature chips that help them to make the conversion quickly.

Further complicating the situation, the Macintosh and Windows operating systems use slightly different palettes. One of the basic ideas behind palettes is that each of the 256 colors on an 8-bit system can potentially be assigned to any one of the 16.7 million possible color values in the RGB color space. However, both the Macintosh and Windows have fixed colors to help ensure that their respective interface elements (such as menu bars and dialog buttons) remain readable. The Macintosh reserves two colors, and Windows reserves 20.

Because browsers are necessarily cross-platform, they have adopted a method of

tive palettes get replaced with what has come to be known as the Web palette: a set of colors chosen for mathematical reasons rather than artistic ones.

Figure 3-2 is a simple animation containing four frames. It comprises two major colors—a burgundy and a green—although there are actually five colors in this animation's adaptive palette. A close-up of one of the frames (Figure 3-3) shows what will be displayed on a system capable of displaying 24-bit color. In this case, the browser employs the capable video card's vast color

dealing with using a standardized palette that has come to be known as the Web palette. When a browser is employed on an 8-bit system, it automatically converts all images, whether 24-bit or 2-bit, displayed within its window to the Web palette. Using a standardized palette allows browsers to quickly make conversions from millions of colors to only 256 colors equitably on the Macintosh as well as the Windows platform.

The downside to the Web palette is that it was chosen more on its mathematical merits than on its visual merits. The Web palette comprises 216 colors. It is a 6×6×6 color cube composed of 20% steps each for red, green, and blue (for example, 20% blue, 40% blue, and so on). These steps are rather large. The result is that the Web palette does not contain a range of colors suited for gradients, and some hues, particularly browns, are not well represented.

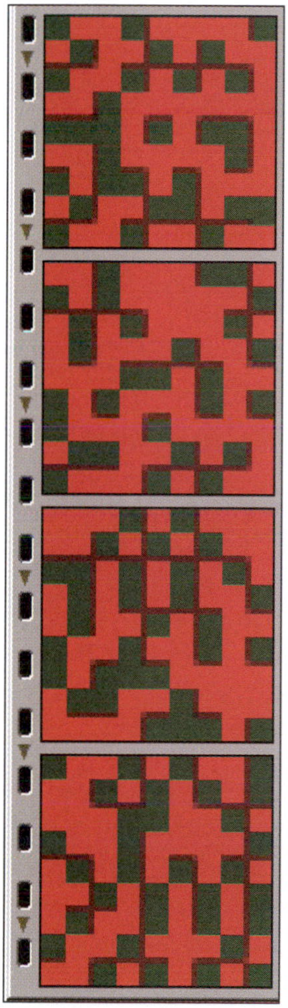

Figure 3-2 This animation is largely composed of two colors, although there are actually five colors in its adaptive palette.

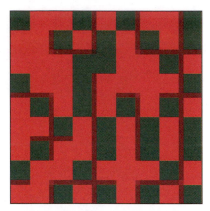

Figure 3-3   A close-up of one of the animation's frames shows how the artwork is displayed on a 24-bit system.

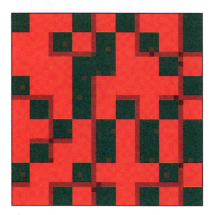

Figure 3-4   The artwork becomes heavily dithered when displayed on an 8-bit system.

range and respects the animation's adaptive color palette. Figure 3-4 shows what happens on an 8-bit system. Because none of the colors in the animation matches the Web palette, the browser must use colors from the Web palette to dither a mix of colors in what is usually a vain attempt at matching the colors in the animation's adaptive palette.

Fortunately, there is an easy solution to this problem: create the animation using colors from the Web palette. If an animation's adaptive palette happens to contain colors that are in the Web palette, the browser won't have to convert those colors; your animation's nice solid colors won't be reduced to a dithered mess. A handy place to access the Web palette is in Photoshop's Swatch palette. Adobe's use of the word *palette* to describe its tabbed/collapsible dialog box is confusing because the "Swatch palette" itself serves to house color palettes. Nevertheless, if you follow these simple steps, you can gain easy access to the colors in the Web palette within Photoshop.

1. Open a new RGB document of any size filled with any color. The only thing that matters is that the document be RGB.

2. Select **Indexed Color** from the Image, Mode menu. Select **Web** from the Palette drop-down menu and press **OK**.

3. Select **Color Table** from the Image, Mode menu. Click **Save** and save the palette with the Adobe Color Table extension (.ACT). Name it **Web.act** and press **OK**.

4. If the Swatch palette isn't open, select **Show Swatches** from the Window menu. Click on the right-pointing arrow in the Swatch palette. At this point you can add the Web palette to the colors in the current swatch by choosing **Load Swatches**, or you can replace the current swatch with

There is an easy way to determine whether a color is part of the Web palette: look at its RGB or Hex color values. A red, green, or blue value of a color in the Web palette can be only one of six numbers: 0, 51, 102, 153, 204, or 255. Similarly, each of the hexadecimal values for red, green, and blue can be only one of six values: 00, 33, 66, 99, CC, or FF. For example, you know that a color with RGB values of 0, 255, 51 is from the Web palette because each RGB value is one of the six possible RGB values. On the other hand, if the RGB values were 1, 254, 52 you can be sure that it's not part of the Web palette because none of those RGB values is among the six possible values for a color in the Web palette.

the Web palette swatch by choosing **Replace Swatches**. Whichever you choose, change the Files of Type field from .ACO to **.ACT**; then find and load the color table you saved in step 3. If you choose **Replace Swatches**, your Photoshop Swatch palette should look like Figure 3-5. If you want to get Photoshop's default color swatch back, select **Reset Swatches** from the Swatch palette's pop-up menu. After you have the Web palette loaded in the Swatch palette, you can use the eyedropper tool to select colors.

Figure 3-5 Photoshop's Swatch palette with the Web palette loaded.

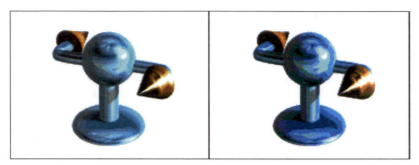

Figure 3-6   The left image employs an adaptive 64-color palette, and the image on the
right is set to the Web palette.

Because there has been a lot of hype about the Web palette among Web designers, you
might assume that you should create all your Web graphics and animations using the Web
palette. Usually, this assumption is nonsense. Figure 3-6 shows a frame from an animation
created by T. Michael Scott using Extreme 3D. The version on the left employs a 64-color
adaptive palette. Although you can see dithering close-up, when viewed at its normal size
the dithering is fairly difficult to see, especially while the animation is playing. The version
on the right was set to the Web palette, which contains 216 colors—or three times as many
colors as the 64-color adaptive palette employed in the other version. Despite the additional colors, the version on the right is clearly banded. Even when the animation is viewed
at 50% of its normal size, the banding is still clearly visible.

Assuming that you don't want to lose that much visual quality, this example demonstrates
that using the Web palette for an animation's global palette is undesirable. People viewing
your animations with 8-bit cards may see your animations this way no matter what, but
why subject the increasing number of 24-bit viewers to such visual torture? It makes sense
to use the Web palette whenever you have a solid color in your animation for which a color
from the Web palette can easily be switched; if you can live with one of the colors in the
Web palette, it's easy to use it. But using the Web palette for the global palettes of all your
GIF animations is simply a formula for a lot of bad-looking animations.

Reducing Colors to Eight Bits

Another important consideration when you produce GIF animations is the overall range
of color contained within the frames. Although many animations fit nicely into a 256-color
palette, it is easy to create a series of frames that does not fit that limitation. Figure 3-7
shows a few frames from an animation created by Scott Balay in Bryce 3D. Notice that its
transparency and color change over time. Also note that the 3-D animation has smooth
and subtle gradients. In Figure 3-8 the animation has been converted to a 256-color GIF

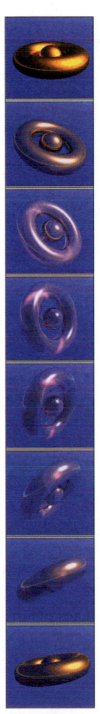

Figure 3-7 The frames from this animation are seen here at 24-bit.

Figure 3-8 The same animation reduced to a 256-color palette.

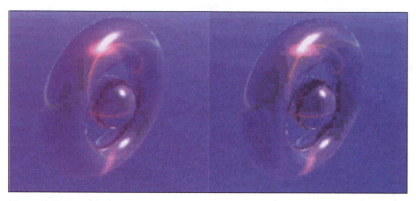

Figure 3-9   The version on the left is 24-bit, and the version on the right is 8-bit.

animation. As shown by a side-by-side comparison of one of the frames (Figure 3-9), each frame has become very blocky. Although the color shift that occurs throughout the 3-D animation is fairly slight, it is too much for the 256-color limitation of an 8-bit palette.

Figure 3-10 shows what happens when one frame of the animation is given preference over the others. In this example, the first frame's contents have been reduced to 256 colors, and then the remaining frames were conformed to the palette. Consequently, the first frame looks nearly as good as in the original 24-bit version, but the rest of the animation is butchered.

Three-dimensional animations typically suffer when reduced to 256 or fewer colors. Their precisely rendered highlights, shadows, reflections, and transparency often result in an increased number of colors per frame compared with other types of animation.

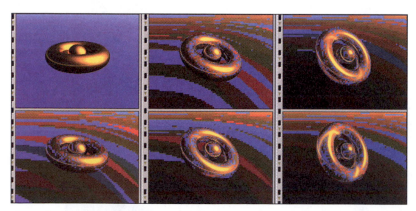

Figure 3-10   When the first frame is given precedence over the other frames in the animation, it looks fine, but the rest of the frames in the animation suffer visibly.

However, you can make it easier for 3-D animations to fit within the 256-color limit. Figure 3-11 shows an animation created by Scott Balay using formZ Renderzone for Eyeland (eyeland.com). This animation has a 64-color adaptive palette. A close-up of one of the frames (Figure 3-12) shows that the visual quality of the 3-D animation doesn't suffer very much from the diminutive palette.

There are several reasons that the quality does not suffer. First, the dimensions of this animation are smaller than those of the animation shown in Figure 3-7 (the Bryce animation). The larger the dimensions of the animation, the more pixels there are in an image and thus the more potential colors contained in the overall animation. Conversely, the smaller an animation, the easier it is to reduce its palette because a by-product of the smaller dimensions is typically that there are fewer colors.

Another important reason that smaller dimensions help is that the gradients are also smaller. The wider a gradient is, the more colors it takes to generate a smooth transition between colors. Smaller animations tend to have smaller gradients, and that translates into fewer colors.

Smaller gradients are another reason that this animation survives a color diet better. Notice that all the moving parts of the animation in Figure 3-11 (the formZ animation) are small and thin. The little rods are so thin that even though they appear 3-D, their dimensionality is achieved with only a few colors.

In addition, the lighting does not result in wide gradients because the transitions between the highlights and shadows are not gradual. Also, note that the results of the color reduction show up most on the inside curves of the silver eye shape, where the gradients are most pronounced; but all the motion is generated by the small blue rods, thus drawing the viewer's eye and distracting from these areas. For a simple technique for reducing gradients, see the sidebar Tightening Gradients with Photoshop's Posterize Filter.

Finally, this animation doesn't change color. The blues are always blue, the reds red, and the silvers silver. Therefore, unlike the animation in Figure 3-7, this animation's palette doesn't have to accommodate a series of color shifts over a range of different gradients. The gradients required for dimensionality in a 3-D image make it tough to reduce 3-D animations to 256 or fewer colors, but when the colors shift from frame to frame you have a unique set of gradients on each frame, exacerbating the problem of color reduction.

TIGHTENING GRADIENTS WITH PHOTOSHOP'S POSTERIZE FILTER

An easy way to tighten gradients slightly is to apply Photoshop's Posterize filter. Appropriate settings depend on the image, but generally you should use a setting that isn't so low that it causes noticeable banding but isn't so high that it has no visible effect. In Figure 3-13 **Posterize** has been applied to the image on the right with **Levels** set to **20**. The result is that the shadows have deepened and the transitions between the gradients are thinned.

Banding is often a result of posterization, but the Posterize tool can give you an added level of control over where the banding will occur. In this example, the banding is more visible along the shading gradients. Because the eye is often drawn toward light (thus the highlights), this tradeoff is a desirable one. In this example, the shadows are sacrificed slightly, but the gradients along the highlights have become thinner without introducing excessive banding. The overall result is a reduced color range for the entire animation. ❯

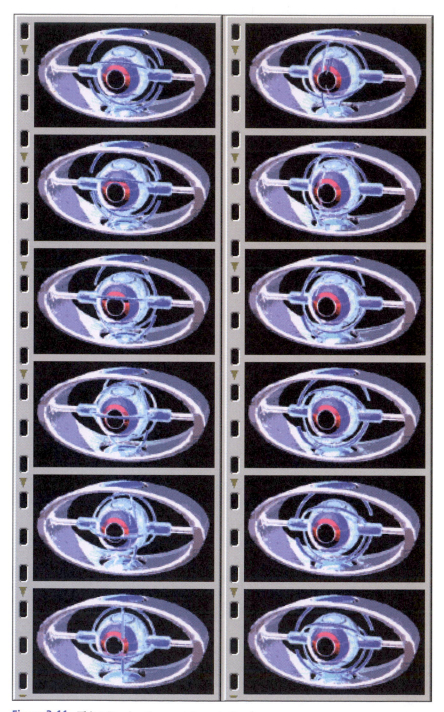

Figure 3-11   This 3-D animation contains only 64 colors.

Figure 3-12   The image quality of the 3-D imagery suffers little despite the small palette.

To fulfill the ideal of keeping colors within a reasonable range, not all frames in an animation need the same colors. Figure 3-14 is an animation from Dreamworks Record's Forest for the Trees site (http://www.dreamworksrec.com/forestforthetrees/) created by Eric Johnson. This animation is an animated collage in which each frame contains a unique subject and the colors used on each frame change abruptly. Although some banding is vaguely noticeable, particularly in frames 3 and 7, overall the animation has weathered the color reduction very well.

The color reduction works because all the frames are kept within a reasonable range of colors. Three of the frames are confined to gray tones, and two of them are limited to browns and tans. The remaining three frames are largely greens and blues with some red and yellow splashes. Also notice that the more-colorful frames alternate with the frames having grays and browns (the progression in Figure 3-14 goes from top to bottom within each row as you go from left to right). The impact of the more-colorful frames is increased because of the contrast, so in a sense the animation appears to be more colorful than it actually is.

Figure 3-13   The image on the right was Posterized in Photoshop to reign in the gradients.

Figure 3-14   This animation, by Eric Johnson, appears to be relatively colorful, and it survives the reduction to 256 colors very well. Courtesy of Eric Johnson, VisionTank.

We have looked at three fundamental techniques for reigning in an animation's palette: make the animation smaller, try to limit the range of the gradients, and keep the colors within reasonable ranges. Now let's look at one final factor you need to consider in relation to the color palette when you are producing an animation: transparency.

Accommodating Transparency

Chapter 4, Frame Cropping and Interframe Transparency Optimization, thoroughly covers transparency, but here we take a quick look at how transparency relates to palettes. Many animation programs not only create a global palette but also automatically generate interframe transparency. However, these automated processes can often be less than ideal, and also you may want to ensure that transparency will occur precisely where you want it to. Let's look at an example.

Figure 3-15 shows an animation that features artwork for a stylized television. Notice that the background and the outline of the TV are the same in every frame. Only the screen and a tiny meter below the screen change from frame to frame. In the interest of maximum compression, the areas of the frames that are always static should always be transparent on every frame except the first one. Figure 3-16 shows the animation as optimized by Ulead's GIF Animator 2.0. The red ellipses show areas where Ulead GIF Animator has fallen down on the job. Small portions of these frames have not been made transparent as they should be, bloating the animation's file size unnecessarily. (Not all GIF animation utilities make

Figure 3-15 A large portion of each frame in this animation is redundant.

this error. For example, GIF Movie Gear, GIFmation, HVS Animator Pro, and ColorWorks: Web 3 all handled the interframe transparency for this example correctly.)

To ensure that the transparency will be handled correctly, you can manually assign the transparency. To do this, you add a color to the color palette that you can select for

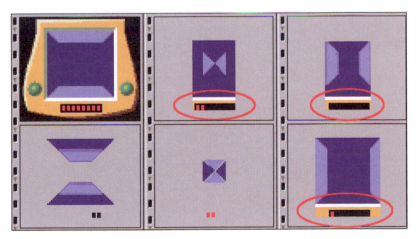

Figure 3-16 Ulead GIF Animator 2.0's auto optimization has failed to make all redundant pixels transparent.

transparency. If you are using Photoshop (or any other program that supports layering), this is easy to do. You simply create a layer that defines the transparency. For example, in Figure 3-17 a layer called Transparency was created. The light blue color covers areas of the animation that do not change from frame to frame.

After creating the Transparency layer over all the other layers, I used it to create all the frames for the animation (except the first frame, which doesn't need to be transparent). For example, to create the second frame I made visible the Transparency layer and the layer with the art for the second frame. Then I selected all, chose **Copy Merged** (from the Edit menu in Photoshop), and then pasted the animation into a new document. (We look at this approach to generating GIF animation frames with Photoshop more closely in Chapter 5, Advanced Animation Techniques in Photoshop.) If you are exporting the frames for your GIF animation manually for utilities that do not allow you to specify the color to be used for transparency (such as GIF Construction Set), you can use Photoshop's GIF89a Export filter to specify the transparency of each frame by selecting the color established by the Transparency layer.

Remember, we're talking here about palettes. The point is that your palette must include any colors that will be used to define transparency. For the purposes of this discussion, the important thing is that you ensure that certain portions of your animation are transparent by setting up your animation's frames as just described. Using this technique, your anima-

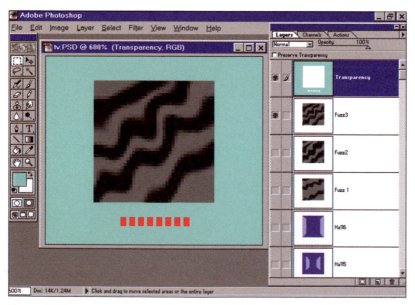

Figure 3-17   A separate layer is filled with the color for transparency to ensure that those portions of the animation's frame are transparent.

tion's global palette will include the color you need for transparency whether or not the animation utility generates your global palette for you.

Most GIF animation utilities allow you to select a color for transparency, and because all the frames after the first one are set to a predefined color, you can easily define the transparency for the animation manually. Whenever you predefine the transparency using this technique, be sure to use a unique color on the transparency layer. The light blue color was chosen because it was not used elsewhere in the animation.

Creating a Global Palette Manually

As we mentioned, many GIF animation utilities create global palettes for you. If your GIF animation program is one that imports layered Photoshop files (such as GIF Movie Gear or GIFmation), this method works well. These programs create a global palette from all the frames in the animation and generally arrive at a respectable global palette. However, these utilities do not let you selectively give preference to portions of the animation when creating the global palette. In many cases, you may want certain portions of the animation to look better. To put it another way, you may be willing to sacrifice certain portions of an animation.

Many animations stop on the first or final frame, so you might want to improve the appearance of the final frame. Also, animations typically have a main subject—something that you want the viewer to focus on—and the rest of animation's contents are peripheral. If so, you might want to give the subject more color preference, sacrificing the surroundings. Because the eye tends to follow the subject, the surroundings tend to receive less scrutiny.

Another reason that you might want to create your own global palette is that some GIF animation utilities use poor approaches to creating global palettes. For example, some utilities make a global palette based on the first frame of the animation. This approach becomes problematic if new colors are introduced after the first frame of the animation.

If you are not using a GIF animation utility that imports layered Photoshop files (such as GIF Construction Set, Ulead GIF Animator, and SPG Web Tools), you must export each frame as a separate GIF. If you do this without first creating a global palette, the GIF animation utility will be at a slight disadvantage when it creates the global palette because each frame has its own palette. If you have a three-frame animation and you export each frame separately without creating a global palette, each frame will have its own palette.

When the GIF animation utility sets out to make the global palette for the three GIF images, it must generate the global palette using only the colors found in the three images,

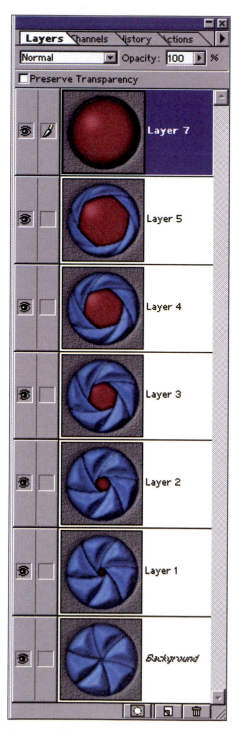

Figure 3-18   These seven layers in Photoshop are the basis for a 14-frame animation.

deriving it from a maximum of 768 colors (256×3). On the other hand, if you create the global palette from all the frames while they're still in 24-bit, the global palette will be derived from a much wider range of colors and potentially will be better.

To manually create a global palette in Photoshop, you arrange all the frames of the animation onto one layer and then index that layer. Figure 3-18 shows the layered frames for an aperture animation in Photoshop. Although the final animation will be 14 frames long (to create the opening and closing motions of the aperture), these seven frames constitute the basic frames of the animation and are all that you need to create the global palette. The animation's size is 80 pixels square.

The following steps assume that you have a series of animated frames on separate layers in Photoshop. Each frame should be fully opaque. In Chapter 5, you will learn how to use Photoshop to create frames for animations. For now, you can follow along by opening the Photoshop file named ap_anim1.psd located in the Chapter 3 directory on this book's companion CD-ROM. Save the document before you proceed. The adjustments to the file made in the following steps need only be temporary. When you are finished, you can select **File: Revert** to restore the file.

1. Increase the canvas size of the document so that all the frames in the animation can be viewed at once. The easiest way to determine how big the canvas should be is to multiply the height or width of the animation in pixels by the number of frames in the animation. In this example, the animation is 80 pixels high, and there are seven frames, so you make the canvas 560 pixels high. It does not matter whether you use the height or width of the document; just choose one. We use height in this example. Select **Image: Canvas Size**, fix the height, change the Anchor to the top middle (as shown in Figure 3-19), and press **OK**.

2. Now all your frames should be at the top of the canvas, one atop the other. Now you need to array each frame so that all of them are visible. You could manually move each frame, but there is an easier way.

   Assuming that one of your animation's frames is on the background layer, select the second layer or frame up from the frame on the background layer. Select the **Offset** filter from the Filter, Other menu. In the Offset filter dialog box, set Horizontal to zero and Vertical to the height of your animation, as shown in Figure 3-20. Again, the sample animation is 80 pixels high, so I set the offset to **0** pixels horizontally and **80** pixels vertically. Note that positive values in the vertical field move the affected layer down.

   After you apply the offset, the second layer or frame is moved directly below the other layer or frames. Now select the next frame or layer up from the background layer and press **Ctrl+F** (PC) or **Command+F** (Mac) two times to reapply the filter. This action moves the next layer into position.

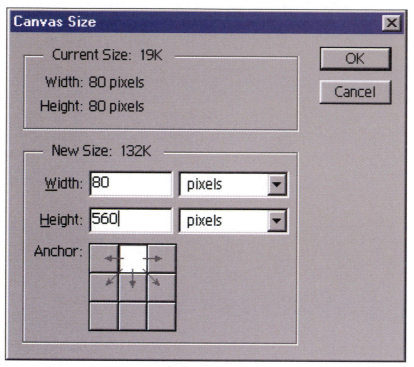

Figure 3-19 Set the anchor point in Photoshop's Canvas Size dialog box to the top center position.

Repeat this process for each layer or frame, increasing the number of times you press the shortcut key to reapply the Offset filter by one each time you go up a layer. When all the layers or frames are visible, choose **Flatten Image** from the layer's palette pop-up menu. Now you have all the frames arrayed on a single layer in Photoshop, as shown in Figure 3-21.

At this point you could create the global palette, but I chose this animation to demonstrate how you can use Photoshop's selections to influence the color selection. When the aperture is fully open in this scene it reveals a burgundy button. This button is shaded, resulting in a lot of gradients. These gradients could easily break apart or become banded when the animation is reduced to 256 colors (or fewer). So we want to give preference to the colors in the button so that it will look as nice as possible.

Fortunately, Photoshop makes it easy for you to give preference to a given area when indexing: you simply place a selection around the area or areas you wish to prioritize. When Photoshop indexes the image to create the palette, it gives precedence to the colors within any selections. Zoom in on the frame that shows the burgundy button

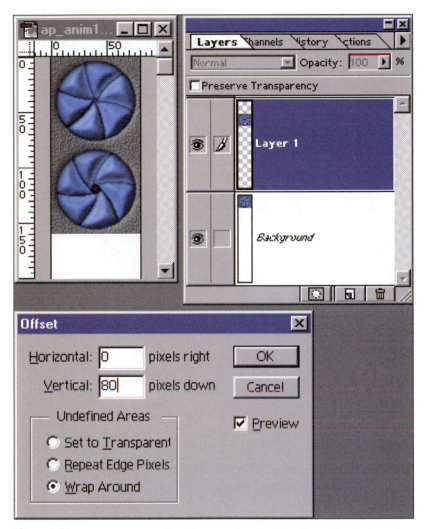

Figure 3-20 Use Photoshop's Offset filter to easily and accurately position the layered frames.

open fully (see Figure 3-22). Next, draw an elliptical marquee around the burgundy button as shown in Figure 3-22. (To get the circular marquee tool, click and hold on the rectangular marquee tool in Photoshop's toolbox and select the circular marquee tool.)

3. Now you have all your layers arrayed on the background of the resized document and have made your selections to influence the selection of colors. It's time to make your global palette. To do this, select **Indexed Color** from the Image, Mode menu. Change the Palette drop-down menu to **Adaptive**, select a bit depth, and set the Dither option

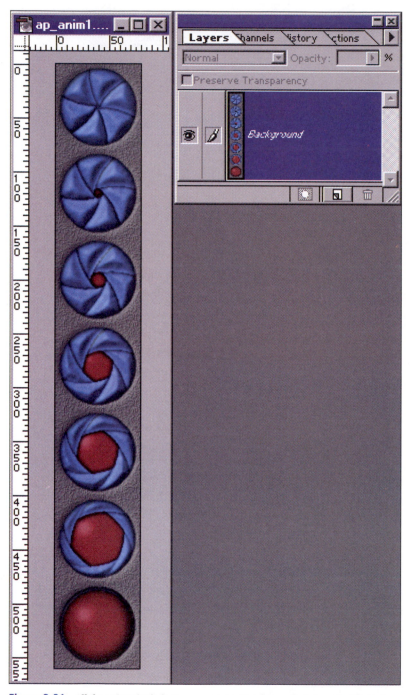

Figure 3-21   All the animation's frames are now arrayed on a single layer in Photoshop, each in full view.

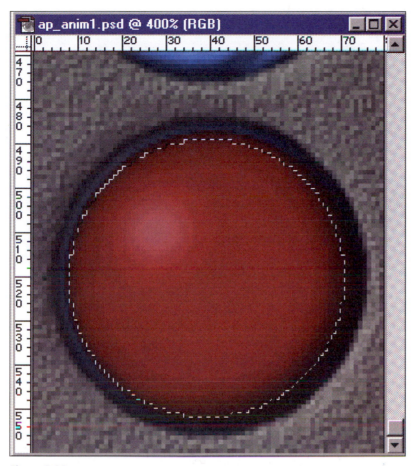

Figure 3-22 During the indexing process Photoshop gives preference to colors within selections.

to **Diffusion**. Set Color Matching to **Best**, and leave Preserve Exact Colors off, as shown in Figure 3-23. You can use a bit depth of 8 bits/pixel, but it's a little smarter to try something smaller, such as 4 bits/pixel (16 colors) or 5 bits/pixel, first. If you don't like the results of the color reduction after you index the file, you can simply undo the process and try again. But if the palette is passable at a low bit depth, you can use the smaller palette.

If your animation already has fewer than 256 colors, Photoshop will default to the **Exact palette** option. Such an animation will likely survive a drop into the lower bit depths easily. If this is the case, try changing the palette option back to **Adaptive** and select a bit depth that has fewer colors than the exact number. For example, if the

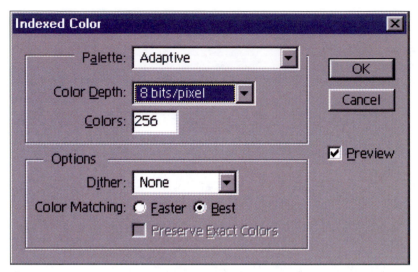

Figure 3-23   When you create global palette, set Photoshop's Palette options to
Adaptive and Dither: None, and set Color Matching to Best in the Indexed
Color dialog box.

Indexed Color dialog box defaults to an exact palette of 75 colors, it means that your
animation has only 75 total colors. In this case, it would be worth trying to get away
with 6-bit (64 colors) or even 5-bit (32 colors). If your animation contains only 64 colors, it certainly doesn't need an 8-bit (256-color) global palette.

Also note that you need not use the number of colors contained within each bit depth.
That is, you don't have to use 256, 128, 64, 32, 16, 8, 4, or 2 colors in your palette. It
can contain 200 colors instead of 256 colors, and the file size of the animation will reflect the smaller number of colors.

4. Apply the Indexed Color dialog box and examine the results. If you approve, select
    Color Table from the Image, Mode menu. Click **Save**, give the palette a recognizable
    name, and save the file with the **.ACT** extension. If you will be importing this global
    palette into an animation utility that supports only the Microsoft Palette .PAL format,
    save the palette in that format. Mac users need not specify an extension, but it's help-
    ful to include the word *palette* in the file name. After you've saved the animation's
    global palette from the Color Table dialog box, cancel out of it and select **Revert** from
    the File menu to revert to the 24-bit layered version of the Photoshop file.

    The remaining steps assume that you are creating frames for a GIF animation pro-
    gram that does not import layered Photoshop files (which means that you need not

export a bunch of GIF frames). If your GIF animation utility doesn't import layered Photoshop files, you must export each frame of the animation using the global palette you just created.

5. Select one of the frames or layers in the document, select all, and copy. Open a new document with the default file size (which should automatically be the size of the frame you just copied). Now paste the frame into the new document and merge to the background.

6. Select **Indexed Color** and choose **Custom** from the Palette menu. Press **OK**, and you will be presented with the Color Table dialog box. If the palette you just created is not already in the Color Table dialog box, select **Load** and find the palette you saved in step 4. Press **OK** to apply the custom palette to the frame in the new document.

    Before you proceed, let's pause a moment and point out what you've just done. When you copied the frame to a new document and merged it to the background, it made a separate file that you could apply a custom index to. You don't want to do this to your layered document because you can't index a layered file (you can, but you lose the layers in the process), and you want to leave your 24-bit layered file alone so that you can come back to it if anything goes wrong. For example, if you have a lot of custom palettes, you might accidentally apply the wrong one. In this case, it will help greatly to have a 24-bit version of the animation's frames if you need to start over.

    So when you created a new document and applied the custom palette to it, you assigned a predefined set of colors to it. This predefined set of colors takes into account the content of all the animation's frames and not just the one you are currently working on. So every time you do this for each frame, you are making sure that each frame uses exactly the same set of colors. Because these colors were derived from all the frames in the animation, this global palette works very well for every frame in the animation.

7. Select **GIF89a Export** from the File, Export menu and export the frame as a GIF file. If you have predefined portions of a frame for transparency as described earlier, select that color in the GIF89a Export Options dialog box. Be sure to save the file using an easy-to-recognize name that allows you to easily determine the sequence of the animation. For example, I named my first frame apertur1.gif, the second one apertur2.gif, and so on.

    You could repeat steps 5 through 7 for each frame, but here's a little shortcut. Photoshop automatically indexes an image when it is pasted into an indexed file. So all you need to do is to copy and paste each frame into the document you created in step 7. Each time you paste the frame into the document and merge it to the background, that frame will be indexed to the global palette. Then you can save the frame as a GIF and then copy and paste the next frame.

Which Adaptive Palette Is Best?

A tremendous amount of time, energy, money, and research has been invested in the effort to develop an optimal approach to creating an adaptive palette. Depending on the assumptions in the algorithms, it is easy to come up with substantially different adaptive color palettes for the same image. Let's take a quick look at some of the basic strategies to arriving at an adaptive palette.

Early programs that performed adaptive palette conversions (including past versions of Photoshop—version 4 and earlier—and Equilibrium's Debabelizer) used a relatively crude technique for generating an adaptive palette. Essentially, these programs would look at an image from a statistical standpoint and choose the colors for the adaptive palette by deciding which colors were most common within the image. So, for example, if the image had 10 pixels with a given RGB value (say, blue) and only two pixels with a different RGB value (say, red), it might toss the red out of the palette and keep blue.

Newer approaches put more emphasis on how the human eye perceives color. Studies show that most people are more sensitive to lightness (also referred to as *value*) in reds and greens than in blues. Also, people are more sensitive to the subtleties in the midtones than in the highlights and shadows. In addition, people's eyes tend to be more offended by banding within gradients than they are by abrupt color shifts at the fringes of areas in an image where the colors change from one color to another.

Many programs, such as Digital Frontiers HVS Color, Boxtop Software's PhotoGIF, and Adobe Photoshop 5, generate adaptive palettes by using algorithms that take these and other important factors into consideration. As a result, these adaptive palettes tend to be technically better than those generated using the more brute force statistical method.

The question is whether "technically better" translates into palettes that are better in practice. That is, can the average viewer see the difference? The idea of using an adaptive palette algorithm that takes human perception into account makes sense to designers who want to be more sensitive to the nuances of human visual perception. However, can the average user see the difference? Should designers who don't use such utilities be worried about the quality of their animations? Let's look at an example.

Figure 3-24 shows two versions of a frame from a GIF animation created by NavWorks (navworks.i-us.com). This image was chosen because of its numerous shades of color and subtle gradients. Both versions of the animation's frame have been indexed to a 64-color

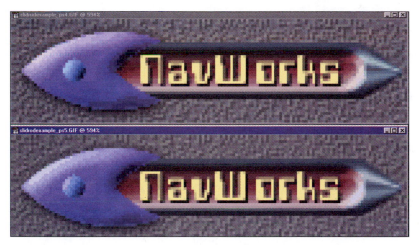

Figure 3-24 An image indexed with Adobe Photoshop 4 (top) and with Adobe Photoshop 5 (bottom).

(6-bit), diffusion-dithered palette. The version on the top was indexed with Adobe Photoshop 4, and the version on the bottom was indexed with Adobe Photoshop 5.

If you compare the two versions, you notice that, if anything, Photoshop 4 seems to have done a better job of indexing, at least in terms of banding. If you look closely at the light blue curved left-pointing arrow element, you see that the Photoshop 4 version has less banding than the Photoshop 5 version even though Photoshop 5 uses an algorithm that is supposed to be more sophisticated.

To be fair, it would probably be easy to find an image that showed very different results. Furthermore, Photoshop 5's algorithm certainly can't lay claim to being the best at taking human visual perception into account. (Look to programs such as HVS ColorGIF, PhotoGIF, and recent versions of Debabelizer for better adaptive palette algorithms.) The point is that you might be justified if you didn't concern yourself with the issue of adaptive color palette algorithms.

For example, although it's not very hard to see the differences between the two versions of the GIF animation frame shown in Figure 3-24, this is because we're looking at it from a zoomed-in perspective. When this animation actually plays, the animation will be much smaller, making it much harder to see such details. Furthermore, the movement of the animation will further distract us from seeing the details.

In any case, it's always best to use the best tools that you have at your disposal. I do not mean to imply here that you shouldn't use utilities or programs that use more-sophisticated adaptive palette algorithms. However, designers who do not have these utilities shouldn't worry that their animations are suffering. In fact, as the example here implies, you might be better off with a utility that uses the older approach to generating adaptive palettes.

Color Locking with Adobe ImageReady

Adobe ImageReady introduced a valuable feature for color reduction of GIF animations: the ability to lock colors during color reduction. Let's look at an example to see what the problem is so that you can understand the benefits of ImageReady's solution. Figure 3-25 shows a series of frames for a small (88×31) banner button animation for i/us Corporation (i-us.com).

Notice that although the animation is fairly colorful, there are only a few colors in the animation. Aside from colors introduced through anti-aliasing, there are mauve, yellow, orange, green, and six shades of blue. This animation is very small, so the subtle details in the anti-aliased portions aren't subject to a great deal of scrutiny. Therefore, this animation should be able to survive color reduction to 32 colors. This would give each major color at least three colors for anti-aliasing, which is more than enough for such a small animation.

Figure 3-26 shows the animation after it has been reduced to a 32-color palette with GIF Movie Gear. If you compare Figure 3-26 with Figure 3-25, you see that there has been some

Figure 3-25   A series of frames for a small banner animation. Copyright © i/us Corp. http://www.i-us.com.

Figure 3-26   The animation after reduction to a 32-color palette. Copyright © i/us Corp. http://www.i-us.com.

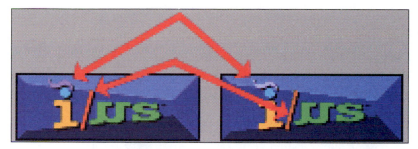

Figure 3-27   A frame from the original 256-color animation (right) and from the 32-color version (left). Arrows indicate changed colors. Copyright © i/us Corp. http://www.i-us.com.

noticeable color shifting. Figure 3-27 compares a frame from the original 256-color animation (on the right) to a frame from the 32-color version (on the left). As you can see, the mauve-colored "tilde" sign has changed color, and the orange slash has changed color.

As would be the case with most corporate logos, this color shift is unacceptable. Using a 64-color palette solves the problem, but it also adds more than 2K to the file size. Fortunately, Adobe ImageReady provides a solution. Adobe ImageReady allows you to select the key colors in an animation and then lock them. If you do this before attempting to reduce the colors in the palette (or attempting to optimize the animation's palette), ImageReady will remove other colors but not the locked colors.

For example, Figure 3-28 shows the eyedropper tool in ImageReady being used to select the orange color on the slash. Notice that the orange color is outlined in the Optimized Colors palette. Figure 3-29 shows a magnified view of ImageReady's Optimized Color

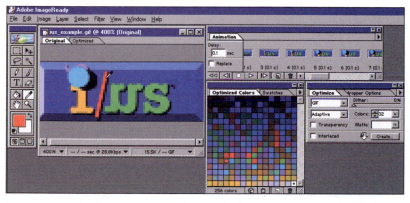

Figure 3-28   Selecting a portion of the image to be locked. Copyright © i/us Corp. http://www.i-us.com.

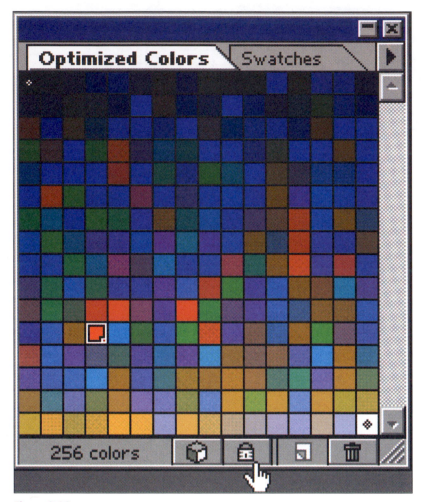

Figure 3-29   The notch indicates that this color has been locked.

palette. The cursor is pointing to the color-locking button. Notice that the orange color swatch in the color palette now has a little white notch in the lower-right corner. This indicates that the color has been locked.

Figure 3-30 shows the two frames from the sample animation magnified 500%. The frame on the left is from the original 256-color version, and the frame on the right is from the 32-color version optimized with Adobe ImageReady's color locking feature. The two frames are virtually indistinguishable even when magnified. So Adobe ImageReady's color locking allows for the best of both worlds—reducing the color palette while maintaining the essential colors for the visual integrity of the animation.

Figure 3-30 The original 256-color version (right) and the 32-color version optimized with the ImageReady color locking feature (left). Copyright © i/us Corp. http://www.i-us.com.

Summary

Taking the time to master the palette can often pay off in drastically reduced file sizes for your animations. Fortunately, you need not settle for ugly animations in the process. Incidentally, in Chapter 6, Seamless Integration, we look at techniques that can essentially get around the 256-color limit by teaming up GIF animations. One animation might be limited to 256 colors, but two animations, together, are not. You can get around the 256-color limit if you seamlessly integrate animations with one another or with static images.

Color reduction is not always the answer. In Chapter 4 we look at using transparency to reduce file sizes. Although color reduction can reduce the file size of an animation, Chapter 4 shows how to achieve even smaller file sizes by using frame cropping and interframe transparency to aid GIF animation's LZW compression. You can achieve maximum optimization when you combine transparency with a masterful approach to creating an animation palette.

Frame Cropping and Interframe Transparency Optimization

Reducing the number of colors may be an effective way to decrease the file size of a GIF animation, but it has an obvious downside. The fewer colors there are in a GIF animation, the more unattractive it can be. Fortunately, there a few lesser-known ways to reduce the file size of a GIF animation that don't involve potentially impairing its visual quality. ◗

Understanding the Benefits of Frame Cropping and Interframe Transparency

Understanding Disposal Methods

Frame Cropping Optimization

Interframe Transparency Optimization

Manual Interframe Transparency Optimization

As we discuss in Chapter 1, a GIF animation works by displaying one frame after another. Put another way, animation works with the GIF format by displaying a sequence of GIF images. The techniques that we discuss in this chapter involve reducing the amount of data required by each of these frames.

Chapter 2 briefly discusses frame cropping optimization (also known as dirty rectangle optimization) and interframe transparency optimization. You learned that frame cropping involves minimizing the dimensions of the frames and that interframe transparency involves using transparency on the frames to aid the LZW compression algorithm used by the GIF format. We look at these two techniques more closely in this chapter.

Understanding the Benefits of Frame Cropping and Interframe Transparency

Both frame cropping optimization and interframe transparency optimization depend on a relatively unknown feature in the GIF format: the disposal method. Disposal methods control how the browser displays frames of a GIF animation. They determine how subsequent frames are displayed over previous frames. Browsers display GIF animations by laying consecutive frames atop one another. With disposal methods, you use contents from previous frames as part of the current frame's visible makeup by cropping part of the current frame or by making portions of the current frame transparent.

Let's review the problem that frame cropping and interframe transparency solve. Figure 4-1 shows a simple animation of a leaky faucet. Each frame shows a little bit more of a drop falling from the faucet. Without taking advantage of frame cropping or interframe transparency, the GIF animation would work as shown in Figure 4-2. Each frame plays on top of the preceding frame. In other words, each new frame completely covers the preceding frame.

This approach is extremely inefficient because only a small portion of the overall image changes from frame to frame. Most of the animation's frame (the faucet, the water at the bottom, and the background) stays the same in each image; only the water droplet changes

Figure 4-1   **A basic animation of a water droplet falling from a leaky faucet.**

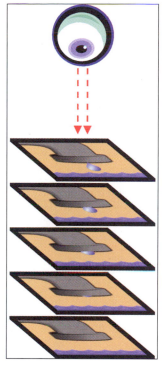 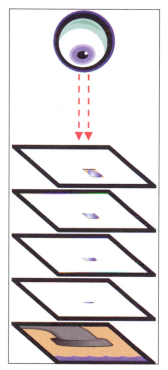

Figure 4-2 Each frame fully covers the preceding frame.

Figure 4-3 When you use frame cropping and interframe transparency, portions of an animation show through to opaque portions of any previous frames.

from frame to frame. Thus, there is an excessive amount of redundant information in the animation. We can remove this redundant information with a combination of frame cropping and interframe transparency.

Figure 4-3 shows the animation with most of the redundant information, or imagery, removed. Only the portions of the image that contain the water droplet are displayed; the rest of each frame's contents are transparent. Because the vast majority of the redundant information has been removed, the animation's file size is drastically reduced.

For example, if you have a two-frame animation in which each frame is 2K, the total animation is 4K. But if you use frame cropping or interframe transparency optimization, you can use only the portion of the second frame—say, 1K—that changes from the first frame, thereby shrinking the animation to 3K. This is explained in more detail in a moment. First, let's look at a few important considerations for employing frame cropping and interframe transparency optimization.

Note two important things in Figure 4-3. First, notice that even the top frame is showing through to the bottom frame. Therefore, the visible contents of frame 5 are made up of frames 1 and 5. Next, notice that each frame overlays only portions of the preceding frame as opposed to fully replacing it. This means that successive frame contents that have changed from the preceding frame must cover the preceding frame's contents; otherwise, the differences will show through.

Let's look at another example to help clarify these points. Figure 4-4 shows a few frames of a classic bouncing ball animation. In this animation, the ball changes position as it drops, and its shadow grows larger as the ball gets closer to the floor. If the animation is constructed as shown in Figure 4-4—that is, if there is no frame cropping or transparency in any of the frames—the animation will look fine. Each frame will cover the preceding one, and the animation will look normal.

However, what if we made everything transparent except for what has changed from the preceding frame, as shown in Figure 4-5? Figure 4-6 demonstrates what we would see on frame 5 of the sample animation if everything except the ball and the shadow were transparent in each frame. As you can see, the contents of each frame show through. Part of the ball in frame 1 shows through in frame 2, the balls from frames 1 and 2 show through in frame 3, and so on until parts of all the balls show through in frame 5. In the case of the ball's shadow, this is OK, because the shadow gets larger in each frame and thus covers the shadow in the preceding frame. The ball's movement, however, means that it only partially covers the ball in the preceding frame. This in turn destroys the illusion of motion because one of the fundamental aspects of motion is that if you move, you no longer occupy the position you held before you moved. For the animation to work properly and for the illusion to fool the viewer's eye, you must set up the frames in a GIF animation so that each frame covers anything that has changed from the preceding frame.

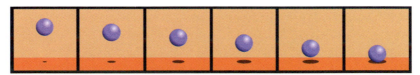

Figure 4-4   A few frames from a simple bouncing ball animation.

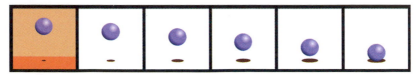

Figure 4-5   Everything except the ball and the shadow is transparent after frame 1.

Figure 4-6 Too much transparency destroys the illusion of motion by showing portions of previous frames.

Figure 4-7 shows proper implementation of transparency for the ball animation. Each frame after the first one contains not only the ball and shadow but also enough of the background to cover the ball from the preceding frame. For example, frame 2 contains enough of the background to fully cover the ball from frame 1. Notice, however, that frame 3 need not have enough of the background to cover the ball in frame 1. It need only cover the ball in frame 2. Frame 2 covers frame 1, frame 3 covers frame 2, and so on.

Understanding Disposal Methods

Now that you understand what we are trying to achieve with frame cropping and inter-frame transparency optimization as well as the benefits that can be realized with these techniques, let's talk about what makes all this possible: a little-known feature called disposal methods.

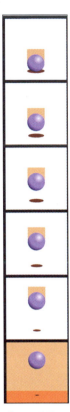

Figure 4-7 Each subsequent frame entirely covers any changes from the preceding frame.

Disposal methods control how the browser displays frames of a GIF animation. They determine how subsequent frames are displayed over previous frames. Browsers display GIF animations by laying consecutive frames atop one another. With disposal methods you can use contents from previous frames as part of the current frame's visible makeup by making portions of the current frame transparent. Disposal methods also allow for other interpretations of frames. For example, you can have the background of the browser, rather than the contents of an earlier frame, show through in the cropped or transparent portions of a given frame.

The GIF file format has four built-in types of disposal methods. (The GIF file format allows for eight types of disposal methods, but four of them are undefined.) Let's look at each of the four disposal methods that are defined by the browser. Note that the names of the disposal methods shown next are the actual names as defined in the GIF format specification. Different GIF animation utilities use different names for these disposal methods.

No Disposal Specified

The "No disposal specified" disposal method essentially says, "Treat the animation frame exactly as you would any other GIF image." In other words, if the current frame is smaller or cropped, then show any part of the preceding frame that the current frame isn't covering or, if the current frame is partially transparent, make the transparent areas show through to what is below.

Figure 4-8 shows what the "No disposal specified" disposal method does to our bouncing ball example. The top two frames in Figure 4-8 show the first two frames of the bouncing ball animation as they are actually constructed in the GIF file. The first frame is fully opaque; that is, there is no frame cropping or transparency built into the first frame. The

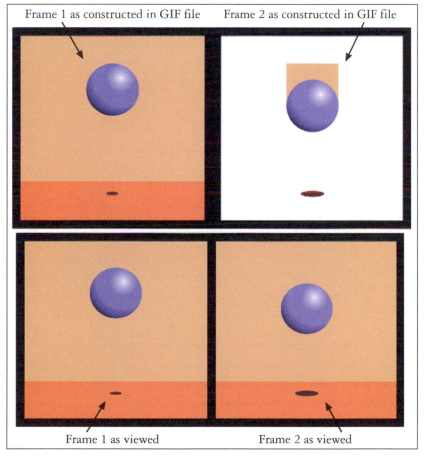

Figure 4-8 The top two images show how the animation is constructed in the GIF animation program; the bottom two images show what you actually see.

second frame has frame cropping built into it, as shown on the top right. The bottom version, however, shows what the viewer actually sees in the animation. The imagery from frame 2 covers part of the imagery from frame 1, so the viewer is actually seeing part of frame 1 when frame 2 displays. The "No disposal specified" disposal method is allowing the cropped portions of frame 2 to show through to frame 1.

One popular misconception about the "No disposal specified" disposal method is that it can be used to override frame cropping and transparency. That is, it is thought that any frames with the "No disposal specified" disposal method will show those frames as fully opaque whether or not they have been cropped or made transparent. This belief is false. There is no such disposal method in the GIF format.

Do Not Dispose

For all practical purposes, the "Do not dispose" disposal method is exactly the same as the "No disposal specified" method. You can use "Do not dispose" interchangeably with "No disposal specified." Therefore, if you want to take advantage of frame cropping and interframe transparency optimization, you should use either "No disposal specified" or "Do not dispose." GIF animation utilities usually have either the "No disposal specified" disposal method or the "Do not dispose" disposal method on by default.

Restore to Background Color

The "Restore to background color" option is something of a special effect. If you have the "Restore to background color" disposal method selected, cropped or transparent portions of a frame will show the background color or texture of a Web browser. In other words, the "Restore to background color" disposal method treats the GIF animation as if the frames are not stacked one atop the other. Each frame fully replaces the preceding frame; if the new frame has cropped portions or has transparency, then these portions of the frame show through to the Web page's background.

Figure 4-9 shows how "Restore to background color" would work with our bouncing ball example. The white areas in the first two frames on the top represent transparent areas. The bottom copies of the two frames show how these frames look over a Web page that has an orange background. The first frame's transparent areas show through to the orange color. When the second frame displays, the first frame is removed and the second frame's transparent areas show through to the orange color.

> The various versions of Netscape Navigator (through version 4.04) contain a small bug with regard to GIF animations that use the "Restore to background color" disposal method. If the first frame of the animation does not contain any transparency, subsequent frames that are assigned to the "Restore to background color" disposal method do not display correctly. Any portions of frames that contain frame cropping or interframe transparency will show black in those areas rather than show the background color or texture. Therefore, if you are using the "Restore to background color" disposal method and you want to be sure that it displays correctly in Netscape as well as Internet Explorer, you must make at least one pixel in the first frame of the animation transparent. ▶

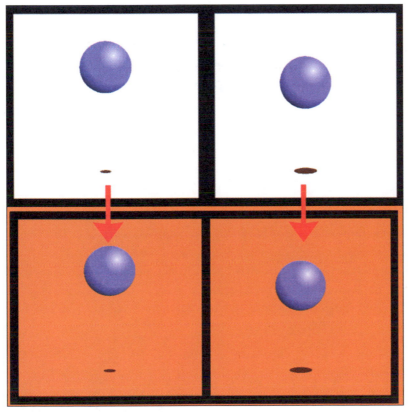

Figure 4-9   The top row shows the frames as they are constructed; the bottom row shows what the viewer actually sees.

Restore to Previous

It's worth noting that Netscape Navigator does not support the "Restore to previous" disposal method, and that explains why this disposal method is seldom used. At the time this book was written, Microsoft has come just short of taking over the known universe, but Web designers are still reticent to use a feature that cannot be seen by all their visitors. Nevertheless, the potential benefits of the "Restore to previous" disposal method make it worth looking at.

It's too confusing to try to explain the "Restore to previous" disposal method in words only, so let's look at an example. Figure 4-10 shows a four-frame animation. The four frames on top show how the animation is constructed (bright green areas indicate transparency), and the four frames on the bottom show what the viewer actually sees (or should see if it weren't for naughty Netscape).

Notice that the stylized text "Click Here" shows up in frame 3 even though that area of the frame is actually transparent. This is due to the "Restore to previous" disposal method. The transparent areas in frame 3 have been restored to the opaque areas in frame 1. This would not be possible with the "No disposal specified" or "Do not dispose" disposal method because frame 2 has opaque areas that cover the "Click Here" text.

So as the animation in Figure 4-10 plays, the words "Click Here" flash on and off while the arrows shoot out from the center. Although this effect would be possible using other disposal methods, the animation's file size is a bit smaller as a result of using the "Restore to previous" disposal method. You will learn why the compression is better in a moment.

Although the results of the "Restore to previous" disposal method show up in frame 3, the "Restore to previous" disposal method has actually been applied to frame 2. This points out two important things. First, you can apply disposal methods to individual frames selectively. (For example, one frame can have the "No disposal specified" disposal method while another has the "Restore to background color" disposal method.) Second, disposal methods affect the subsequent frames; that is, when you apply a disposal method to a frame, it determines what happens to the next frame.

Most GIF animation utilities let you choose which disposal method to use. In GIF Movie Gear, the "No disposal specified" option is on by default, but it is called "No Disposal method" (see Figure 4-11). In GIFBuilder, it is called "Do Not Dispose." Whatever it is called in the utility you use, you want the disposal method that allows any pixels not covered by

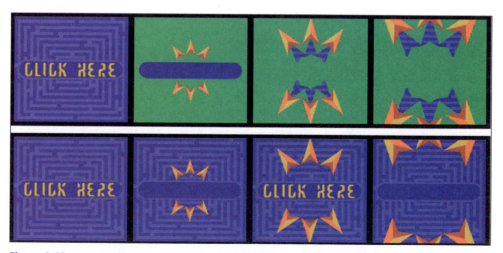

Figure 4-10   Frame 3 shows through to frame 1 with the "Restore to previous" disposal method on.

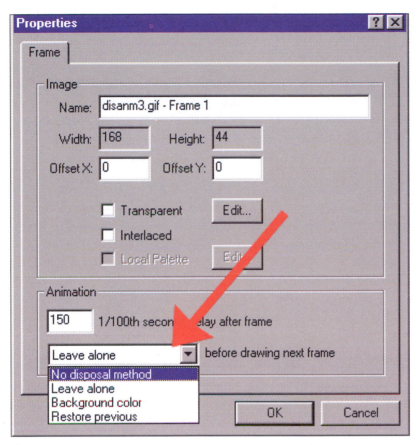

Figure 4-11   In GIF Movie Gear, you can select disposal methods from the Frame
Properties or the Global Properties dialog box. (Arrow added.)

any subsequent frames to continue to display. In other words, transparent areas of the current frame should be allowed to show through to previous frames. Figure 4-8 shows how the "Leave Alone" or "Do Not Dispose" disposal method works. Only the portions of the image that contain the water droplet are displayed, and the rest of each frame's contents are transparent.

Frame Cropping Optimization

In Chapter 2 we looked at frame cropping optimization (also known as dirty rectangle optimization). Frame cropping refers to a mode of optimization that involves cropping frames in a GIF animation to their smallest needed rectangle. The unnecessary, or redundant, portions of the frames are cropped. Each frame after frame 1 is actually a smaller GIF file. The smaller GIF files are displayed over the first frame using pixel coordinates for their placement. Because the smaller GIF images cover the first frame only partially, you can still see parts of the original frame as the animation plays.

Let's look at an example. Figure 4-12 shows a 24-frame animation of a stylized TV screen with a colorful spiral pattern playing on the monitor. Note that parts of the animation never change. Most of the motion occurs within the TV screen and in a little meter below it. Otherwise, the remainder of the contents of all the frames stays the same or is redundant from frame to frame. With a 32-color (5-bit) palette, this animation's file size is 21,309, or 22.7K.

Now let's apply frame cropping to this animation. In GIF Movie Gear (GMG) this is done in the Optimize Animation dialog box, shown in Figure 4-13. The option that performs the frame cropping optimization in GMG is called **Shrink frames to smallest needed rectangle**. The name says it all. This feature compares the animation's frames to one another and crops redundant portions of any of the frames. Notice that the Optimize Animation dialog box indicates that the file size of the animation will be reduced from 21,309 bytes to only 4,417 bytes. Frame cropping optimization reduces the file size to almost one-fifth its original size.

Figure 4-12   Portions of this 24-frame animation do not change.

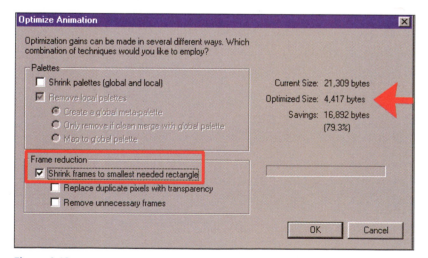

Figure 4-13   Cropping redundant portions reduces the file size by almost 80%.

Figure 4-14 shows the results of the frame cropping optimization in GMG. The gray areas in all the frames after frame 1 indicate cropped portions of those frames; that is, each frame after frame 1 is now a smaller GIF file in terms of dimensions. Don't confuse this with transparency. When frame 2 displays, the gray areas of frame 2 do not show through to frame 1 because those areas are transparent. Rather, they show through to frame 1 because the contents of frame 2 only partially cover frame 1.

It is easy to verify that the contents of frames 2–24 are now smaller, cropped GIF files. Figure 4-15 shows GMG's frame Properties dialog box for frame 2. I have zoomed into frame 2, and GMG has outlined the selected frame in red. The red arrow at the bottom points to the animation's overall dimensions, which are 72 pixels wide by 62 pixels high. However, the red arrow in the Properties dialog box shows that the currently selected frame's dimensions (frame 2) are 16 pixels wide by 36 pixels high. So frame 2 is actually a 16×36 image placed on top of a 72×62 pixel image.

The 16×36 image in frame 2 is positioned using coordinates. You can see the coordinates in Figure 4-15 in the Properties box directly below the dimensions. The **Offset X:** is 33 pixels, and the **Offset Y:** is 20 pixels. Pixel coordinates correspond to the left and top of the frame's image. So the image in frame 2 of this example is positioned 33 pixels to the right of the left edge and 20 pixels down from the top.

Notice that GMG allows you to enter new pixel coordinates for a frame's image (you can even change the coordinates of the contents of the first frame of the animation). Figure 4-16 shows what happens if the coordinates of frame 2 are changed to zero for both the X and Y offsets. Now the image in frame 2 is positioned at the upper left.

Normally you wouldn't want to mess with the coordinates of a GIF animation frame. When GIF animation utilities position the contents of each frame after performing frame cropping optimization, they always position the images correctly. Although you can conceivably get wild animation effects by manipulating the coordinates of an optimized animation, you would normally leave them alone.

The main reason for pointing out the pixel coordinates here is to demonstrate that frame cropping, or dirty rectangle optimization, involves cropping the contents of a GIF animation's

Figure 4-14   The results of frame cropping optimization in GMG.

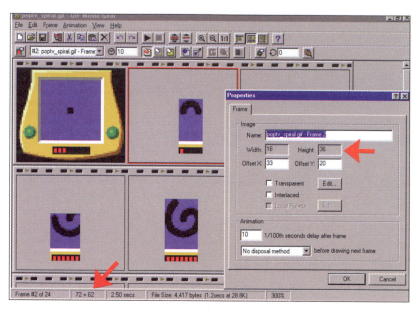

Figure 4-15   The Properties dialog box verifies that frame 2 has been cropped.

frames. Cropping results in reduced file size because the animation no longer contains numerous full-sized GIF images. When the dimensions of the frames are reduced, you reduce the amount of data that must be stored in the overall GIF animation file. When you reduce the dimensions of a GIF image or the dimensions of GIF images within a GIF animation, it almost always results in file size reduction. In a moment we talk about why we say "almost always."

You can take advantage of the fact that you can change these pixel coordinates to generate animation. For example, Figure 4-17 shows an animation I created by editing the pixel co-

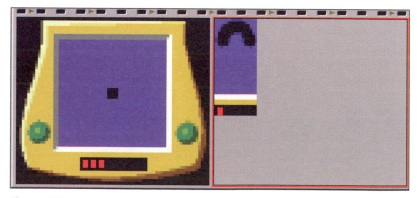

Figure 4-16   Changing the frame's pixel coordinates changes the position of the image.

ordinates of the frame. First, I created a 100-pixel-square rich yellow GIF image and imported it into GMG. Then I created a 40-pixel-square GIF file with an image of a blue ball over the same rich color. I then imported the 40-pixel-square image into GMG.

As Figure 4-17 shows, GMG imported the 40-pixel-square image using the same coordinates as frame 1; that is, frame 1's coordinates are zero for the X and Y offset, and so are frame 2's. To create the animation shown in Figure 4-17, I made eight copies of frame 2 and edited the coordinates of each of the copies independently. For example, the Properties dialog box in Figure 4-17 shows the coordinates as 30 by 30. GIF Movie Gear's Preview Animation dialog box shows what the frames look like on the final frame—after all the frames have played. The resulting animation is basically an animated pattern all of which was created by duplicating frame 2 and manipulating the coordinates of the copies.

Not all GIF animation utilities allow you to perform frame cropping. For example, GIF Construction Set does not support frame cropping optimization. Also, not all GIF animation utilities allow you to perform frame cropping independently of the next GIF animation optimization technique that we talk about: interframe transparency. For example, Ulead's GIF Animator 2.0 and Boxtop Software's GIFmation only allow you to perform frame cropping and interframe transparency optimization at the same time. Now let's take a closer look at interframe transparency optimization.

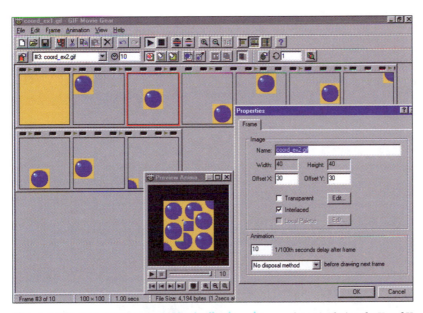

Figure 4-17   An animation created by duplicating a frame and manipulating the X and Y coordinates of the copies.

▣ Interframe Transparency Optimization

The term *interframe transparency* is hardly standard. Some utilities refer to this form of optimization as *frame differencing*. However, as the term *interframe transparency* implies, this form of optimization involves using transparency to achieve file size savings. As with frame cropping, the idea is to compare the frames within an animation, except that with interframe transparency redundant pixels are made transparent (whenever possible) rather than being cropped. Interframe transparency optimization is typically done at the same time as frame cropping, although some utilities (such as GMG and the GIF animator that comes with SPG Web Tools for Photoshop) allow you to perform frame cropping and interframe transparency optimization independently.

Let's look at an example. Figure 4-18 shows most of the frames from a much larger (in terms of the number of frames) version of the TV animation we used earlier to discuss frame cropping. This version of the animation has 83 frames, and it has a 64-color palette to accommodate the additional colors. Unoptimized, the file size of the animation in Figure 4-18 is 81,294 bytes (79.3K). When this animation was optimized with frame cropping, the file size dropped to 23,771 bytes (not shown). Note that even though some GIF animation utilities allow you to perform frame cropping optimization without interframe transparency optimization, no GIF animation utility allows you to perform interframe transparency optimization without frame cropping optimization. (As we will see later, you can perform interframe transparency optimization manually, and that, in effect, allows you to perform interframe transparency without frame cropping.)

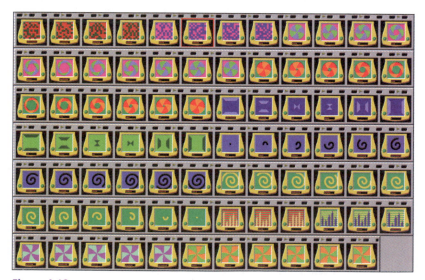

Figure 4-18   This unoptimized animation is 79.3K.

Many of the newer GIF animation programs, such as GIF Movie Gear, GIFmation, HVS Animator Pro, and Ulead GIF Animator, contain features that perform interframe transparency optimization for you. The process varies among the programs. Depending on the animation, some programs do better than others. GIF Movie Gear's interframe transparency optimization is about average. You apply it using the Optimize Animation dialog box (the same one used for frame cropping optimization). The feature that performs interframe transparency optimization in GMG is called **Replace duplicate pixels with transparency** (shown in Figure 4-19).

Figure 4-20 shows the results of the interframe transparency optimization. All transparent pixels have been turned to white. GIF Movie Gear has compared the frames of the animation to one another and has converted all redundant pixels of the animation transparency. In Figure 4-20, all the frames after the first frame look garbled. However, when a browser displays the animation, frame 2 will cover frame 1, and all transparent portions of frame 2 will show through to frame 1. This will continue as each frame covers the preceding one.

As Figure 4-19 shows, when interframe transparency optimization is employed, the sample animation is reduced to 19,904 bytes (19.4K), which is just short of 4K from the file size achieved with frame cropping optimization. With frame cropping and interframe transparency optimization together, the animation's file size was reduced from 79.3K to only 19.4K, a file size savings of almost 60K.

With the animation's original 256-color palette, the animation was 87,277 bytes. Reducing it to the 64-color palette shrank the animation's file size only by 5,983 bytes (a savings

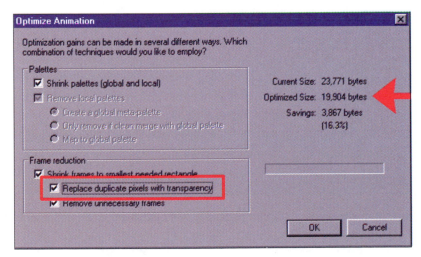

Figure 4-19   GMG supports interframe transparency optimization through the Optimize Animation dialog box. (Arrow and highlight added.)

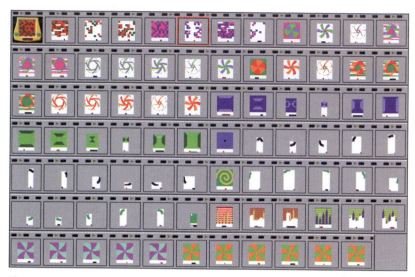

Figure 4-20   White portions in each frame indicate transparency portions.

of 81,294 bytes). So for this example, using frame cropping and interframe transparency optimization resulted in compression that was 10 times better than the compression achieved by reducing the number of colors.

In some situations frame cropping optimization cannot be performed, so you must rely more on interframe transparency optimization (and color reduction) to reduce the file size of the animation. For example, Figure 4-21 shows an animation that benefits very little from frame cropping. The top row is the unoptimized version of the animation. The bottom row has been optimized with frame cropping (cropped areas are medium gray) and interframe transparency (transparent pixels are white). In this example, frame cropping reduced the animation by only about 200 bytes, and interframe transparency was able to lop off an additional 400 bytes. Neither frame cropping nor interframe transparency optimization, in this example, performs very well because the motion between frames takes up a large area; that is, there is relatively little redundant information between frames. And because very little can be cropped, interframe transparency outperforms frame cropping.

▣ Manual Interframe Transparency Optimization

As noted earlier, not all GIF animation utilities perform interframe transparency optimization. If you use a GIF animation utility such as GIF Construction Set or GIFBuilder, you must perform interframe transparency optimization manually. If your utility performs only frame

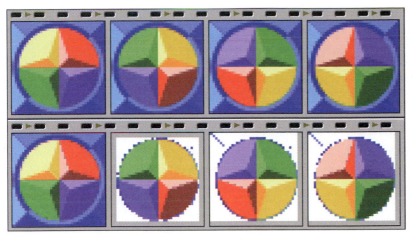

Figure 4-21   Relatively little is gained when this unoptimized animation (top) is
optimized with frame cropping and interframe transparency (bottom),
although the latter performs somewhat better.

cropping optimization, you can often improve on it by performing manual interframe transparency optimization. Furthermore, even when these approaches are performed by software, the optimization isn't always perfect. In some cases you might want to exchange the results of your utility's interframe transparency optimization for your own on a frame-by-frame basis.

When you work with interframe transparency optimization, the objective is almost always to keep the GIF animation's file size as small as possible. To do that, you take advantage of disposal methods in the GIF format that allow you to use animated frames that contain only the portion of the image that has changed from any previous frame or frames. The guiding principle is the fact that GIF transparency is either on or off.

> The following technique is useful only if your GIF animation utility allows you to select disposal methods. GIF animation utilities that do not support this option, notably GIF Construction Set, cannot be used for manual interframe transparency optimization. In addition, the tool must let you select a color for transparency. ▶

There can be no 99% transparent areas. So you must generate a *transparency mask* for the GIF animation frame that covers the preceding frame and yet results in as little of the frame showing as possible. In other words, you want as much of the frame as possible to be transparent while maintaining coverage of the preceding frame.

Figure 4-22 shows an animation that demonstrates manual interframe transparency optimization. The animation starts with a diamond shape that has a slight drop shadow over a subtle blue texture. This same texture is used as the background texture for the Web page that this animation was intended for. As the animation progresses, the diamond shape splits in two. Each half moves away from the center, revealing a circular shape in the center

Figure 4-22   The diamond splits apart, and the triangles spread out to reveal a small circular shape. Then they come back together to form the diamond shape again.

between the two triangular shapes. Midway through the animation, the triangles begin coming back together; then the animation loops back to the beginning as the triangles rejoin to form a diamond shape.

The animation takes place over a textured background and features a drop shadow. We must define the transparency for each frame so that it accounts not only for the movement of the triangle shapes but also for the shadows that they cast over the background texture. To do this, we must create a *mask* for each frame. We fill this mask with a single color that we can use to define the transparency when we export each frame to a separate GIF file.

The background texture used with this animation is naturally seamless (see Chapter 6, Seamless Integration, for tips on generating naturally seamless textures). This means that we add transparency to the first frame because we do not need to be concerned about whether the texture in the animation blends seamlessly with the background texture on the Web page. ❯

Figure 4-23 shows the layers in Photoshop used to create the animation in Figure 4-22. If you would like to follow along with this discussion more closely, this Photoshop file is located on the companion CD-ROM in the Chapter 4 directory. The file is called diambase.psd. Each of the layers (except the background layer) shown in Figure 4-23 is named to correspond to the frame that it will be used to create. For example, the layer named Frame 1 was used to create frame 1 of the animation, the layer named Frame 2 was used to create frame 2, and so on.

Notice that we have one background layer. Each frame's artwork is on a different layer. When we create each of the frames we use the same background texture layer for each frame, thereby ensuring that each frame's background has exactly the same texture. However, as you will see, there is another reason that the artwork for each of the frames is on a separate layer: it allows us to easily define the transparency for each frame.

Follow these steps to define the transparency for the frame 1 of the sample animation.

1. Turn off the visibility of all the layers except the background layer and the frame 1 layer. Select frame 1, hold down the **Ctrl** key (PC) or **Command** key (Mac), and then click on the thumbnail of frame 1 in the Layers palette. This action loads the layer's *transparency channel*. Alternatively, choose **Load Selection** from the Select menu to

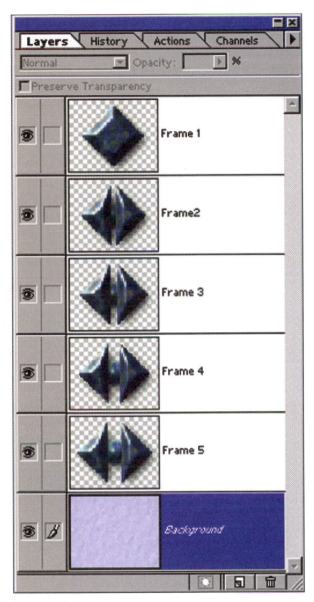

Figure 4-23   This is the layered Photoshop document used to generate the animation in Figure 4-22.

open the Load Selection dialog box. The Channel pop-up menu defaults to the layer's transparency channel, as shown in Figure 4-24. Press **OK** to apply the frame 1 transparency channel to the Frame 1 layer.

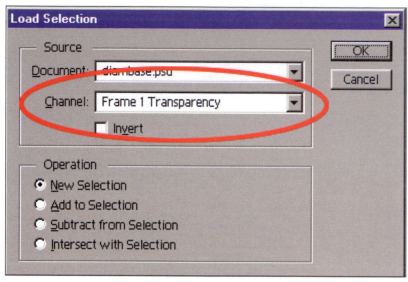

Figure 4-24   The Load Selection dialog box defaults to the selected layer's transparency channel. (Highlight added.)

2. Choose **Save Selection** from the Select menu. Open the Channels palette and rename the new channel to the name of your frame (**Frame 1** in this case).

    Figure 4-25 shows the transparency mask for the layer; this is the mask that is used to describe the opacity and transparency of the layer for the contents of the Frame 1 layer. White areas indicate fully opaque pixels, and black areas indicate fully transparent pixels. Grayscale areas indicate partially opaque and partially transparent pixels. This is an 8-bit mask. This means that the mask has 256 possible levels of opacity or transparency.

    Right now this mask doesn't suit our purposes. Recall that the GIF format does not support 8-bit transparency; this format allows only pixels that are either fully opaque or fully transparent. We can't have any partially transparent pixels, so we must alter this mask so that it is fully black and white with no grayscale pixels.

3. With the new channel selected, choose **Image, Adjust, Threshold**. Apply the **Threshold** filter with a value of **1** and then invert the channel (**Image, Adjust, Invert** or **Ctrl+I/Command+I**).

    Using the threshold feature turns all the gray values to white, making all the pixels in the channel either black or white. In other words, with a threshold value of 1, even the darkest grays will turn white, as shown in Figure 4-26. Because the grays in the channel translate into the all-transparent areas in the layer, this operation creates a mask that encases

Figure 4-25 The transparency channel for Frame 1, saved as a channel in the Channels palette, contains grayscale values that cannot be used for GIF transparency.

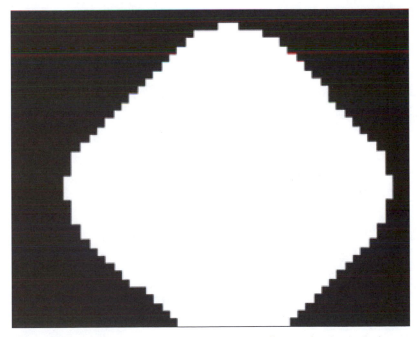

Figure 4-26 Use Photoshop's threshold feature to turn all grayscale values in the frame 1 channel to white.

every pixel that has changed from the preceding frame. (In the case of frame 1, nothing has changed from a "preceding frame," but we can still make portions of the frame transparent because of the random background pattern as mentioned earlier.) Now we have a mask that we can use for the interframe transparency optimization of frame 1.

4. Go back to the Layers palette and select the **Frame 1** layer. Load the frame 1 channel as a selection (choose **Load selection** from the Select menu and choose **Frame 1** from the Channel pop-up menu). Fill the selection with a bright red color, as shown in Figure 4-27.

We fill the selection with red because it is the color we will use to define the transparency for frame 1 in the GIF animation. Choose a color that is easy to select. In other words, it should be a color that doesn't exist elsewhere in the animation. Red was used in this example because the objects and background are made up of shades of green and blue.

5. Now you are ready to create the first frame of the animation. With the **Frame 1** layer selected, choose **Select all** from the Select menu (**Ctrl+A/Command+A**). Make sure that all the other layers in the diambase.psd file are invisible except for the background layer. Choose **Copy Merged** from the Edit menu. Open a new document and press **OK** (the new document will default to the size of the contents of the clipboard). Paste in the new frame and merge it to the background.

Photoshop's **Copy Merged** option creates a copy of the visible layers within a selection, so it is an easy way to merge the contents of the Frame 1 layer with the background layer.

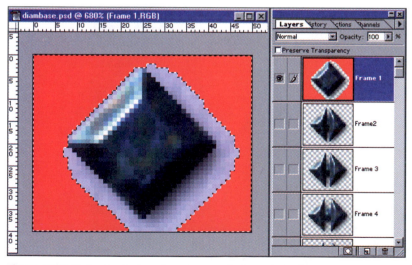

Figure 4-27 To begin the interframe transparency optimization, select the frame 1 channel and fill it with bright red.

You paste the results into a new document so that you can come back to the original document if there are any problems. Also, you will index the new document (change the color mode from RGB to Indexed Color) so that you can export it to a GIF, and you can't index a layered Photoshop file. Note that you are disregarding the issue of global palettes for the moment. See Chapter 3, Mastering the Palette, for instructions on how to create a global palette manually.

6. Choose **Index Color** from the Image, Mode menu and convert the new document to a 128 or 7-bit adaptive palette. Next, export the image using **GIF89a Export**.

    Don't worry about assigning transparency here. Some GIF animation utilities do not recognize transparency defined by other programs, so the best way to be sure that transparency is defined correctly is to define the transparency of the frame within your GIF animation utility.

7. Open the GIF image in your GIF animation utility and choose the red color as the color for transparency.

Each GIF animation utility has its own way of allowing you to specify a color for transparency. Figure 4-28 shows the Pick Transparency Index dialog box in GIF Movie Gear. I used the eyedropper tool to select the red color for transparency. In GMG's Pick Transparency Index preview window I changed the background to orange to make it easier to

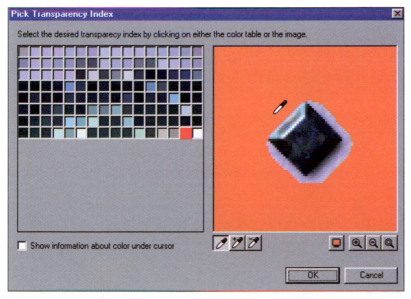

Figure 4-28   In GMG, you use the Pick Transparency Index dialog box to specify a color for transparency.

see what portions of the frame have been made transparent. The orange areas indicate these portions of the frame.

Repeat this process to create the next four frames of this animation. The resulting GIF animation frames should look similar to Figure 4-29 (again, orange depicts transparency). Because the two triangles are moving apart from each other, each of the first five frames covers the preceding frame successively. However, in frame 6 the triangles start going back toward each other. So if the technique used for frames 1–5 were to be used for frames 6, 7, and 8, parts of frame 5 would show through during frame 6, parts of frames 5 *and* 6 would show through during frame 7, and so on.

The solution is simple. Let's look at frame 6. By frame 5, the animation has reached its apex, so in frame 6 the triangles are moving back toward each other. Therefore, the artwork for frame 6 is the same as the artwork for frame 4 and we can use frame 4's artwork for frame 6. However, the artwork for frame 6 must cover the outer edges of frame 5. How do we get a mask that will cover frame 5's contents? It's simple: combine a copy of frame 5 and frame 4 and use the combined artwork's transparency mask for frame 6. To do this, simply create copies of the layers for frame 5 and frame 4 (delete any transparency-defining colors) and merge the copies (see Figure 4-30).

Then you use the transparency mask of the combined layers to create the channel for defining frame 6's transparency. The process is the same for frames 7 and 8 except that you combine frames 3 and 4 for frame 7 and combine frames 3 and 2 for frame 8. Figure 4-31 shows all the Photoshop layers used to create the animation with their transparency specified in red.

Again, to generate the example from this point the background and each frame's layer (one frame at a time) were made visible. I selected all, copy merged, created a new document, and pasted the clipboard's contents into the document. I repeated this process for each frame, copying each frame into the new document; after I had all the frames in the new document, I saved the document. Then I used these frames to create the global palette manually, as described in Chapter 3. When I had the global palette, I selected **Revert** from the File menu, copied and pasted each frame into a new temporary document, and indexed the new document to the global palette. Remember that if the temporary document is al-

Figure 4-29   The resulting GIF animation.

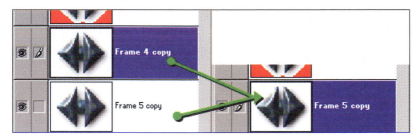

Figure 4-30   Merge copies of frame 4 and frame 5 and use the resultant layer's transparency mask for frame 6. (Arrow added.)

ready indexed, Photoshop will automatically index the new frame when you paste it into the temporary document. Finally, I exported each frame with the GIF89a Export filter, opened the files in my GIF animation utility, and then used the red color to define transparency for each frame.

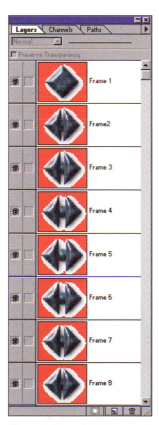

Figure 4-31   All the layers with a color added for transparency.

Now let's see whether all this effort pays off in file size savings. For comparison, I first generated a version of this animation without any frame cropping or interframe transparency optimization. The file size for the unoptimized animation was 12.3K. Performing the optimization with GIFBuilder's frame cropping optimization resulted in a size of 9.2K (shown in Figure 4-32). So 9.2K is the best GIFBuilder can do by itself because it does not support interframe transparency optimization. Next, I created a version of the animation with GIFBuilder using the manual interframe transparency optimization. The resulting file size was only 4.87K. By performing the manual interframe transparency optimization, I achieved nearly 50% more file size savings over GIFBuilder's optimization.

The manual approach to interframe transparency optimization can be beneficial even for GIF animation programs that support pixel-level transparency optimization. For example, GIFmation is one of the better GIF animation utilities at interframe transparency optimization. To test whether the manual approach to interframe transparency optimization could improve on GIFmation's approach, I imported a version of the sample animation that did not contain any manually built-in interframe transparency optimization. Then I optimized this animation with GIFmation's interframe transparency optimization feature and saved the animation. The file size of the animation with GIFmation's interframe transparency optimization was 6.8K (6,957 bytes).

Next, I imported the version of the animation that had manual interframe transparency already added using the earlier techniques. When I exported this version, adding GIFmation's interframe transparency optimization to the mix, the file size dropped to 5.8K (5,993 bytes). By using the manual interframe transparency optimization technique, I was able to augment GIFmation's already excellent optimization.

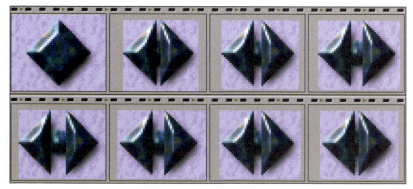

Figure 4-32   GIFBuilder's frame cropping optimization results in a 9.2K file size compared with 4.87K achieved with the manual technique.

Admittedly, saving 1K is scant reward for the amount of effort involved in generating interframe transparency optimization manually. However, if you have multiple animations, the savings can add up. Also note that if you have a program, such as GIFmation or GIF Movie Gear, that imports layered Photoshop files, you can save yourself a few steps, making the extra effort more feasible.

It should be noted that using frame cropping and interframe transparency optimization does not always reduce the file size of an animation. Small animations or animations that fluctuate wildly in color from frame to frame, for example, might actually have their file size increased if subjected to the automated transparency optimization features available in many current GIF animation utilities. Remember that the compression is largely due to GIF's ability to compress contiguous strings of same-color pixels. If the "optimization" results in too many noncontiguous strings of transparent pixels, the file size of the animation may increase instead of decrease.

For this reason, it is always handy to create an unoptimized version of the animation first and then compare it to optimized versions of the animation. Then you can check optimized animations against the unoptimized version to ensure that you have achieved a smaller file size.

▦ Summary

Mastering frame cropping and interframe transparency optimization can be a huge weapon in the arsenal of techniques that you use to minimize the download requirements of your animations. By using disposal methods and palette optimization techniques, you can deliver your animations to your audience more quickly. Also, better compression techniques free you to develop more-ambitious animations because you don't have to be concerned as much with how much the animations will add to the bandwidth taken up by your Web pages. It may seem like a lot of work, but making your animation three times smaller than it was originally means that your viewers see it three times faster. At the very least, it'll get bandwidth conservation types off your back.

CHAPTER 5

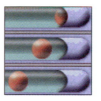

Advanced Animation Techniques in Photoshop

In Chapters 2, 3, and 4 we look at how to generate a basic GIF animation, how to optimize the palette, and how to optimize a GIF animation with frame cropping and interframe transparency optimization. In this chapter we take a step back and talk about efficient techniques for creating the individual frames of an animation. ◗

One of the defining premises of this chapter is that animation's basic requirement is a series of frames. These frames must be carefully crafted or else the illusion of animation will be lost or severely impaired. It's true that craftsmanship's biggest investment is often lots and lots of time but there are a lot of inherent roadblocks to the creation of a compelling animation.

In Chapter 1 we talk about the advantages of cel-based animation techniques. Professional animators have always enjoyed the benefits of these techniques. Because these benefits have a direct bearing on this chapter, let's quickly review the production issues that make cel-based animation techniques valuable. Refer to Figure 1-5 in Chapter 1. Figure 1-5 shows four layered cels that make up a single frame of animation. Cel A contains artwork of a tree and is on the top layer. Below it is cei B, which has imagery of a green monster. Next is cel C, which contains the main subject of the animation: a jolly little doofus skipping along with a bucket in his hand. Finally, cel D is on the bottom layer and contains the background art.

Now imagine that this scene is one frame of an animated 15-second sequence that we must create. In this sequence the boy skips down the path and then gets gobbled up by the monster ("Yummy—but needs a little salt"). Now suppose that we are animating at only 20 frames per second (it's a low-budget production). This means that we must generate 300 frames of animation for our 15-second sequence. That's a lot of frames for something that plays in the amount of time it takes to sharpen a pencil. Fortunately, if we use a cel-based approach to the animated sequence we should be able to stay under budget and meet our outrageous (isn't it always?) deadline.

THE IMPORTANCE OF REGISTRATION

In some animations, a tree or a background scene might move (for example, if you were trying to create the effect of an earthquake or an explosion), but in this case the tree and the background layer stay stationary. So one important aspect of these cels is that we must be able to accurately *register* them each time. Every time we add a different cel for the boy's motion or the monster's motion, we must be able to reposition the tree and background exactly where they were before. Cel-based animation relies on a variety of techniques to facilitate this requirement, all of which are unimportant for our discussion. Be aware, though, that registration of elements between frames is also an important issue in animation.

Our sequence has several recurring or redundant elements that stay stationary—namely, the tree in cel A and the background imagery in cel D. Placing these elements on separate layers does several things. First, we need to draw the art for the tree and the background only once rather than 300 times. Also, if we had to draw the same tree and background over and over again, it would be difficult to make sure that they looked exactly the same from frame to frame. By using the same tree and background images for all 300 frames, we are assured of consistency between cels.

Now let's look at the two moving elements: the boy and the monster. Most of the motion in this sequence is generated by the boy skipping down the path. Because he is on a separate layer/cel, we can concentrate on drawing the skipping motion rather than draw the skipping motion while worrying about how the boy integrates with the background. The same thing goes for the monster. As long as the monster is on one layer and the tree that the monster is hiding behind is on another layer, we don't have to worry about how the monster integrates with the tree cel in front of him. Furthermore, we don't have to worry about drawing the parts of the monster that are behind the tree, because any part of the monster that's behind the tree isn't visible.

So cel-based animation minimizes the work of generating the illusion of animation, and it helps solve many other problems, such as keeping static elements consistent-looking. It also removes the problem of having to integrate static and moving elements as you create each frame. Fortunately, most Web animations are rarely 300 frames long, although that doesn't reduce the need for efficient animation techniques. Cel-based animation techniques are just as valuable for creating Web animations as they are for creating animations for the big screen.

In this chapter we talk about how you can use Photoshop's layers to emulate cel-based animation techniques. Furthermore, we discuss an effective and efficient approach to animation that will give you the flexibility you need to let your imagination run wild. When the time commitment and the hassle inherent in creating animation are minimized, compelling animations become feasible.

Animations can be richly diverse, so we don't establish any prefab animation formulas here. Instead, we look at essential tools and techniques with an eye toward decreasing the amount of time and effort it takes to create high-quality Web animations.

Why Use Photoshop?

When you create static art you have to worry about only one image, whereas with Web animation you deal with perhaps dozens of images. To create or process multiple digital images you need a program that can handle multiple images, preferably one that can handle multiple images, within the same file. Although digital video and animation programs are designed to process multiple images, many of them do not have the array of drawing and editing tools that are found in image editors such as Adobe Photoshop. With the advent of advanced features such as layers, multiple undo, and scripting, it often makes sense to perform much of the image processing for an animation within image editors that typically are used for manipulating static images.

Although art for animation can be created or compiled using any combination of digital graphics tools, one of the best general-purpose animation tools is Adobe Photoshop. Photoshop's layers, channels, guides, and actions, coupled with its robust third-party plug-in market and overall high-quality bitmap manipulation tools, make it a popular choice among Web animators. To be sure, Photoshop is lacking in some areas. Its color indexing leaves much to be desired (although it has been improved in Photoshop 5), and its unimpressive GIF and JPEG compression schemes have spawned a cottage industry—including Equilibrium's Debabelizer, HVS Web Focus, Ulead's Smartsavers, and WebVise Totality—of software dedicated to superior compression.

Despite these shortcomings, Photoshop remains the standard as well as the de facto bitmap manipulation environment, so this chapter focuses on taking advantage of its features for creating Web animations. This chapter should prove useful even if you don't use Photoshop. Most of the competing image manipulation programs have followed Adobe's lead. If you know your tool, many of the methods used in this chapter should be easily translated into your application of choice.

Using Layers

Adobe introduced *layers* to Photoshop in version 3. It's hard to state strongly enough the value of layers to the process of creating Web animations, particularly GIF animations. Layers provide two advantages for generating Web animation. First, each layer can be equal to a single GIF animation frame; that is, you can have a series of fully opaque layers, each of which contains artwork for a frame in your animation. This means that you can store and edit multiple frames in one document.

For example, Figure 5-1 shows seven frames for an animation of an electronic switch. Each frame is on a separate layer inside Photoshop. Although the artwork for the animation was created (by Scott Balay of infinitefish.com) in formZ Renderzone, the frames were imported into Photoshop to adjust the curves and make other minor edits.

Some GIF animation utilities make it easy to create an animation from a layered Photoshop file such as this one. For example, GIF Movie Gear, GIFBuilder, and GIFmation all allow you to import layered Photoshop files. These utilities take each layer in Photoshop and turn it into a GIF animation frame. They also generate a global palette for you on-the-fly. The ability to directly import layered Photoshop files to create a GIF animation is a tremendous time-saver. Almost all the GIF animations featured in this book were generated in this way. If your GIF animation utility does not import layered Photoshop files, you will have to export each frame or layer as a GIF file and then import the GIF files into the GIF animation utility.

The second valuable aspect of Photoshop layers is that layers allow you to emulate cell animation techniques. Layers can be partially or fully transparent. When you stack a series of partially transparent layers, it can be very similar to stacking a series of animation cels.

Figure 5-2 shows Photoshop's Layers palette, which contains the artwork for a spiral animation in Photoshop. One of the tutorials on the CD contains detailed steps on how to create a spiral animation from scratch with Photoshop, but for now we're interested

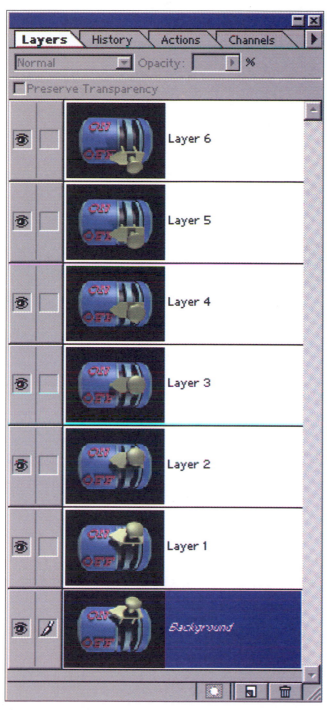

Figure 5-1 Each frame for this 3-D electronic switch animation is on a separate layer in Photoshop.

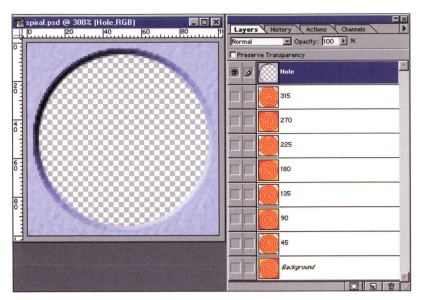

Figure 5-2   The top layer in this Photoshop file contains a transparent hole that shows through to a series of spiral layers, all of which are in various states of rotation.

in how to emulate cel animation techniques using layered Photoshop files. You can inspect the Photoshop file for this example more closely. It is located on the companion CD-ROM (spiral.psd).

The Photoshop file shown in Figure 5-2 contains nine layers. Notice that the top layer contains imagery with a transparent hole. All the layers except the top layer have been turned off. By default, Photoshop shows a white and gray checkerboard pattern for any transparent portions of a layer. The remaining eight layers in the file contain the spiral artwork. The artwork has been rotated 45 degrees in each frame, so the eight layers contain artwork of the spiral rotating 360 degrees. In the final animation we want the rotating spiral to show or play within the hole.

The layers in the Photoshop file for the spiral animation have been constructed in this way to maintain as much flexibility as possible. To make this point, let's talk about an inefficient way to proceed with this animation. In this animation, the hole will be a constant in every frame. In other words, the hole never moves. Only the spiral, as seen through the hole, changes from frame to frame. We could take the Hole layer, make seven copies of it, and then merge each copy of the hole to each of the spiral layers. Why is this a bad idea? Aside from the fact that it's a lot of work, what if we finish the animation, preview it, and then realize that there's something wrong with the animation? We'd pretty much have to start over. Instead, we should save this document and then make a new document for creating the animation.

Now let's look at a more efficient approach for creating the spiral animation. We need to make fully opaque layers for each frame of the animation. If there is any transparency on any layer, GIF animation utilities that import layered Photoshop files typically merge the transparent portions of any frame to the background layer of the Photoshop document.

> It's a good idea to make multiple copies of your layered Photoshop animation documents so that you don't have to start over again if you change your mind or make a mistake. Remember, we're working in low resolution here. These files aren't very big. The more copies you make of the work in progress, the more flexibility you have. ▶

For example, Figure 5-3 shows what happens when the Photoshop file shown in Figure 5-2 is imported into GIF Movie Gear. The frames in the animation start with the lowest layers and then move up. So the background, or first layer, becomes frame 1, the second layer up from the bottom becomes frame 2, and so on. Look at the final frame. Whereas the final frame had a transparent hole in the layered Photoshop file, in GMG the contents of the Hole layer were merged with the first or background layer to form the final frame of the animation. If you look closely you see that the spiral in the final frame is in the same position or state of rotation as the spiral in the first frame.

> Don't confuse the term *transparency* as it is used in association with layers with the way it is used in relation to GIF files. Transparency on Photoshop layers does not translate into transparency in GIF animation frames—at least not without the manual interframe transparency technique detailed in Chapter 4, Frame Cropping and Interframe Transparency Optimization. ▶

So, once again, we need a series of fully opaque layers for the spiral GIF animation. Here's the basic process for creating a Photoshop file that contains a fully opaque layer for each frame of the animation. First, notice in Figure 5-4 that the Hole layer is the very top layer. If we turn off the visibility of each of the layers except the background and the Hole layer, as shown in Figure 5-4, the spiral on the background layer shows through the hole in the Hole layer.

To make a copy of the combined content of the Hole layer and the background, choose **Select,All**, and then choose **Copy Merged** (the shortcuts for these two operations are particularly valuable). **Copy Merged** will not be available unless you have selected one of the visible layers.

Now we need to open a new document. When you choose **New** from the File menu after having copied something to the clipboard, the document's dimensions in the New dialog

Figure 5-3   **The layered Photoshop file from Figure 5.2 imported into GIF Movie Gear.**

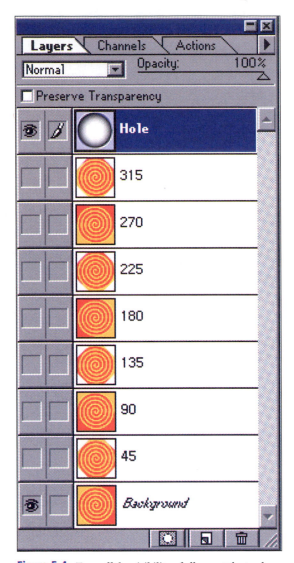

Figure 5-4   Turn off the visibility of all except the top layer and bottom layer.

box default to the size of the contents of the clipboard. We accept the defaults and then paste in the contents of the new document. Pasting in this first frame of the animation results in a new layer in the new document. We don't need one of the frames of the animation to be a big white square, so we merge this first new layer to the background.

What we have just done is analogous to traditional cel-based animations. Each Photoshop layer in the original spiral Photoshop file is like an animation cel. We created the first frame of the animation by copying the cels we need for frame 1 using the **Copy Merge** function. We essentially took a picture of the cels for frame 1 using the **Copy Merged** feature.

Placing the copy into a new document is similar to adding a frame of traditional animation to film. In traditional animation, animators take pictures of cels and then add the picture to a roll of film for the final animation. We took a picture (copy merged the layers) of the cels (the various layers) and added the picture (the copy) to the film (the new document). Also notice that when we make one layer in a Photoshop file visible (in this case we're talking about the original spiral Photoshop file) and make another one invisible, it is like adding and removing traditional celluloid sheets.

This process also provides us with some of the timesaving benefits of traditional cel-based animation. Static or repeating elements have been placed on a separate layer from the moving or changing elements. This means that we do not have to create this artwork over and over again for each frame. Furthermore, we don't have to worry about the positioning of the static elements. They remain in exactly the same place in each frame because we are making copies of the same static elements over and over again.

To create the rest of the frames of the animation, all we need to do is to make the next spiral layer visible, choose **Copy Merged**, and copy and paste the next frame into the new document. For example, to create the second frame, we make the layer named 45 visible, select the 45 layer, choose **Copy Merged**, and paste the file into the new document. The result of repeating this operation for all the rotated spiral layers is shown in Figure 5-5. As you can see, the hole is in the same place in every frame, each frame is on its own layer, and each frame is fully opaque. To make this file into a GIF animation using GIF animation utilities such as GIF Movie Gear or Gifmation, we need only save this file as a Photoshop file and then import it. Each layer will be made into a separate frame, as shown in Figure 5-6.

Incidentally, the approach that we are describing here is essentially the same one used by Adobe ImageReady for creating GIF animations. ImageReady has a Layers palette very similar to Photoshop's, as shown in Figure 5-7. You create animations in ImageReady using the Animation palette, which opens by default with a single frame. You add frames to ImageReady's Animation palette by clicking on the **Duplicate Current Frame** icon (the small page icon to the left of the trash can icon). ImageReady then populates, or fills, this new frame with the contents of the currently visible frames. In other words, ImageReady takes the lump sum of whatever frames are visible in the Layers palette and places it in the new frame.

You make an animation in ImageReady by creating a new frame and then turning on and off the visibility of layers (or manipulating the contents of layers) according to what you want the frame to look like. You repeat this process for all the frames of your animation. This means that the flat frames of the animation are created in the Animation palette, but

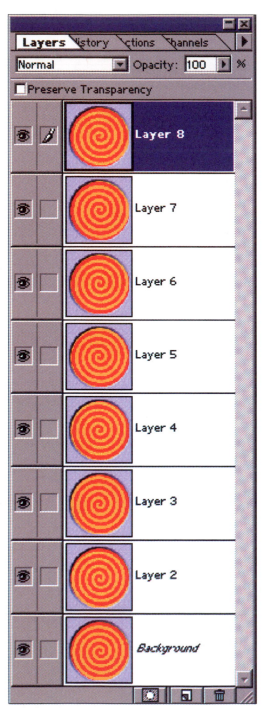

Figure 5-5   Paste the merged frames into a new Photoshop document. Each frame is fully
opaque and on its own layer.

Figure 5-6 Programs such as **GIF** Movie Gear, **GIF**mation, and GIFBuilder automatically create GIF animation frames from layered Photoshop documents.

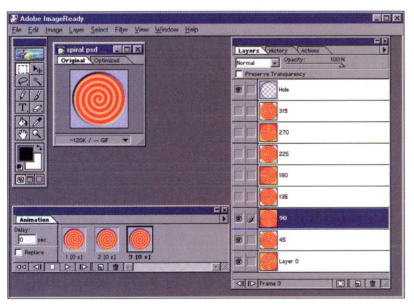

Figure 5-7 Adobe ImageReady uses an approach to creating animation frames that is very similar to the technique described in this chapter for Adobe Photoshop.

the artwork used to create those frames is still on various layers. Complete flexibility is maintained because the static frames of the animation are kept separate from the layered imagery used to create those frames. If you ever decide that one of the frames isn't right, all you need to do is click on that frame and then edit or turn on and off the layers until the problem is fixed.

This process is similar to the one just described using Photoshop. One Photoshop document contains the layered components used to create the various frames of the animation, and the other document contains a series of fully opaque layers that represent the individual frames of the animation. If you ever detect a mistake or otherwise need to change the frames of the animation, you can always go back to the layered Photoshop file that contains the individual components and fix the problem without having to start from scratch.

The spiral animation is a basic example, so let's look at a slightly more complex animation so that we can talk about other important issues. Figure 5-8 shows an animation of a small orange ball traveling through a translucent tube. If you look closely you notice that each ball is not spaced very evenly. Fortunately, using layered Photoshop files makes this problem easy to solve.

Figure 5-9 shows the layered Photoshop file used to create the animation in Figure 5-8. You can inspect this Photoshop file (Tubel.psd) for yourself. It is located in the Chapter 5

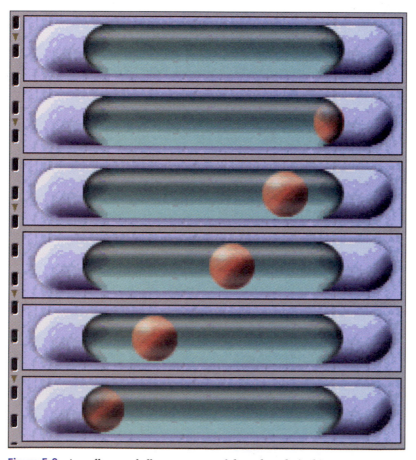

Figure 5-8   A small orange ball appears to travel through a tube in this animation.

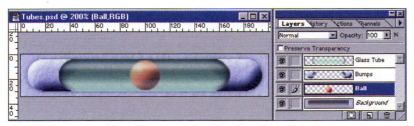

Figure 5-9   Making the ball's motion smooth is difficult when we move a single Ball layer for each frame of the animation.

directory on the companion CD-ROM. The animation was created using layers. However, the animation in Figure 5-8 was created using a single copy of the Ball layer. On each frame, I moved the Ball layer, selected all, copy merged, and pasted into a new document. This required me to eyeball the appropriate position of the ball for each frame. Because I had no frame of reference, I was unable to position the balls on each layer very accurately. As a result, the ball's movement is somewhat jerky.

I created the animation in Figure 5-10 by making copies of the Ball layer (see the section on creating layers for tips on creating new layers). I then positioned each copy of the Ball layer at an incremental location underneath the layer containing the graphics for the tube imagery (the Glass Tube layer is partially transparent), as shown in Figure 5-11. By making copies of the ball, arraying them in their respective positions, and then turning on all the copies, I found it easy to nudge each copy into position so that the motion appears more natural and fluid. To create the animation, I simply turned off all the Ball layers and then turned on each layer one at a time. I used **Copy Merged** to copy each frame into a new document, saved the Photoshop document, and then opened the Photoshop document in GIF Movie Gear.

The advantage of using layers goes beyond the ability to adjust the ball layers independently. After I created this animation, I decided I wanted to adjust the contrast of the Bumps layer and the color of the tube. This was no problem because each element was on a separate layer. Although I had created the Bumps layer using the same texture as the background, adjusting the contrast on the Bumps layer did not affect the background layer, which contains a texture designed to integrate seamlessly with a seamless Web background texture.

Speaking of transparency, note that layers have adjustable opacity. This means that you can emulate onionskinning with Photoshop layers. The term *onionskinning* comes from traditional animation technique. Animators would draw sketches for animations on partially transparent paper (called onionskin). This allowed them to see the position of previous drawings or frames, providing them with a point of reference as they drew a new frame. Figure 5-12 demonstrates the basic idea of onionskinning. In this example, the top layer,

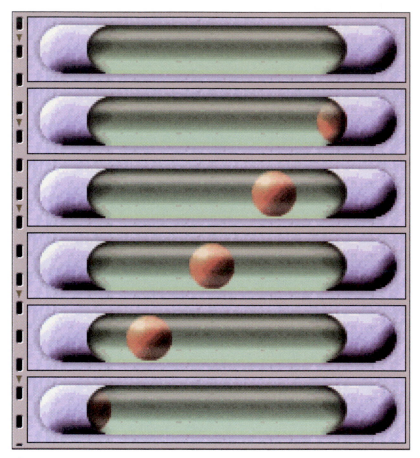

Figure 5-10 In this version of the tube/ball animation, the balls are more evenly spaced, facilitating a more fluid motion.

layer 6, has been made fully transparent. The next three frames are partially transparent: Layer 5 is 30% opaque, layer 4 is 65% opaque, and the remaining layers are all fully opaque. The result is that you can see how the frames on layers 3–5 interact. Onionskinning can be a valuable way to check the status of your work in progress.

Creating Layers

Creating animations using Photoshop's layers means making copies of layers very often. It's worth looking into the various methods of making a layer in Photoshop so that you can determine which method is more efficient in a given situation. Here are the various ways you can make a new layer from an existing layer in Photoshop.

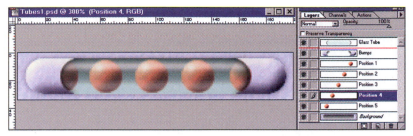

Figure 5-11   With more copies of the Ball layer, it was easy to array them evenly.

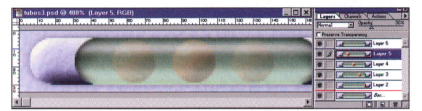

Figure 5-12   Photoshop's layer opacity settings make it easy perform crude onionskinning, allowing you to compare animation frames to one another.

▶ Copy and paste.

▶ Drag an existing layer to the **Create New Layer** icon in the Layers palette.

▶ Right-click on a layer (PC) or click and hold (Mac) and select **Duplicate Layer** from the pop-up menu.

▶ Select **Duplicate Layer** from the Layer menu.

▶ Drag and drop from another document.

▶ Use the Photoshop *action* feature to copy a layer.

Copy and paste is typically the fastest approach. Photoshop automatically creates and names a new layer when you copy and paste. If the size of the pasted contents is smaller than the size of the entire document, Photoshop centers the pasted contents. Therefore, when the contents of the clipboard (the place where the image is stored when you copy) are the same size as the document, the copies are registered to the same position as in the original layer. However, when the contents of the document in the clipboard are larger or smaller, they are centered on the new layer. If you want to make multiple copies of a layer, you can paste it multiple times.

For example, Figure 5-13 shows a blue ball and its shadow on a separate layer over the spiral background. Let's say that we want to make a series of duplicate layers from the Ball

Figure 5-13   There are two layers in this image: the spiral background on one layer and the blue ball and its shadow on another layer.

layer that are located in the same position as the original layer. Using the copy and paste method wouldn't work, as shown in Figure 5-14. As you can see, the ball has been centered. The reason is that the ball is smaller than the overall document, so Photoshop automatically centers the new copy of the Ball layer whether you like it or not.

Later, when we look at Photoshop's actions, we talk about a workaround for this problem, so we also talk later about using actions to copy existing layers.

Another way to create a duplicate copy of a layer is to drag the layer to the **Create New Layer** icon in the Layers palette. This method can get tedious if done repetitively, especially when you have a large number of layers. Also, because the icon is small, it is easy to inadvertently drag the layer to the **Delete Current Layer** icon or the **Add Layer Mask** icon. Nevertheless, this is usually the method of choice in the example described earlier. Layers duplicated with this method are precisely positioned to their original location and not centered. In the

Figure 5-14 When you create a new layer by pasting it into the document, Photoshop centers the new layer.

example of the blue ball over the spiral background, dragging the ball's layer to the **Create New Layer** icon in the Layers palette would result in a duplicate of the Ball layer directly over the original.

The next two methods (right-clicking on a layer and then selecting **Duplicate layer** from the pop-up menu and selecting **Duplicate Layer** from the Layer menu) slow the process by prompting you to name the new layer. Although naming layers appropriately can help you stay oriented and keep you from inadvertently applying edits to the wrong layer, it's often best to go to the trouble of naming a layer only after you've finished editing it. If you make an error while editing a layer, the fix is usually to make a duplicate layer. This can occur multiple times, and naming the layer every time only slows you down.

Dragging and dropping from another Photoshop document is often a handy way to create a new layer, especially when you want to avoid reinventing the wheel by using art from another Photoshop document. The operation requires that you simply drag a layer from one document onto another document.

You might have noticed that the spiral in the earlier example looks odd around the perimeter. There's kind of a yin/yang thing going on there. Let's cover up that part of the animation. Rather than create the art from scratch, though, let's use art from an existing animation.

In Figure 5-15, you can see that a problem can arise when you drag and drop layers between documents. In this example, the new layer is not in the correct position because when you drag and drop between layers, the new layer's contents are centered around the position your cursor occupied when you released the mouse button. For example, in Figure 5-16 the version on the left was the result of releasing the mouse at approximately the upper-left corner of the document, whereas the image on the right was the result of releasing the mouse at approximately the lower-right corner of the document.

Fortunately, holding down the **Shift** key while you drag and drop between documents centers the new layer. In this case, the new layer's contents are kept centered in the new document, as it was in its original document, as shown in Figure 5-17.

The final technique—using an action to copy a layer—is discussed in a later section, Automation with Actions.

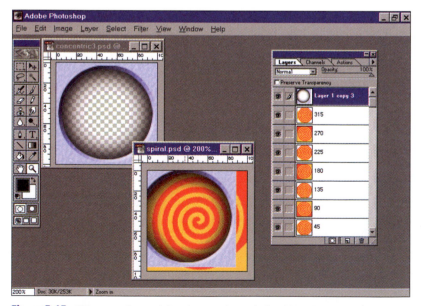

Figure 5-15   When you drag and drop between layered Photoshop documents, Photoshop centers a new layer's contents around the position of your cursor.

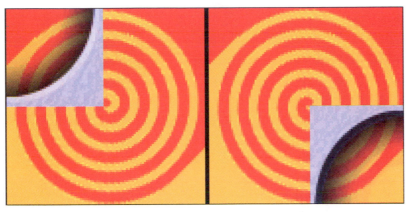

Figure 5-16   With the drag-and-drop method between Photoshop documents, the cursor was located close to the upper-left corner (for the version on the right) and close to the lower-right corner (for the version on the left).

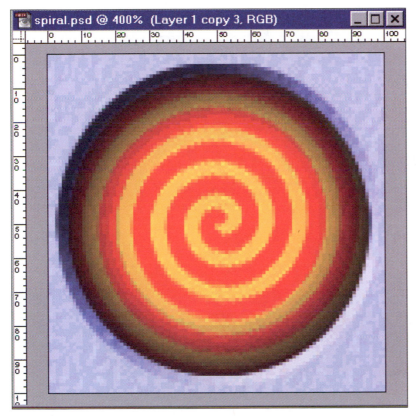

Figure 5-17   If you hold down the **Shift** key while performing the drag-and-drop operation, Photoshop centers the new layer within the new document.

▦ Using Guides

Another valuable asset for creating animation in Photoshop is *guides*. When the motion in the animation is linear (as in the tube example), you can usually position each frame by either nudging the layers into position or moving them with the Move tool while holding down the **Shift** key (which constrains the movement horizontally or vertically). However, when the animation requires more-complex motion, guides can come in handy.

Figure 5-18 shows a Photoshop file for a classic slide puzzle animation. Each puzzle piece was placed on a separate layer, as shown in Figure 5-19. The movement of this animation was designed to be both horizontal and vertical, so guides were employed to help keep the motion consistent and ease the animation process.

Figure 5-18   Each puzzle piece for this example was precisely positioned using Photoshop's guides.

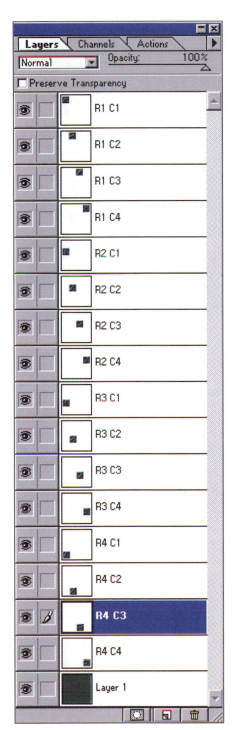

Figure 5-19   Each puzzle piece is on a separate Photoshop layer.

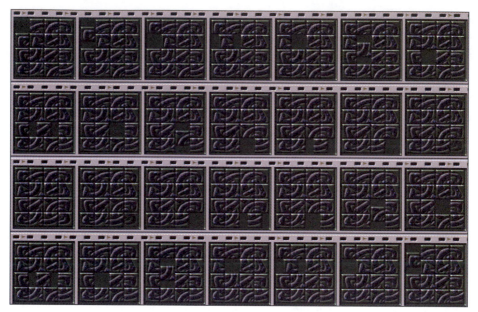

Figure 5-20   In the final animation, each puzzle piece moves progressively in a linear pattern.

Figure 5-20 shows the final animation. It starts with the blocks out of position. The blocks then move into position in a stairstep pattern and finally move again out of position. Despite the large number of layers used to create this animation and the higher-than-average number of frames (for a GIF animation), it was easy to create using Photoshop's guides. I positioned each piece using the guides with the **Snap to Guide** option on. If you look carefully at each frame you see that the motion for each puzzle piece has only three positions. Each piece starts in its original position. In the next frame, the piece moves halfway between its original and final position. In the third frame, the piece is in its final position.

Photoshop's guides snap to the edges of a layer's contents. After you create a layer you can position guides for it by turning on the ruler and then dragging from the ruler to position the guide. The guide snaps to the layer at the left and right horizontal and top and bottom vertical points where the layer becomes fully transparent. Guides also snap to selections. For example, if you make a marquee selection, you can easily position guides to it because the guides snap to the edges of the selection. ▶

The motion of each puzzle piece in this animation is totally linear. The pieces move either up, down, right, or left. Each piece is either exactly within a square as defined by the guides or is exactly in between two squares as defined by the guides. Positioning was easy because not only do layer contents snap to guides but also their center point snaps to guides. So each piece was either snapped into a square when dragged or snapped in between squares (at its center) when dragged. See Chapter 6 for more on using Photoshop guides with Web animations.

▦ Automation with Actions

Animation is often a repetitive process. Whenever you are doing something repeatedly in Photoshop, think "Actions." *Actions* are effectively macros. You can record commands and play them back on any image to automate the application of a series of commands. Let's look at a simple example of how actions can come in handy when you create animations.

Figure 5-21 shows a somewhat mesmerizing wave animation created in Photoshop. As you can see, the hole is similar to the one used in the earlier spiral animation. Originally, the graphics used to create the waves were black and white, as shown in Figure 5-22. After creating each graphic I decided I wanted to colorize each frame using Photoshop's Hue/Saturation dialog box. Rather than open, arrange the settings, and apply **Hue/Saturation** seven times, I created an action to reduce the hassle.

Creating the action was straightforward. I simply selected the Action palette, clicked on the little right-pointing triangle (the Actions palette Options menu), and selected the **New Action** option. In the Action Options dialog box I named the action **Quick Hue/Saturation**, assigned the **F10** key to it, and applied the color red to it, as shown in Figure 5-23. When you click **OK**, Photoshop starts recording. So I turned off a few of the layers so that I could see a layer on which I could clearly see the colorize effect as I adjusted the settings. Then I selected **Hue/Saturation** from the Image, Adjust menu, adjusted the settings, applied the effect, and then stopped the recording (see Figure 5-24).

There are four ways you can apply an action.

1. Click on the **play** button at the bottom of the Actions palette when an action is selected.

2. Switch to Button mode and click on the action's button.

3. Assign a shortcut key.

4. Run an action within another action (this is called a *nested* action).

Figure 5-21 This animation has the same hole as the one used in the earlier spiral example.

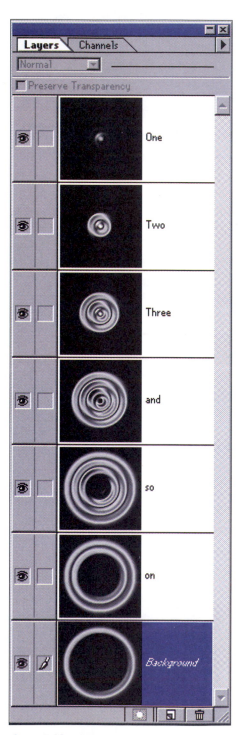

Figure 5-22   The imagery seen through the hole was originally black and white.

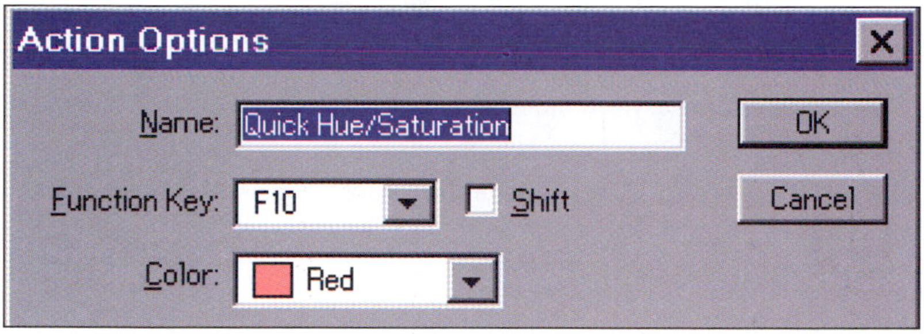

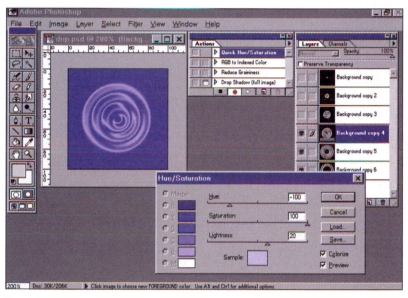

Figure 5-23 Photoshop lets you apply shortcut keys and colors to actions.

Figure 5-24 Photoshop's Hue/Saturation feature was used to colorize the black and white imagery.

For this example, I simply selected each of the remaining noncolorized layers and pressed **F10** to run the **Quick Hue/Saturation** action on it. That was easier than selecting each layer, opening Hue/Saturation, remembering what settings I used the first time, entering them, applying them, and then repeating the process for the rest of the layers. Not only is it easier, but it also ensures consistency. As you can see in Figure 5-24, I used a setting of **–100** for the **Hue** option in the Hue/Saturation dialog box. If I had a dollar for every time I forgot to put a minus sign in front of my entries in one of these dialog boxes, I certainly wouldn't be sitting here writing this book. Using actions ensures that you use the same settings for each frame.

If you have used up all the shortcut keys for actions (and if you're using actions that much, good for you), you might want to apply the actions via Button mode. To turn on Button mode, select the **Button Mode** option from the Actions palette Options menu. The Actions palette will look similar to Figure 5-25. Notice that the button named "Quick Hue/Saturation" is pink. This makes it easy to distinguish from the other buttons. Normally, the Actions palette is housed in the tabbed dialog box with the Layers and Channels palettes. To easily apply an action with Button mode to a series of layers, simply click on the **Actions** tab and drag the Actions palette out and away from the Layers and Channels palettes, as shown in Figure 5-24. Now, if you set the Actions palette next to the Layers palette you can simply select each layer and then press the action's button in the Actions palette.

Actions can make many common animation tasks much easier. For example, earlier we mentioned that if you choose **Duplicate Layer** from the Layer menu, you will get a dialog box prompting you to name the layer. Putting the **Duplicate Layer** command in an action eliminates the tedium of having to stop and name each layer. If you make **Duplicate Layer** an action, that pesky dialog box doesn't show up. You can make **Duplicate Layer** an action with a keyboard shortcut, press the key a few times, and start animating.

Actions are also great for moving layers. Why manually move or even nudge layers when you can move them with precision by using Photoshop's Offset filter located in the Filter, Other menu? If you can duplicate a layer in an action and you can move that layer with an action, then you can create an action that duplicates a layer and then moves it. You can be creating an animation with a few clicks of a keyboard shortcut.

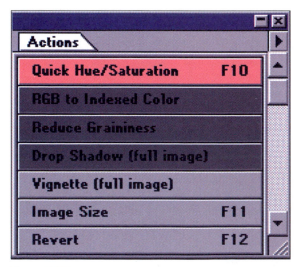

Figure 5-25 With Button mode on, you can apply actions simply by clicking on the action's button.

📽 Auto-Generated Animation Effects

Many kinds of animation can be automated. At this point, we depart from our discussion of creating animations in Photoshop to talk about auto-generated animation effects that are available in various GIF animation utilities. Although it's valuable to learn how to use Photoshop to generate animations, it's also important to know when to let your animation utility do the animation for you.

Many GIF animation utilities generate animation automatically. For example, Ulead GIF Animator 2.0, SPG Web Tools for Photoshop, and InterDimensions' GIFX all include a variety of computer-generated animation effects. For the most part, these effects are transition effects such as wipes, fades, and slides that have no adjustable parameters. These effects are generally low-quality and are more valuable to the vendors, who can say they have animated effects in their program, than they are to animators. Some GIF animation utilities offer slightly better auto-generated animation effects. For example, GIFX provides adjustable parameters for its auto-generated effects, which include waves, art effects (such as Monet), and the ability to animate resolution changes. SPG Web Tools offers some excellent 3-D and flare special effects. With the GIF animator in SPG Web Tools, you can apply the animated 3-D text, buttons, simple 3-D models, and flare effects directly to existing GIF animations (see Figure 5-26).

A new breed of animation tools, including Extensis PhotoAnimator and Paceworks GIF Dancer, has emerged that generates more-sophisticated effects for Web animations. These tools allow you to build your animations in a 24-bit layered environment similar to Photoshop. However, with these tools you can apply effects to specific layers across multiple

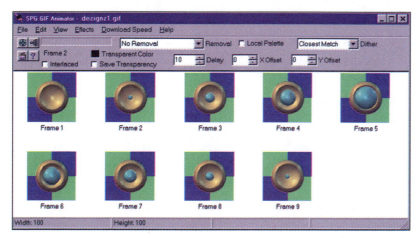

Figure 5-26   The GIF animator in SPG Web Tools can generate 3-D animation effects on-the-fly over existing GIF animation frames.

frames. After you have processed your animation, both programs export fully optimized GIF animations for the Web.

For example, Figure 5-27 shows the Extensis PhotoAnimator interface. Notice that the upper-left window (called the Layers pane) is similar to Photoshop's Layers palette. Below this window is a layered filmstrip area (called the Filmstrip pane). The layers on the Filmstrip pane correspond to the layers in the Layers pane. Layers on the Filmstrip pane contain what Extensis calls "cells." Each cell can have multiple frames, and each layer can have multiple cells. To create animations in Extensis PhotoAnimator, you can apply simple animation effects—such as resize, rotate, and move to objects—directly to cells.

PhotoAnimator allows you to apply more-complicated effects, such as transitions or animated masking effects, nondestructively. You apply the effects to separate cells on separate layers below the layers or cells you wish to be affected. For example, the bottom layer in the Filmstrip pane shown in Figure 5-27 affects the filmstrip layer above.

For more-sophisticated auto-generated animation effects, you can always turn to digital video and animation-capable 3-D programs, such as Adobe After Effects and Adobe Premiere, or animation-capable 3-D programs such as Metacreation's Bryce 3-D. Although these programs weren't exactly designed for Web animation, they are great sources for

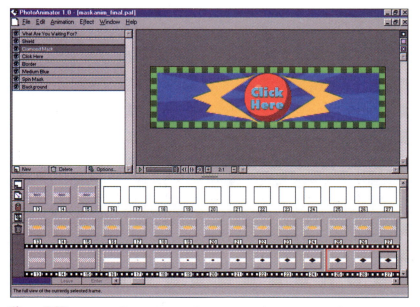

Figure 5-27   Extensis PhotoAnimator allows you to apply auto-generated animation
effects to specific layered elements nondestructively.

auto-generated animation effects. The tools offer a wide range of adjustable, professional-quality animation effects. Adobe also provides free GIF animation export plug-ins for both After Effects and Premiere. This means that you can easily create GIF animations from digital video (see Figure 5-28).

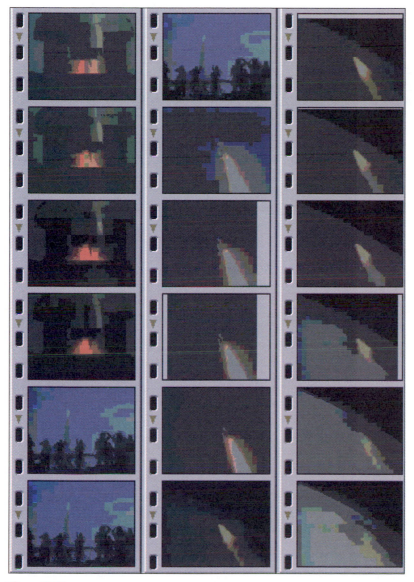

Figure 5-28 This animation was exported straight from an AVI file in Adobe Premiere using the free GIF animation export plug-in available for download from Adobe's site.

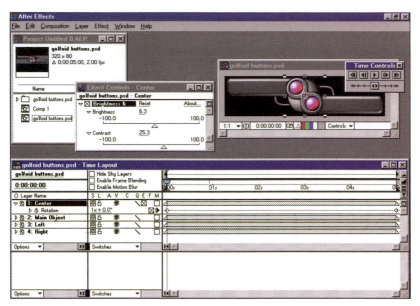

Figure 5-29   **After Effects allows you to apply special effects and image manipulations (such as brightness and contrast) over time to specific elements on separate layers.**

If you can afford it, After Effects is particularly good for creating Web animation. Much like Photoshop, After Effects allows you to create animations using layers. Unlike Photoshop, After Effects allows you to animate on a timeline. Using key frames, you can apply effects at various stages along the timeline and After Effects creates the in-between frames for you (Figure 5-29). When you create Web animation in programs such as Adobe After Effects, bear in mind that these advanced digital video applications are generally geared toward output that's closer to broadcast quality. Frame rates of 15–30 frames per second, used with most digital video, are usually overkill for Web animation. You can set up After Effects to any screen size and frame rate, so you can set up your projects to be more appropriate for Web animation.

▣ Summary

Animation is a time-consuming prospect, but you can substantially reduce the amount of time and frustration involved by using Photoshop's layers to emulate traditional cel animation techniques. If you take advantage of features such as guides and actions, you can simplify the process even more. You should take advantage of any auto-generated animation effects offered by your animation utility whenever appropriate. You can always touch up auto-generated animations in Photoshop to make them more unique.

CHAPTER 6

Seamless Integration

One of the most effective ways to add to the impact of animations is to integrate them seamlessly into the overall design of a Web page. Animations have a limited effect when they stand alone. When individual animations are a part of the big picture, however, they benefit from the overall design, essentially increasing their impact and perceived depth. ▶

Integration with a Background Texture

Using HTML Tables with Animation

Slicing Up an Image in Photoshop

Assembling the Pieces in HTML

Correcting Seams Between GIF and JPEG Images

Integration with Other Web Multimedia Technologies

▣ Integration with a Background Texture

A simple way to integrate an animation with a Web page is to blend the animation into or onto the page's background texture. Seamless tiled backgrounds are commonly used in Web design. Often, you can use these textures within the animation to make it appear that the animation is part of the background. For example, Figure 6-1 shows three animations from NavWorks (navworks.i-us.com). All three of the animations integrate seamlessly over the same noisy gray background texture. You cannot see the edges of the animations because they appear to blend in perfectly with the background texture.

The key to this effect lies in the texture, which is so random that it is naturally seamless. No extra effort was required to make the tile into a seamless texture. These animations blend into the background because the same texture used for the Web page was used as the background for the animations.

It is easy to create a naturally seamless texture with almost any bitmap editor, such as Photoshop, using the Add Noise filter, which creates random noise patterns. These patterns are almost always so random that no additional steps are required to make them seamless.

There are several ways to employ the Add Noise filter to get a naturally seamless texture. For example, you can fill a document of any size with a color and then apply the Add Noise filter with the Monochromatic setting. This technique results in a random noisy pattern in the color you chose. If you want the noisy pattern to have additional hues, try applying Add Noise (with the Monochromatic option on) to different colors on different layers and then combine the layers using various layer modes. To create a random bumpy texture,

Figure 6-1   All these animations from NavWorks integrate seamlessly with the Web page's background.

apply the Add Noise filter to a white background and then blur and emboss the results. Next, colorize the bumpy gray texture using Hue/Saturation with the Colorize option.

There are basically two ways to integrate a background texture into an animation. All the animations shown in Figure 6-1 use the same basic approach for integrating the texture used on the Web page into the actual animation. Figure 6-2 shows the Photoshop file used to create one of the animations shown in Figure 6-1.

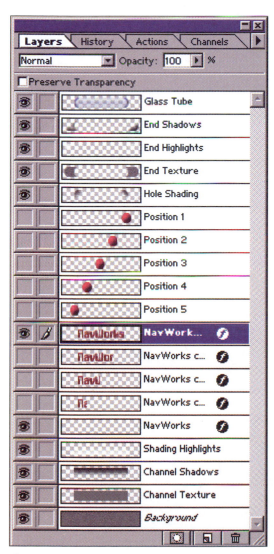

Figure 6-2 The background texture is on a separate layer from the rest of the graphic elements used to generate the sample animation.

Notice that all the graphic elements used to create the animation are set on layers above the background layer. The background layer is filled with the same texture that was used on the Web page. When I created this animation, I started by opening the noisy gray background texture tile used for the Web page. In Photoshop, I chose **Select All** and then defined the texture as a pattern (**Edit, Define Pattern**). Next, I used the **Fill** feature (also located in the Edit menu) to fill the background layer with the pattern. I then made each frame of the animation using the background layer as the background for the entire animation. (See Chapter 5, Advanced Animation Techniques in Photoshop, for a discussion on how to create animations from layered Photoshop documents.)

This approach is versatile because you can easily change the texture in the background layer to make the animation play over a different texture.

In this first approach to building a naturally seamless texture into an animation, you make it the background and then put all the other animation components above the background. However, this approach may not work for some animations. Figure 6-3 shows a series of animations that require a second, slightly different approach. All these animations appear to be embedded, or cut into, the Web page.

Figure 6-4 shows the Photoshop file used to create one of the animations shown in Figure 6-3. The layer called Top Texture contains a hole that shows through to the layers below it. The motion takes place within this hole. So, for this example, the naturally seamless texture must be placed on a layer above the background layer. To create such an effect, you can fill a layer with the texture you want and then delete or cut out a hole. However, when I created this Photoshop file, I cut out the hole before filling the layer with the final texture that was needed to blend in the Web page's background. Even when the layer has transparent

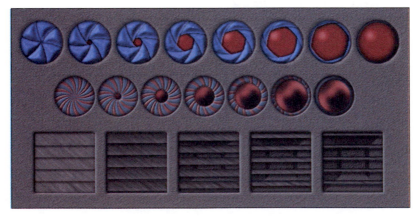

Figure 6-3   These animations look as if they are holes that have been cut into the Web page.

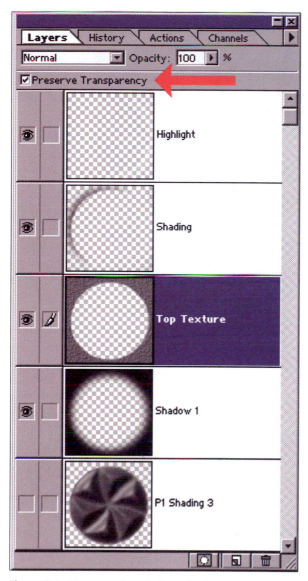

Figure 6-4   The texture layer is above the elements used to generate the animated effects.
(Arrow added.)

portions, it is easy to fill the layer with a new texture. All you have to do is to turn on the
Preserve Transparency option. Then, when you use the **Fill** feature to fill the layer with
the texture, the texture fills only the opaque areas of the layer.

When a texture is not naturally seamless, you must go to a little extra effort to integrate
an animation over the background. Figure 6-5 shows an animation created by Scott Balay

Figure 6-5   This animation spins over, and independently of, a dark gray, rocky background texture.

of Infinitefish productions. The animation is set over a dark gray texture created by a seamless tile used as the background for the Web page. The background texture is not naturally seamless—that is, it is not random. Therefore, using it as background for the animation would not work because it would be difficult or impossible to blend the animation's texture seamlessly with the texture on the background of the Web page.

To get the animation to appear to blend over the dark gray texture, Balay created the graphics for the animation on a black background. Then he made all the pixels around the spinning graphic transparent. Figure 6-6 shows all the frames of the animation. All the gray areas around the colorful spinning graphic are transparent. Each frame actually has a black seam around the edges of the graphic, but because the background texture of the Web page is dark gray, this seam is barely apparent.

When you want to blend an animation over a background texture that is not naturally seamless, you create the animation over a color that will be similar to the dominant color in the background texture. All the images will be anti-aliased to the background color. Therefore, when you make all the outlying areas transparent, as shown in Figure 6-4, the fringes will roughly match the background texture and the animation will appear to integrate seamlessly over the background.

If your Web page has a solid-color background, your job is even easier. Simply use that color as the animation's background color. This, however, can be a problem in some cases. Sometimes, animation utilities shift the colors within an animation. Figure 6-7 shows an animation set over a green background. The animation's background color is slightly off from the Web page's background color. Figure 6-8 shows a close-up of the animation. If you look carefully where the arrows are pointing, you see a slight color shift along the animation's

Figure 6-6   The dark gray portions of these frames are transparent so that those portions show through the background texture of the Web page.

boundaries. Figure 6-9 shows all the frames of the animation. The same light green color is built into each of the frames, so the unsightly seam is visible throughout the entire animation.

One way to fix this problem is to use Adobe ImageReady's color locking feature.(Macromedia Fireworks version 2 also has this feature.) ImageReady makes it easy to preserve colors in a GIF animation by allowing you to lock them (see Figure 6-10). All you have to do is to use the eyedropper tool to select the color. When you do this, the color becomes selected in the Optimized Colors palette (up arrow). Then you click on the little lock icon to lock the color (down arrow). After you lock the color, it will not shift to a different color or be deleted when you perform color reduction or optimization.

If you do not have ImageReady, there is another approach you can take. After you create your animation, open the GIF file in Photoshop and use the eyedropper tool to find out what color the background is. Then create a new document. Make the document 50–100 pixels square and then fill the document with the color you sampled from the GIF

Figure 6-7   The background color of the animation differs slightly from the background color of the Web page.

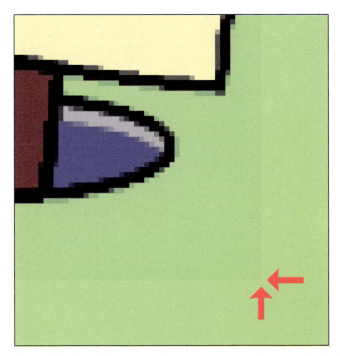

Figure 6-8   The difference in color results in a noticeable "seam" (indicated by the arrows) between the animation and the background of the Web page.

Figure 6-9   All the frames of the animation have the same background color.

animation. Then save this file as a GIF and use it as the Web page's background tile. If you optimize the GIF file (it has only one color, so the GIF's palette should be no larger than 1-bit), the file will be very small and won't add much to the overall download of the Web page. If the color of your Web page's background matches the background color in your GIF animation, the GIF animation will appear to blend in seamlessly with the Web page.

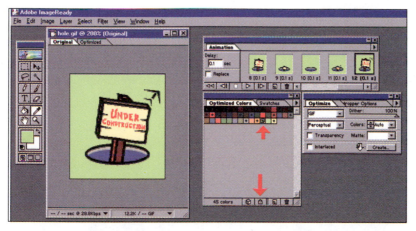

Figure 6-10   Adobe ImageReady allows you to lock colors so that they remain the same during color reduction. This means that the background color of the animation will match the color of the Web page.

▦ Using HTML Tables with Animation

In Chapter 2, GIF Animation: Basics and Beyond, we looked at how several animations can be placed next to one another so that they appear to be a single animation. You learned how several animations could be combined to increase the overall impact. If you can combine animations, you can logically merge animations with still images or with a combination of still images and other animations.

Tiling, or combining images on a Web page, allows you to isolate sections of an image and use them to blend dynamic Web elements such as GIF animations, JavaScript mouseover events, Java applets, and Shockwave movies along with static images. Furthermore, you can position JPEG images next to GIF images, a technique that can help keep the file size down when parts of an overall design compress better in JPEG and other parts compress better in GIF.

Basic HTML is fine for stringing together a series of images and/or animations that are the same size as long as they are in single row. Even creating multiple rows of images is fine as long as all the pieces share a common height. However, when you need to puzzle together pieces that have different heights, you often want to turn to HTML *tables* for the solution. The trick to this approach lies in careful preparation and precise implementation.

Figure 6-11 shows a banner ad window from jumplist.com. JumpList is a Web links program created by Jim Shaw. This banner ad window was designed to have a beveled border around the banner ad as well as a small button bar below the window. The button bar was designed to hold a maximum of three buttons, although only one button is shown in Figure 6-11. Notice that there is no gap between the beveled borders and the banner ad (which is a GIF animation). The entire element looks as if it is one unit. In reality, there are nine separate images. These nine images were combined seamlessly using HTML tables.

Aside from creating the graphics, animations, or other elements, tiling images with HTML tables is essentially a two-step process:

1. Slice the graphic into pieces.

2. Assemble the pieces with HTML tables.

Figure 6-11   A border with an attached button bar encases this standard 468 × 60 pixel banner ad. Copyright © i-us Corp. http://www.i-us.com.

It helps a great deal to create or compile the images in a comprehensive bitmap-editing program such as Adobe Photoshop. Essentially, the object is to avoid unsightly gaps when the image is ultimately displayed, so Photoshop's ability to precisely isolate portions of a bitmap image with guides and selections, in addition to the ability to layer elements, makes it the perfect central processing center for this technique.

Figure 6-12 shows the three layers used for the banner ad frame and button bar for JumpList. Notice that the difference between each layer is in the button bar below the banner ad frame. Shaw designed this button bar to dynamically change depending on where it is displayed. On some pages you see all three buttons, and on others you see only the middle button. Also, all three buttons were designed to have rollovers. Note that the blank rectangular area within the borders is where the animated GIF banner ads are displayed. This area was designed to fit a standard 468×60 banner ad. So the border pieces surrounding this hole had to be exactly the right size to fit the ad.

It is best to set HTML tables in rows and columns. The more organized the rows and columns, the easier it is to create the table. Usually, the object is to try to break the image into as few rows and columns as possible, although the rows and columns must be defined by the intricacies of the image.

Let's look at how this image was broken apart. The red lines in Figure 6-13 show how the pieces were sliced up. There are three rows. The top row is a long thin piece of the top border. The second row contains three pieces: the left border piece, the center area (no image

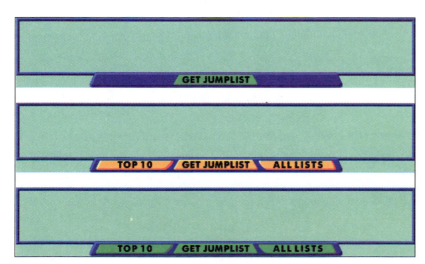

Figure 6-12   Three different layered images were used to generate the graphic elements.
Copyright © i/us Corp. http://www.i-us.com.

Figure 6-13   The red lines outline the borders of all the pieces. Copyright © i/us Corp.
http://www.i-us.com.

was saved for this area because it was designed to contain a banner ad), and the right border piece. The third row contains five pieces: the left and right bottom corners and three pieces for the buttons.

Slicing Up an Image in Photoshop

When cutting up an image, you should not cut up the original image. Instead, you should make copies of the various pieces and then save them as separate pieces. You make an accurate selection of each piece, copy it, paste it into a new document, and then save each piece as a GIF or JPEG.

When it comes to sectioning off individual pieces of the graphic, precise selections are crucial because the image won't look right in the browser if each piece isn't perfectly sized. Photoshop's guides (with **Snap To Guides** on) and Info box may help you manage this requirement. However, it is all too easy to create imprecise guides with Photoshop.

Figure 6-14 demonstrates what can happen when the guides are not precisely aligned. It is a zoomed-in view of the upper-right corner of the sample image from jumplist.com. In 100% view, I placed a guideline by trying to eyeball it. The guideline needed to be directly over the border between the vertical dark blue pixels and the mint green pixels. It looked dead on at 100%, but, as you can see, when zoomed in the vertical red guide is way off. (I changed the guides from the default light blue to red to make them easier to see.) Now notice the black and blue dotted lines. This is a marquee selection that I made with the **Snap To Guides** feature on.

The problem is that Photoshop's selections snap to the nearest pixel borders regardless of where you position the guidelines. Because guides can be positioned anywhere, more often than not they are over the top of a pixel rather than over the pixel boundaries. A pixel is the smallest unit of a bitmap image, so you can't cut a pixel in half. Inaccurate selections are therefore often the result when guides that are not positioned over pixel boundaries are

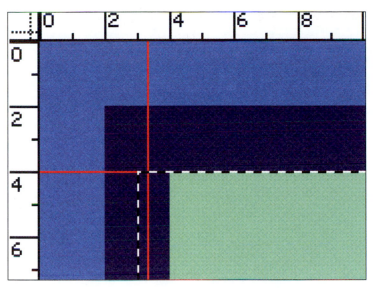

Figure 6-14   Marquee selections in Photoshop snap to the closest pixel boundaries when a guideline is over the top of pixels, resulting in inaccurate selections.

employed to help make selections. Pieces of the resultant image typically are a single pixel too wide, thin, high, or short.

Fortunately, there is an easy way to precisely position guides over pixel boundaries: you hold down the **Shift** key as you position the guidelines. To position guidelines, you turn on the rulers (located in the View menu) and then use the Move tool to click and drag guidelines from the ruler. Hold down the **Shift** key as you drag, and the guidelines will snap to pixel boundaries. It also helps to zoom in a little to make sure that the guidelines are snapping to the desired position. Figure 6-15 shows all the guides that were used for

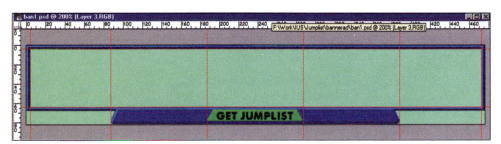

Figure 6-15   The guidelines used to break the animation into pieces. Copyright © i/us Corp. http://www.i-us.com.

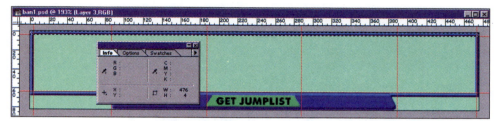

Figure 6-16   Get the accurate dimensions for each piece from the Info palette. Copyright © i/us Corp. http://www.i-us.com.

the sample (again, the guides have been changed from the default light blue to red to make them easier to see).

Browsers display an image at whatever height and width you specify in the HEIGHT and WIDTH image tag attributes even if the dimensions of the image are really a different size from the size you have specified, so it is always a good idea to get accurate image dimensions for each graphic, animation, or other integrated element. You can access this information when you make each selection. Open the Info palette (ensure that units are set to pixels) and find the height and width of each selection in the lower-right quadrant, as shown in Figure 6-16. Make a note of this information to use later when you write the HTML <IMG> tags for each piece.

After the guidelines have been positioned precisely, it's time to save the pieces as separate images. All the images used in this example are GIFs. With the **Snap To Guides** feature on, it's a simple matter of making selections and copying them to a new document. Notice that the overall image has very few colors. Furthermore, when you cut up an image, each piece often does not have as many colors as the overall image. This was the case with this example. I was able to save each piece with a separate optimized GIF palette, resulting in a small file size savings.

For example, the first piece that I made was the top bar piece shown in Figure 6-16. When the whole image for the JumpList banner ad bar is indexed, it has 115 total colors. However, when I copied and pasted the top bar piece to a new document and then indexed it, the top bar piece contained only five colors. I was able to achieve a tiny amount of file size savings by saving the piece with five colors in its GIF palette rather than with 115 colors. I repeated this process (make selection, copy, paste into new document, optimize, and save) for all the other pieces for the banner ad bar.

Remember that the sample image actually has several images that need to be generated for the buttons. Each of the buttons has default and rollover states, and blank images are required for the positions representing the left and right buttons when only the center button is displayed. Because this artwork was on a different layer within the same Photoshop File, all the guidelines were already positioned for the various button pieces. All I needed to do was to select the layers that contained the different button states and follow the same steps described earlier to make the pieces for the buttons.

Assembling the Pieces in HTML

After you've cut up all the pieces, it's time to put them back together with HTML tables. It is assumed that you understand the basics of HTML tables, such as how to establish a table in HTML with the table (`<TABLE>`), table row (`<TR>`), and table data (`<TD>`) tags. You should also be familiar with how to write a proper image tag (`<IMG...>`), complete with `HEIGHT` and `WIDTH` information.

There are several keys to creating seamlessly tiled images within an HTML table. First, you must set the `BORDER`, `CELL-PADDING`, and `CELLSPACING` attributes of the `<TABLE>` tag to zero (`"0"`). Merely leaving these attributes to their defaults will result in a single-pixel gap between each cell. Additionally, you

> All the image tags are on a single line. They wrap around as shown here because of the word wrapping requirements of this book, but in the actual HTML, all these lines would be on a single line extending far out to the right. ▶

need not set the `WIDTH` attribute of the `<TABLE>` tag because the browser will read the `HEIGHT` and `WIDTH` attributes of the image tags, which essentially designate the size of the table when the image tags are combined. (See the table code that follows.) It doesn't hurt to set the `BORDERS` attribute in the image tags to equal zero (`BORDERS=0`).

Following is the table that was used for the JumpList banner ad bar (unrelated elements, such as JavaScript and name attributes, have been removed for clarity):

```
<TABLE BORDER="0" CELLSPACING="0" CELLPADDING="0">

  <TR>
    <TD><img src="topbar.gif" width=476 height=4 border=0></TD>
  </TR>


  <TR>
    <TD><img src="leftbar.gif" width=4 height=60 border=0><img src=
"banadph.gif" width=468 height=60 border=0><img src="rightbar.gif" width=4
height=60 border=0></TD>
  </TR>


  <TR>
    <TD><img src="botleft.gif" width=87 height=18 border=0><img
src="b1_blank.gif" width=100 height=18 border=0><img src="b2_def.gif"
width=100 height=18 border=0><img src="b3_blank.gif" width=101 height=18
border=0><img src="botright.gif" width=88 height=18 border=0></TD>
```

```
</TR>
</TABLE>
```

Let's get oriented. This table has three rows, which are defined by the `<TR>` tags. The first row contains one image, the second row contains three images, and the last row contains five images. The table is relatively simple. It is defined by the `<TABLE>` tag (note that the `BORDER`, `CELLSPACING`, and `CELLPADDING` attributes are all set to zero). Each cell is defined by the table row (`<TR>`) and table definition (`<TD>`) tags. However, there are some subtle, important things to point out.

HTML tables can quickly become difficult to read (curiously, that principle also applies to discussions of HTML tables). Web designers commonly add spaces or hard returns between the `<TR>` and `<TD>` tags to help make the overall table more legible and editable. So, for example, notice that there are spaces after each `</TR>` tag. This helps make the table easier to read and edit. Similarly, if there were multiple `<TD>` tags within the `<TR>` and `</TR>` tags, you could place a hard return after each `</TD>` tag to make it easier to read and edit the tags. However, to keep the position of the images seamlessly together, you must make sure that there are no spaces between any tags *within* any given `<TD>` tag. To see this, let's zoom in on the second row:

```
<TR>
    <TD><img src="leftbar.gif" width=4 height=60 border=0><img src=
"banadph.gif" width=468 height=60 border=0><img src="rightbar.gif" width=4
height=60 border=0></TD>
    </TR>
```

As mentioned, the second row contains three images. There are no spaces or hard returns between the image tags used to define the images. If there were a space between the image tags, the browser would display the image with gaps between the pieces, as shown in Figure 6-17.

It's also important to notice that all the `</TD>` tags are on the same line as the image tags. If you put a hard return after the last image tag that is between the `<TD>` and `</TD>` tags, the

Figure 6-17   The red arrows point to the gaps that result from adding spaces between the image tags in the second row of the example. Copyright © i/us Corp. http://www.i-us.com.

result would be a gap. In other words, suppose that the second row of the example looked like this:

```
<TR>
    <TD><img src="leftbar.gif" width=4 height=60 border=0><img src=
"banadph.gif" width=468 height=60 border=0><img src="rightbar.gif" width=4
height=60 border=0>
</TD>
</TR>
```

The </TD> tag is on a separate line from the image tags, and the result would be the gap shown in Figure 6-18.

Beyond constructing a logical HTML table with BORDER, CELLPADDING, and CELLSPACING set to zero, the main secret to putting images together seamlessly within tables is to ensure that there are no spaces between HTML tags of any kind that are within table definition tags (<TD>) and that the closing table definition tags are on the same line as the image tags.

Cutting up pieces of images and then reassembling them with HTML tables can be tedious work. Not only is it time-consuming, but it's also mistake-prone. The more complex the table is, the more difficult and time-consuming it is to do it all by hand. Fortunately, there are several tools that do the work for you, including Macromedia Fireworks, SPG Web Tools, and Adobe ImageReady.

> When you're coding a complex table or series of tables, it can be difficult to pick out various images from one another when you're looking at line after line of HTML. Because browsers aren't particular about how and where you place attributes within tags, you can place the source attribute (SRC="...") before the HEIGHT and WIDTH attributes for images that are always static, and after them for images that change (such as the animated GIFs and rollover buttons in the example). Techniques such as this one make it easier to come back later and customize pieces within the table. ▶

The table-cutting capabilities of Macromedia Fireworks are the best because Fireworks allows you to cut up pieces in any odd arrangement you choose; it writes JavaScript rollover script for you at the same time. By contrast, SPG Web Tools and Adobe ImageReady cut pieces only along guidelines. It is easy to see why the latter approach is less than ideal.

Figure 6-18 Closing table definition tags (</TD>) must be on the same line as the image tags or a gap will result, as shown here by the arrow. Copyright © i/us Corp. http://www.i-us.com.

For example, look again at Figure 6-15. If SPG Web Tools and Adobe ImageReady were to use the guidelines shown in Figure 6-15 to cut up the image, the image would have 21 pieces instead of only nine pieces because these tools offer no way to override cuts in given areas. If there's a guideline running through a portion of an image, SPG Web Tools and Adobe ImageReady dice it up according to the guidelines. For example, the top bar would be cut into seven pieces instead of only one piece because there are five guidelines running through it.

Macromedia Fireworks takes a different approach. Figure 6-19 shows an interface from NavWorks (navworks.i-us.com). The interface is designed to have eight rollover buttons and as many as three interactive animations. The buttons change from dark blue to yellow when the user moves the cursor over them. Figure 6-20 shows the animation that plays in the center of the interface, and Figure 6-21 shows one of the two screen animations. Notice that the buttons and the animations don't line up exactly into neat rows and columns. It would be extremely difficult to cut up and code this interface by hand.

Macromedia Fireworks makes it easy. Figure 6-22 shows the interface in Fireworks. Notice that there a lot of guides, but they are not what Fireworks uses to cut up the image. Instead, these guides are used to help make selections with Fireworks' Slice tool. The shaded portions

> Macromedia has a bad habit of not documenting important features in its paper manuals. You must go the Macromedia Web site (www.macromedia.com) to find documentation on how to fully use the table-cutting features in Macromedia Fireworks. ▶

Figure 6-19   This interface from NavWorks features eight buttons and three animations.

Figure 6-20   This animation plays in the center of the interface.

Figure 6-21   One of two interactive screen animations.

Figure 6-22   The shaded areas tell Fireworks what portions of the image to isolate with the HTML table. This is all Fireworks needs to automatically cut up the pieces and generate the HTML code for you.

are areas that have been selected (portions of the image that have either JavaScript rollovers or animations). Fireworks cuts up the pieces and writes the HTML according to the areas selected by the Slice tool. You need only select the areas that need to be isolated for JavaScript or animations, and Fireworks takes care of the rest.

🎞 Correcting Seams Between GIF and JPEG Images

When you can easily see a difference between a GIF and an adjacent JPEG, you usually still want to use the JPEG because of the file size advantages, but you don't want an unsightly seam. To avoid having a seam, convert the pieces to GIF and then back to RGB; then export them as JPEGs and they will match the GIF images. Figure 6-23, a page from Riven Journals—a site designed by Organic Online for Cyan and Broderbund to promote Riven: Sequel to Myst—demonstrates this strategy in action. This page attempts to create the effect of a journal whose pages contain a magical porthole through which viewers can see images of the topics discussed in the journal.

The porthole features an animation of a whale-like creature. The animation does not fill the entire porthole. Because the remaining portion of the porthole was colorful and full of texture (from the rocks and the water), that portion compressed far better as a JPEG than as a GIF. However, because JPEG allows for millions of colors and GIF only 256 colors, there would have been an obvious seam between the (GIF) animated portion of the porthole and the JPEG portion. By indexing the Photoshop file used to create all the graphics on this page before exporting the pieces as GIFs and JPEGs, Organic ensured that the JPEG and GIFs shared the same dither patterns and colors.

Figure 6-23   **This porthole animation from the Riven Journals Web site is adjacent to a series of static JPEG images. Copyright © Cyan, Inc.**

Figure 6-24 Static GIFs were employed next to the JPEGs to take advantage of GIF transparency. Copyright © Cyan, Inc.

Incidentally, integrating GIF animations is not the only example of a need you might have to match a JPEG to a GIF. Because JPEG doesn't support transparency, you might also want to use GIF to make portions of the overall tabled graphic transparent. This technique was also employed by Organic Online, as Figure 6-24 illustrates. Note that the GIF images on the top, bottom, left, and right contain large areas of gray. This denotes the portions of the GIF images that are transparent. Using transparency at the edges of the JPEG images and the GIF animation allows the porthole to blend seamlessly over the paper texture that is used as the background tile for the Web page. Using transparency on these GIF images also results in significantly reduced file sizes.

Integration with Other Web Multimedia Technologies

Almost any Web multimedia technology can easily be interwoven with still images on a Web page. The key is to ensure that the background of the Shockwave, Flash, or Java applet matches the still images that will surround the new element. Figure 6-25 shows a

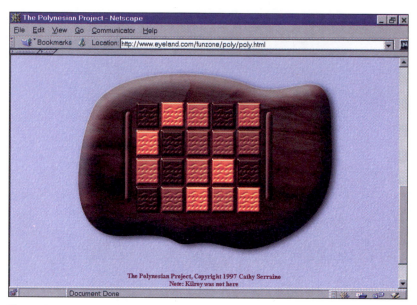

The Polynesian Project, Copyright 1997 Cathy Serraino
Note: Kilroy was not here

Figure 6-25   The Polynesian Project, a Shockwave game, is surrounded by four static JPEG images.

Shockwave game animation called The Polynesian Project, by Cathy Serraino of the Home Shocking Network. It is encased within four static JPEG images. The background of the Shockwave game was derived from the same image used to create the JPEG images, as shown in Figure 6-26.

Most popular Web multimedia technologies are implemented with a combination of <EMBED> (Netscape) and <OBJECT> tags. These tags often have a lot of parameters, usually written on different lines within the HTML. However, if you want to table an <EMBED> or <OBJECT> element within images, you must make sure that all the attributes of the <EMBED> and <OBJECT> tags are on one line.

For example, Figure 6-27 shows a game made using Parable Corporation's ThingMaker. The actual ThingMaker game occupies only the center of the image; the surrounding imagery—the little blue creature taking a nap by a tree and all the imagery for the thought bubble—is composed of still GIF images that have been tabled together around the ThingMaker game.

Here is the table code for the game shown in Figure 6-27:

```
<TABLE border=0 cellpadding=0 cellspacing=0>
<TR>
<TD><img src="left.gif" width=145 height=321 border=0></TD>
```

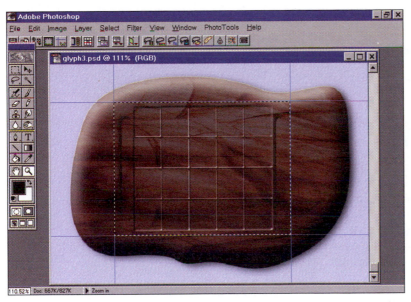

Figure 6-26   The same image used to create the JPEG static images was used to create the background for the Shockwave game.

```
<TD><img src="top.gif" width=255 height=40 border=0><br>

<OBJECT id="dream" name="dream" classid="CLSID:F2D71283-BEE3-11d0-90AE-
00A0C9270D87" codebase="http://www.thingworld.com/download/ie/
ThingViewer.cab" width=255 height=230><param name="SceneFile"
value="dream.tms"><param name="bgcolor" value="#ffffff"><EMBED type=
application/x-Parable-Thing SceneFile="dream.tms" width=255 height=230
bgcolor="#ffffff" pluginspage="http://www.thingworld.com/download/netscape"
name="dream"></object><br>

<img src="bottom.gif" width=255 height=52 border=0></TD>

<TD><img src="right.gif" width=84 height=321 border=0></TD>

<TR>

</TABLE>
```

Word wrap has forced the lines to wrap here; all the contents of the <OBJECT> and <EMBED> tags (the <EMBED> tag is within the <OBJECT> tag) are written on one line. There are no hard returns. If there were hard returns after the various parameters in the <OBJECT> tags of the attributes of the <EMBED> tag, there would be a gap between the static GIF images and the ThingMaker game in the browser window.

Although loading the Web multimedia element may take longer than loading the still images (with the notable exception of many Flash animations), you can substantially reduce the file size of these Web multimedia elements by minimizing the stage area. The whole point is that you can make the smaller Web multimedia element (Shockwave, Java,

Figure 6-27   In this image, an animated game is tabled within four images that border it on the top, bottom, left, and right.

and so on) not *look* so small by mixing it with a series of other elements such as GIF animations and static images.

Summary

Fundamentally, successful integration of Web elements—whether still images, animations, Shockwave, or Java (or anything else)—is a matter of breaking the elements into logical units and then plugging the units into HTML. Each mechanism has its own set of important details to bear in mind, but all the basic concepts are the same. Careful planning, combined with precise sizing of the elements, is more than half the battle. After you have the elements and their dimensions, the code all but writes itself.

PART **II**

JavaScript

CHAPTER 7

Interactive Animations with JavaScript

Implementing interactivity is one of the better ways to add depth to an animation. Indeed, interactivity is one of the primary appeals of the Web. The ability to interactively navigate the Internet by clicking on hyperlinks is one of the fundamental factors that has contributed to the Web's success. When you integrate interactivity with animation, you add a level to the user experience that not even Hollywood or broadcast television can provide: the ability to manipulate the motion. ▶

Basic Rollover with GIF Animations

Using JavaScript to Animate Images

Using Image Maps with JavaScript Animations

Object-Oriented Animation with JavaScript

The highest level of interactivity offered by HTML is the ability to click on a link that sends the browser to the document or file specified in the link. You can use this aspect of HTML to simulate a rudimentary interactivity. Figure 7-1 shows an interface created by Andy Evans for his site www.andyart.com. To avoid any incompatibilities with plug-ins or JavaScript versions, Evans created the interface using six interwoven GIF animations. The animations are combined with still images using HTML tables (see Chapter 6). The interface serves as a navigational unit for the Web site. Because the animations potentially distract visitors from information or from viewing other images at the site, Evans added a way to turn the animations off. An image near the bottom, which looks like a classic electric switch, is a link to another version of the interface. This version has no animations; they have been replaced with still images. The same images from the animated version are used on the non-animated version, so only the still images must load. The overall effect is an interactive on and off switch for the animated interface.

Although providing a way to turn off GIF animations is thoughtful, it isn't very exciting. To implement a more compelling interactivity, we need something that will allow us to show multiple images on a given Web page without requiring that a new page be loaded. HTML merely responds to mouse clicks. We need a technology that does something if the mouse cursor rolls over or away from a given image.

All this is beyond the scope of standard HTML. Fortunately, JavaScript has become a standard scripting language on the Web. With JavaScript, not only can you generate animation but you can also make the animations interactive. We look at several examples in this chapter, explaining the scripts step by step. The scripts shown in this chapter are also available on the CD-ROM (located in the "NarWorks/Anipack1/chrome" directory) that comes with this book.

JavaScript 1.0, supported by Netscape 2.0 and Internet Explorer 3.0, does not support image handling. Image handling was introduced in JavaScript 1.1, which is supported by Netscape 3 and later and Internet Explorer 4.

All the techniques that we discuss in this chapter have a prerequisite. The JavaScript in this chapter does not work for browsers earlier than Internet Explorer 3.0 or Netscape 2.0. Such browsers are out of date and are in use less and less, but if you expect your site's visitors to be using old browsers, you might want to avoid using the techniques in this chapter.

Basic Rollover with GIF Animations

There are several ways to implement interaction with GIF animations using JavaScript. The simplest way is to add a mouseover or rollover event to a GIF animation. Let's look at an example. Figure 7-2 and Figure 7-3 show the two animations used for this example. In Figure 7-2 we have a simple animation that shows animated liquid as if seen through a hole on the Web page. This animation is playing when you first see the page. This image could

Figure 7-1   A link to a non-animated version serves as an on and off switch for this interface. © Courtesy of Andy Evans.

be referred to as the animation for the "off" state; that is, this animation is visible when the visitor's mouse cursor is off or not over the animation. When the mouse rolls over the animation, the animation in Figure 7-2 is replaced with the animation in Figure 7-3, indicating the "over" or "on" state. The overall effect is that you have disturbed the water when you rolled the mouse over it. This is a basic mouseover or rollover event: one animation is replaced with another.

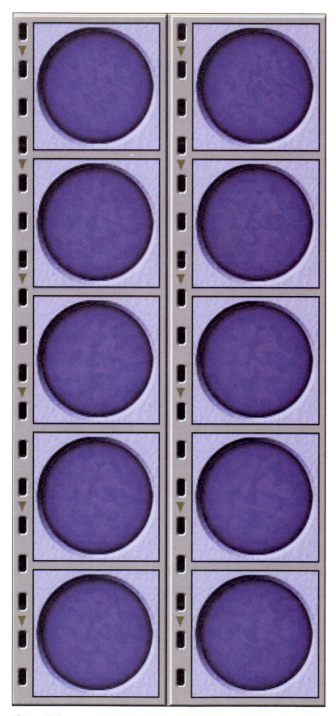

Figure 7-2   During the "off" state of the rollover event, the viewer sees this liquid
animation.

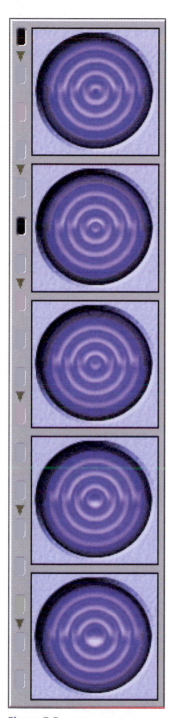

Figure 7-3 During the "on" state of the rollover event, the viewer sees this wavy animation.

Implementing this effect is relatively easy with JavaScript. Here is the JavaScript and HTML used to power the rollover event:

```
<HTML><HEAD>

<SCRIPT LANGUAGE="javascript">

 if (document.images) {
  {
  on = new Image (100,100);
  on.src = "watron.gif";

  off = new Image (100,100);
  off.src = "watroff.gif";
  }
    }
 function swapimage (imagename, target)
  {
  if (document.images)
   document.images[imagename].src = target.src;
  }
</SCRIPT>

</HEAD>
<BODY BACKGROUND=bump.gif><CENTER>
<A HREF="javascript:void(0);" onMouseOver="swapimage('water',on);"
onMouseOut="swapimage('water',off);"><IMG SRC="watroff.gif" WIDTH=100
HEIGHT=100 BORDER=0 NAME=water></A>
</BODY></HTML>
```

We start with the if statement. Because browsers prior to Netscape 3 and Internet Explorer 4 do not support the document.images object, this if statement acts as a browser check. If the browser supports images, the script between the brackets is run; if it does not, all the JavaScript on the page is ignored. Next, we set up two image objects by defining them as "on" and "off." By establishing the source and size of these image objects, we effectively pre-load these images. This is particularly important for the on image, because we want it to be in the browser cache when we call on it. If it isn't, the image will be downloaded over the Internet only after the rollover event occurs, and that would result in an awkward pause. If the Internet is too slow, the user may never realize that a rollover event is occurring.

Next, we create the function `swapimage`, which contains two parameters, or arguments: `imagename` and `target`. All that matters here is the order in which they are listed: `imagename` first, `target` second. After the `if` statement, which again acts as a browser check, the code reads as follows:

```
document.images[imagename].src = target.src;
```

This line powers the whole function. The left side of the equal sign effectively says, "Look at all the images in the document and find one that matches `[imagename].src`." This is the name of the image to change. The image to change is established with the `name` attribute in the image tag (`name=water`). On the right side of the equal sign is the image to switch to.

Within the image tag there are two JavaScript event handlers: `onMouseOut` and `onMouseOver`. The `onMouseOut` event handler calls the `swapimage` function and defines the parameters as (`'water',off`). `water` is the `imagename`, and `off` is the `target`. Because the mouse cursor is normally not over the image or is normally away from the image, this is the default position. The image named `water` by the `name` attribute of the `image` tag is, in fact, the watroff.gif file. So the `OnMouseOut` event handler is effectively being called by default, or whenever the mouse is not over the watroff.gif image.

When the mouse rolls over the watroff.gif image, the `onMouseOver` event handler is called. In this case, the `swapimage` function defines the parameters as (`'water',on`). `water` is the `imagename`, and `on` is the `target`. Because `on` corresponds to the watron.gif image, this serves to swap watroff.gif for watron.gif. So, in this case, both `onMouseOver` and `onMouseOut` "modify" the water image, but one replaces it with the `on` GIF and the other replaces it with the `off`. This example uses animations in both states: on and off. You could make either state static by using a non-animated GIF or JPEG.

Multiple Rollovers with JavaScript

You may be wondering why we didn't use the name `water` instead of `imagename`. Using the latter name allows for the code to expand and be more versatile because it allows us to potentially add more rollovers by adding new sets of paired images. If it's fun to swap one set of images, it'll be twice as fun to swap two sets of images, especially if we can do it using only one JavaScript function. With this code, that is simply a matter of defining more images and adding the `image` tag code complete with the event handlers. Then, as long as the two `image` tags define a different name via the `name` attribute, one function can power both rollovers.

For example, if we had two sets of water animations, each with its own animations for the on and off events, we could use one JavaScript function to power the rollover events for both sets of animations simply by giving each set a different `imagename`. One set could have the imagename `water1`, and the other set could have the imagename `water2`. Then we could make both sets work with the same function by giving each its own `OnMouseOver` and `OnMouseOut` event handlers. The code for the first set would look like this:

```
onMouseOver="swapimage('water1',on);" onMouseOut="swapimage('water1',off);
```

The code for the second set would look like this:

```
onMouseOver="swapimage('water2',on);" onMouseOut="swapimage('water2',off);
```

Having multiple JavaScript rollover events opens the door to a different type of interactive animation. Figure 7-4 shows a Web interface for Lingo programmer Cathy Serraino's Home Shocking Network (homeshocking.com/hsn.html), which employs multiple rollover events. The JavaScript for this interface was written by Scott Balay of Infinitefish Productions (infinitefish.com). Each ball and corresponding HTML text has a set of `onMouseOver` and `onMouseOut` JavaScript event handlers attached to it. As shown in Figure 7-5, when the mouse rolls over a ball or its companion channel name, four separate events occur. One of the more interesting events is an interactive dial animation. The dial turns as you roll over the links. Each rollover event turns the dial. Because the dial movement is tied to the rollover events, the dial moves as fast or as slow as the cursor moves.

To discuss this effect, we'll number these events. In event 1, the blue ball is exchanged for a green ball. For event 2, the image on the screen changes to an image that reflects the topic

Figure 7-4   All the mouseover events for this interface from the Home Shocking Network are in the "off" state.

Figure 7-5   When a mouse cursor rolls over a ball or its corresponding link, four events
occur: the ball changes color, an image displays on the screen, a number
appears under the screen, and the dial rotates.

of the channel. The channel number changes in event 3, and in event 4 the dial below the
channel number rotates. All these events occur simultaneously.

Each channel has its own set of events. For events 2 and 3, all the images are different. Event
1 uses the same two images every time (the blue ball and the green ball). Event 4, however,
uses three images. Because the spokes on the dial occur every 30 degrees, a spinning dial
effect was achieved with only three frames of animation, each frame distinguished by 10
degrees of rotation. The `onMouseOver` events on the channels cycle through these three frames.

So as you roll your mouse from top to bottom, frame 1 for the dial changes to frame 2, then
to frame 3, then back to frame 1 and so on. The result is that the dial rotates interactively
as you roll over the links. At the same time, the television appears to be changing channels
because the channel number changes in unison with the changing screen images.

This series of multiple rollover events is powered using a slightly different approach
from the one noted earlier. As with the preceding script, there is a `swapimage` function
(in this script Balay called it `switchimage`). However, Balay did not call the same
`switchimage` function by using different names for the `NAME` attribute of the `IMG` tag for
each set of animations or images. Instead, he used two separate functions that call

switchimage for each of the respective rollover events. These functions are called rollover and rollout. The rollover function contains four function calls to the switchimage function, each of which calls switchimage for a different rollover event. In other words, one function call in the rollover function calls switchimage to switch the screen images, another one calls switchimage to switch the channel number images, another one calls switchimage to switch the dial images, and yet another one calls switchimage to switch the ball images.

The reason for using this approach is that not all the rollover events act the same. For example, all the balls by the various links are the same image; that is, when the cursor isn't over any of the links or balls, each link has a blue ball next to it. When the cursor rolls over any link, the corresponding ball for that link turns green. The same two blue and green ball images are used for all 10 links, so the JavaScript function need only switch between the blue and green ball images for the rollover event.

The animated dial is a little different. Three images are used for the interactive dial animation (see Figures 7-6, 7-7, and 7-8), so the JavaScript must be able to match the dial images with the appropriate links or else the animated effect will not look right. Let's look at the JavaScript that Balay used to generate the interactive dial animation effect. First, he wrote a variable:

```
var dialfiles = new Array ("dial1.jpg", "dial2.jpg", "dial3.jpg");
```

This variable, dialfiles, defines an array of three images. The order of the images in the array is important. The rotation of the dials is in 10-degree increments, so dial2.jpg has been rotated 10 degrees from the position of dial1.jpg, and dial3.jpg has been rotated 10 degrees from the position of dial2.jpg. So if the order of the images in the array were dial1, dial3, dial2, for example, the animation would not work properly.

Next, Balay wrote a for loop to define the images:

```
for (count=0; count<3; count++)
{
dialimages[count] = new Image (52, 40);
dialimages[count].src = dialfiles[count];
}
```

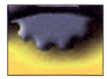

Figure 7-6 This is the first dial image.

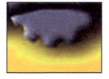

Figure 7-7 This is the second dial image.

Figure 7-8 This is the third dial image.

All for loops have three sections, called **arguments**. The first argument establishes what should be done initially, the second one dictates what the conditions are for continuing to run the for loop, and the third argument determines what will happen after the for loop runs each time. This for loop contains three arguments: count=0, count<3, and count++. The count=0 argument essentially says, "Start count at zero." The count<3 argument says, "If count is less than 3. . . ." The count++ argument says, "Then increase count by 1." The count++ argument is tied to the preceding argument. If the preceding count<3 argument is true, then the count++ argument is invoked. So the three arguments of the for loop say, "Start at zero and count up. After you have counted, check to see whether the count is less than 3. If the count is less than 3, start over, increasing the count by 1."

The count number is then fed into the lines of code that follow the for loop. The for loop starts with count at 0, so the 0 is fed into all the portions of the code that have count in brackets. So in the first pass of the loop the code

```
dialimages[count] = new Image (52, 40);
dialimages[count].src = dialfiles[count];
```

becomes

```
dialimages[0] = new Image (52, 40);
dialimages[0].src = dialfiles[0];
```

This process is repeated until count equals 3. When count equals 3, the argument count<3 is no longer true, so the for loop stops. This code defines each of the dial images with its height and width attributes and assigns a number and source image to each of the dial images. This not only provides JavaScript with a way to refer to each of the dial images, but it also preloads the dial images so that they will already be in the cache when rollover events occur (assuming that the whole page's contents have been loaded), ensuring that the animation effect will run smoothly.

To this point, we've covered how the dial images are defined. Now let's look at what makes them move. We are concerned only with the dial images in this discussion, so all the parameters for the other rollover events have been removed so that we can focus on the code that powers the interactive dial animation. The switchimage function is written and works essentially the same as the swapimage function described earlier:

```
function switchimage (imagename, target)
{
if (ns) document.images[imagename].src = target;
}
```

Following this switchimage function are two functions: rollover and rollout. Each of these functions contains a series of function calls to switchimage. Each of the function calls corresponds to the individual `rollover` events (one for the screen images, one for the channel images, and so on). Here is the `rollover` function with the `switchimage` function call for the dial images:

```
function rollover (number)
{
switchimage ("dial", dialfiles[number%3]);
}
```

The `number` argument of the `rollover` function corresponds to each link. When the cursor rolls over the first link, Sci Fi, it feeds the number 0 (JavaScript starts counting at 0) into the `rollover` function argument. When the cursor rolls over the second link, Mystery, it feeds the number 1 into the `rollover` function argument, and so on. Next, the `switchimage` function is called. It has two arguments: `imagename` and `target`. Each time this call to `switchimage` is made, the `imagename` argument is always `dial`. However, this call to `switchimage` must go through a small calculation to come up with the designation for the `target` argument of the `switchimage` tag. Here is the calculation:

```
number%3
```

Again, `number` is the number of the link. The percent sign means "Divide by and give the remainder of the division." This calculation divides the number of the link by 3 and leaves the remainder. For example, if the cursor is over the fifth link, the Commercial link, the `number` for this calculation equals 5, so 5 is divided by 3. The remainder is 2, so the resulting number of this calculation is 2. As a result, the second argument would be `dialfiles[2]` which would be the dial3.jpg image.

In case you missed high school math, what happens when 0, 1, and 2 are divided by 3? When 0 is divided by 3 the result is zero with a remainder of zero; when 1 is divided by 3 the result is 0 with a remainder of 1; when 2 is divided by 3 the result is zero with a remainder of 2. So the results of this calculation are always the numbers 0, 1, or 2, because the remainders are always either 0, 1, or 2. Conveniently, those are the numbers of the `dialfiles`:

```
dialfiles[0]=dial1.jpg
dialfiles[1]=dial2.jpg
dialfiles[2]=dial3.jpg
```

There is one final aspect to this JavaScript that makes the interactive dial work. Unlike all the other JavaScript events on this interface, there is no call to the `switchimage` function for the dial in the `rollout` function. In other words, when the mouse rolls off the link, whatever dial image was last swapped in is the one that stays visible.

Let's recap this dial animation effect now that we have looked at the JavaScript that powers it. When the interface first loads, the dial1.jpg file is used. If you roll your mouse down from the top, the first link (Sci Fi) corresponds to dial1.jpg, so nothing appears to happen. However, when you roll your mouse over the second link from the top, Mystery, dial2.jpg is swapped in. When you roll your mouse over the third link, dial3.jpg is swapped in. When you roll your mouse over the fourth link, dial1.jpg is swapped in, and so on. If you roll your mouse from the fourth link to the third link, dial1.jpg will change to dial3.jpg, so the effect works whether you roll your mouse up or down.

There is a slight gap between each link. When you are between links, the rollout function is invoked for the other events, but because there is no call to switchimage for the dial event, the dial image stays put. The overall effect is that as you roll your mouse up and down, the dial turns according to your movement.

Using JavaScript to Animate Images

JavaScript can also be used to generate animation. In other words, JavaScript can sequentially display a series of images. Let's look at a simple example. Figure 7-9 shows five JPEG images that are used to create a basic animated loop. Frames 1 through 5 are displayed sequentially over and over again. There is no interactivity.

Now let's look at the code. Here is the HTML and JavaScript code for this example:

```
<html>
<head>
<script language="javascript">
<!--

var frame=1;
function cycle()
    {
if (!document.images) return;
document.chrome.src = "chrome"+frame+".jpg";
if (frame >= 5) frame = 1;
else frame++;
setTimeout ("cycle();", 100);
    }

//-->
</script>
</head>
<body onLoad="cycle();">
```

```
<center>
<img width=100 height=100 src="chrome1.jpg" border=0 name=chrome>

<script language="javascript">
<!--
var imgslist = new Array(
"chrome2.jpg",
"chrome3.jpg",
"chrome4.jpg",
"chrome5.jpg"
);

var imgs=new Array();
if (document.images)
for (x=0; x {imgs[x]=new Image(); imgs[x].src = imgslist[x];}

//-->

</body></html>
```

Let's look at how this code works. First, there is a variable that defines frame as 1. This essentially starts the animation on frame 1. Next, we have the cycle() function:

```
function cycle()
{
if (!document.images) return;
document.chrome.src = "chrome"+frame+".jpg";
if (frame >= 5) frame = 1;
else frame++;
setTimeout ("cycle();", 100);
}
```

Figure 7-9   These five JPEG images are used to create a basic animated loop using JavaScript.

The `cycle` function starts with an `if` statement that works as a browser check, much as described in the earlier examples. The exclamation point in front of the `document.images` stands for "not." This `if` statement essentially says, "If the browser does not support `document.images`, then ignore everything else in this function." If the browser supports `document.images`, the code within the `if` statement is executed.

Next, we have the line of code that works with the `image` array (which shows up later in the code) to preload the images and declare the images as objects so that the JavaScript can manipulate the images. The `"chrome"+frame+"jpg"` contains the `frame` variable, which starts as 1 during the first pass through the `cycle` function. So `"chrome"+frame+"jpg"` is equal to `"chrome1.jpg"`.

Next, there is another `if` statement. It says, "If the `frame` variable is greater than or equal to 5, then `frame` equals 1." In other words, this `if` statement redefines the `frame` variable to equal 1 after the `frame` variable becomes 5. How would it get to 5? That's what the `else` statement does. If the `frame` variable is not equal to or greater than 5, the `else` statement is invoked. The `else` statement does two things. First, it increases the variable `frame` by 1 (`frame++`). Second, there is a recursive `setTimeout` line. "Recursive" means that the function calls itself. This is done in the first parameter of the `setTimeout` line: `cycle()`. The second parameter in the `setTimeout` line dictates the pace at which the function will run. Numbers are in thousandths of a second, so this function is set to run every 100/1000ths of a second (or 10 times per second).

So starting from the beginning, the `cycle` function checks to see whether the browser supports the necessary JavaScript. If the browser supports the JavaScript, the first image for `document.chrome.src` is defined as chrome1.jpg, so chrome1.jpg is displayed. Next, the `cycle` function checks to see whether the value of the `frame` variable is equal to or greater than 5. If it is not, it increases the `frame` variable by 1 (if the `frame=1`, then the `frame` variable is changed to 2, and so on). Then the `cycle` function is called again (at the rate of 10 times per second) and the whole process starts again. Because the `frame` variable is now 2, the image for `document.chrome.src` is defined as chrome2.jpg, and so on. When the `frame` variable reaches 5 it is redefined to 1, so the function continues playing indefinitely. Note that if you wish to customize this code to use with other images you can increase or decrease the number of `frames` that the JavaScript will animate. For example, if you wish to use six images, change the numeral 5 in the line `if (frame >= 5) frame = 1;` to 6 (and don't forget to add a sixth image to the image array).

This is not the only JavaScript that powers this code. Note, for example, that there is an `onLoad` command in the body tag. This `onLoad` command waits until the page is loaded before starting the `cycle` function for the first time. This technique helps avoid display problems or JavaScript errors because it ensures that all the necessary code is loaded before it starts to run the JavaScript. Also notice that the `<img>` tag contains a `name` attribute. This `name` attribute is what is referenced with `document.chrome.src`. It therefore ties the contents of the `<img>` tag to the JavaScript.

Now let's talk about the `image` array:

```
var imgslist = new Array(
"chrome2.jpg",
"chrome3.jpg",
"chrome4.jpg",
"chrome5.jpg"
);
```

It is here that we define the images we will use in the JavaScript animation. Note that one of the images is missing; only four images are defined here. That is because chrome1.jpg is defined within the `<img>` tag. If you want to use different images with this code, you would enter the names of those images here as well as in the `src` parameter of the `<img>` tag. The remaining code is used to define the images. We forgo explaining how it works because there is nothing you need to do with it. Just remember that this code cannot be removed.

JavaScript animations have some advantages over GIF animations beyond the fact that JavaScript animations can be interactive. Among the key advantages is that JavaScript can be used to animate JPEG images. Also, you can reuse frames in JavaScript animations and save valuable bandwidth. In the following example you will see how JavaScript can be used to create different animations from the same set of images.

Figure 7-10 shows eight JPEG animation frames used for an interactive JavaScript animation from NavWorks (navworks.i-us.com). These eight images were used to generate three separate animations. The first five images form a seamless looping animation. This animation is the default, or off, state. In other words, when the mouse cursor is not over the animation, the first five frames shown in Figure 7-10 loop endlessly.

When the cursor rolls over the animation, the animation stops looping the same five frames over and over. The JavaScript checks to see which of the five frames in the five-frame loop is currently displayed. Then the JavaScript starts with the next frame and

Figure 7-10   These eight images are used to generate three animations.

sequentially displays the rest of the frames shown in Figure 7-9. When the eighth frame is displayed, the animation stops. For example, if the browser is displaying the third frame of the animation when the cursor rolls over the animation, the JavaScript starts with frame 4 and sequentially displays the remaining frames, finishing with frame 8. Finally, when the mouse rolls off the animation, the JavaScript displays frame 8, 7, and 6 before beginning the five-frame loop again.

So, in effect, this example has three animations: a five-frame loop, a nonlooping animation that goes from a variable frame up to frame 8, and then a nonlooping animation that goes from frame 8 to frame 6. If this effect were attempted with GIF animations it would require 16 frames of animation (5+8+3). But with JavaScript, only eight frames are needed. Furthermore, when the three animations are saved as optimized GIF animations, they total more than 88K, whereas the eight JPEG frames used for this example total slightly less than 27K.

Here is the JavaScript and HTML used to power the interactive animation.

```
<html>
<head>
<script language="javascript">
<!--
var frame = 1;
var onbutton = false;
function cycle()
{
if (!document.images) return;
document.chrome.src = "chrome"+frame+".jpg";
if (!onbutton)
{
if (frame == 5) frame = 1;
else if (frame > 5)
{
frame--;
}
else frame++;
}
else
{
frame++;
if (frame > 8) frame = 8;
```

```
    }
  setTimeout ("cycle();", 100);
  }
//-->
</script>
</head>
<body background=nw-back.gif onLoad="cycle();">

<MAP NAME="MAP">
<AREA SHAPE=CIRCLE COORDS="50,49,42" href="javascript:void(0);"
onMouseOver="onbutton=true;" onMouseOut="onbutton=false;">
</MAP>

<center>
<img width=100 height=100 src="chrome1.jpg" border=0
name=chrome usemap=#MAP>

<script language="javascript">
<!--

var imgslist = new Array(
"chrome2.jpg",
"chrome3.jpg",
"chrome4.jpg",
"chrome5.jpg",
"chrome6.jpg",
"chrome7.jpg",
"chrome8.jpg"
);
var imgs=new Array();
if (document.images)
for (x=0; x {imgs[x]=new Image(); imgs[x].src = imgslist[x];}

//-->
</script>

</body></html>
```

This code is very similar to the code shown in the basic JavaScript animation example because that code was extracted from this code. Many elements in this example work in the same way as described earlier. Note, however, that the `image` array contains more images. Another minor difference is that this HTML code employs an image map to help isolate the circular area for the interactivity. Otherwise, the main differences between this script and the first example are the interactivity and the animation effects associated with the interactivity.

Like the first example, the JavaScript here starts by defining the `frame` variable as 1. Next, another variable, `onbutton`, is defined as false. We talk about `onbutton` more in a moment. What follows these two variables is a somewhat familiar `cycle` function. The first two lines of the `cycle` function are exactly the same as described in the preceding example. However, this version of `cycle` begins to deviate in the third line: `if !onbutton`. This `if` statement basically says, "If the `onbutton` variable is not true (false) . . . ." The `onbutton` variable is initially defined as false, so the next line is invoked.

The remaining lines in the `cycle` function are a bit hard to explain, so let's first look at what each line says and then how it works. We skip the `setTimeout` line because it is the same as in the preceding example. Here are the remaining lines:

```
{
if (frame == 5) frame = 1;
else if (frame > 5)
{
frame--;
}
else frame++;
}
else
{
frame++;
if (frame > 8) frame = 8;
}
```

Let's work through these lines one at a time.

- `if (frame == 5) frame = 1;`   This line says, "If the `frame` variable is equal to 5, then redefine the `frame` variable as 1."

- `else if (frame > 5)`   This line says, "If the `frame` variable is not equal to 5, then check to see whether `frame` is greater than 5."

- ▶ `frame--;`   This line says, "If the `frame` variable is greater than 5, then decrease `frame` by 1."

- ▶ `else frame++;`   This line says, "If the `frame` variable is not equal to 5 and not greater than 5, then increase `frame` by 1."

- ▶ `if (frame > 8) frame = 8;`   This line says, "If the `frame` variable is greater than 8, then redefine `frame` as 8."

Let's walk through the `cycle` function. When the `onbutton` variable is false (as it is by default), `cycle` checks to see whether the `frame` variable is equal to 5; if it is, it is reset to 1. Note that this is exactly like the animation loop in the first example. If the `frame` variable is not equal to 5, `cycle` checks to see whether `frame` is greater than 5. If it is, it is decreased by 1. If it is not, it is increased by 1. Going back up a few lines, if the `onbutton` variable is true, the `frame` variable is increased by 1 and continues to be increased by 1 until it reaches 8, where it stays.

In real terms, the `cycle` function works like this: Initially, the animation loops from the chrome1.jpg image through to the chrome5.jpg image. When the mouse rolls over the area defined by the image map, the images climb from whatever image is displayed at the time up to the chrome8.jpg image, which is continuously displayed as long as the mouse is over the area defined by the image map. If, for example, the cursor rolls over the animation while the chrome3.jpg image is being displayed, the animation will proceed to display the chrome images from 4 to 8. When the cursor rolls off the image, the images from 8 to 6 are displayed and the animation begins to loop again.

The way this script works demonstrates another benefit of using JavaScript rather than GIF animations. The smooth transitions generated by this JavaScript might be possible using GIF animations, but they would be excessively complex. In addition, the download requirements for the range of required GIF animations would be prohibitive.

▦ Using Image Maps with JavaScript Animations

We briefly noted that the preceding example employed an image map to isolate the circular area for the animation. Image maps may no longer be cutting edge Web technology, but they are still a valuable tool for Web developers and even Web animators. We finish this chapter by looking at another JavaScript animation that is fundamentally reliant on image maps. Figure 7-11 shows a series of animation frames for a whimsical electronic switch created by Scott Balay using formZ Renderzone.

Figure 7-11   Frames from an interactive switch animation by Scott Balay.

Although nonlooping GIF animations could have been used to accomplish this effect, it would have been inefficient in terms of bandwidth. It would require two GIF animations: one to animate the switch to the on position, and another one to animate it to the off position. All told, the effect would require 14 images. But with JavaScript only seven frames were needed.

Balay wanted this electric switch to emulate the way an electric switch works in the real world: you grab the handle and move it to the on position to turn on the switch, and vice versa to turn it off. JavaScript doesn't support click-and-drag operations, but it can generate the effect with rollover events.

Balay wanted to make the animation so that when the mouse cursor rolled over the top half of the switch, the switch image would move up to the on position. Conversely, he wanted to make it so that when the mouse rolled over the bottom half of the image, the switch image would move down to the off position. The solution was to employ image maps to designate the top and bottom halves of the switch images for the on and off switch positions.

Let's look at the code used to power the interactive electronic switch:

```
<HTML>
<HEAD>
<script language="javascript">

<!--
var switchon = false;
var imglist = new Array
("switch0.gif","switch1.gif","switch2.gif","switch3.gif","switch4.gif",
"switch5.gif","switch6.gif");
var imgs = new Array();

var count;
for (count=0; count<imglist.length; count++)
{imgs[count]=new Image(); imgs[count].src=imglist[count];}
```

```
function on(img)
{
if (switchon) return;
if (!document.images) return;

document.images["switch"].src = imglist[img];
if (img<6)
setTimeout ("on("+(img+1)+");", 50);
else
switchon = true;
}


function off(img)
{
if (!switchon) return;
if (!document.images) return;

document.images["switch"].src = imglist[img];
if (img>0)
setTimeout ("off("+(img-1)+");", 50);
else
switchon = false;
}


// -->


</script>
</HEAD>
<BODY BACKGROUND="rock1.jpg">


<map name="themap">
<area shape="RECT" coords="0,0,157,69" href="switch.html" onMouseOver=
"on(2);">
<area shape="RECT" coords="0,70,157,139" href="switch.html" onMouseOver=
"off(6);">
</map>
```

```
<img width=158 height=140 src="switch0.gif" name=switch usemap="#themap"
border=0>

</BODY>

</HTML>
```

Let's look at the code piece by piece. Here's the first part:

```
var switchon = false;

var imglist = new Array

("switch0.gif","switch1.gif","switch2.gif","switch3.gif","switch4.gif",
"switch5.gif","switch6.gif");

var imgs = new Array();
```

This code starts by defining a variable called `switchon` as false. Next, a new array called `imglist` is created. This array includes all the images that will be used in the animation. Note that the images have been named to reflect how JavaScript counts, starting at 0. Next, the `imglist` and `imgs` variables may appear to do the same thing because each of them is equal to new `Array`. However, the variable `imglist` serves to create a series of strings (in other words, it keeps track of the actual image names), whereas `imgs` serves to define an array of image objects.

Although we have an array full of strings, the images actually haven't yet been defined. Here's the code that performs that function:

```
var count;

for (count=0; count<imglist.length; count++)

{imgs[count]=new Image(); imgs[count].src=imglist[count];}
```

First, yet another variable is established called `count`. Next, a `for` loop is created. It is very similar to the `for` loop used for the interactive dial example discussed earlier in this chapter. This `for` loop starts the variable `count` at 0. The second argument of the `for` loop continues the `for` loop if `count` is less than the number of images in the `imglist` variable. The third section tells `count` to increase by 1 after completing each cycle through the `for` loop. Because there are seven images in the `imglist` variable, this `for` loop counts from 1 to 7 and then stops.

Each time the `for` loop goes through its cycle, it runs the code following it. The first part, `imgs[count]=new Image();`, defines a new `image` object for each image in the array. The second part, `imgs[count].src=imglist[count];`, takes the `image` defined in the first part and links it to an actual image by matching the `count` to the sequence of images in the `image` array. This code, then, defines the images in the array and effectively preloads the images that will be used in the animation.

It may seem that we've done a lot of coding just to set up our images, but JavaScript must deal with separate objects for each image. Now that we have defined the `image` array and the images within it, it's time to animate. The following code makes it work. Let's look at the code that moves the switch to the on posiiton from its default off position. The function that powers the animation to the off position from the on position is effectively the inverse of the following code:

```
function on(img)
{
if (switchon) return;
if (!document.images) return;

document.images["switch"].src = imglist[img];
if (img<6)
setTimeout ("on("+(img+1)+");", 50);
else
switchon = true;
}
```

This code creates a function called on with one argument: the `img` variable. Next, there are two `if` statements. The first `if` statement checks the status of `switchon`, which is off by default. If it's on, it means that the switch is already in the on position, so there's no need to run the animation. The second `if` statement is another browser check. If the browser does not support image objects, this statement prevents the function from running. As mentioned, this function powers the animation of the switch to the on position, but these `if` statements control under what conditions the animation will occur.

The next line powers the whole on animation: `document.images["switch"].src = imglist[img];`. This line should look familiar. It's very similar to a line in the code described earlier for the rollover events. As in that code, the left side of the equal sign effectively says, "Look at all the images in the document and find one that matches `["switch"].src`." This is the name of the image to change. The image to change is established with the `name` attribute that is in the `image` tag (`name=switch`). On the right side of the equal sign is the image to switch to.

However, unlike the `mouseover` JavaScript engine, this engine has some conditions established by an `if` statement. (The term "JavaScript engine" is used to indicate that a specific portion of the script is being used to power a given functionality.) The `if` statement starts by saying, "If the `img` variable is less than 6. . . ." (Again, the 6 equals the seventh object in the array because JavaScript starts counting at 0.) The file switch0.gif shows the switch in the fully off position (see Figure 7-12). It is the first image in the array, so JavaScript sees it as

Figure 7-12   The switch0.gif file shows the switch in the fully off position.

object 0 in the `imglist` array. The file switch6.gif shows the switch in the fully on position (See Figure 7-13). It is the final image in the array, so JavaScript sees it as object 6. If the `if (img<6)` statement runs and returns true, then the code assumes that the switch is in the off position. If the switch is in the fully on position, then `img` will equal 6, which means that the code following the `if (img<6)` statement will be ignored.

In this case, the ensuing code is a recursive `setTimeout` line. "Recursive" means that the function calls itself. In other words, the on function contains a line that calls or runs itself. The first parameter of `setTimeout` calls the on function, adding 1 to the `img` variable. This

Figure 7-13   The switch6.gif file shows the switch in the fully on position.

basically runs the `on` function using the next image within the `img` array. The second parameter in the `setTimeout` line dictates the pace at which the function will run. Numbers are in thousandths of a second, so this function is set to run every 50/1000ths of a second (or 20 times per second). This repeats until the `img` variable is no longer less than 6. When `img` variable equals 6, the variable `switchon` is redefined as true.

So this function moves the switch into the on position if the switch is in the off position and if the browser supports the `image` object. When the cursor rolls over the on position, the `on` function is called multiple times, replacing the switch images at a rate of 20 images per second until the switch is in its fully on position or, in other words, until the final image in the arrary or the seventh object in the `imglist` array is displayed.

The `off` function works in the opposite direction. It looks to see whether the `switchon` variable is true; if it is, it runs its subsequent code. The `if` statement that follows starts by saying "If the `img` variable is greater than 0, then run the following code." When the `img` variable is equal to zero, then the `switchon` variable is redefined as false.

Now let's talk about the JavaScript event handlers that call these functions. First, however, note that the event handlers are contained within a client-side image map and not within the image tag (as with the JavaScript for the basic rollover event described earlier). The image map defines two areas: the on area and the off area. It establishes the area that is associated with the on position of the electronic switch and the area that is associated with the off position of the switch.

Within each area there are two JavaScript `onMouseOver` event handlers. The first `onMouseOver` event handler calls the `on` function, giving it a parameter of 2. The second `onMouseOver` event handler calls the `off` function, giving it a parameter of 6. Finally, after the image map is created a basic `Image` tag is created using the switch0.gif (the GIF image that shows the switch in the off position). The `name` attribute of the image tag is defined as `switch`, and the `usemap` attribute tells the browser to use the `#themap` image map for the image within this image tag.

Now let's recap what all this code does. First, the browser is told at the beginning of the code that the switch is off. When the mouse rolls over the area established by the image map's coordinates for the on position, the function `on` is called and is fed the parameter 2 for the `img` variable. The function starts running using the second image in the `image` array (switch1.gif). Then the function is run over and over at a rate of 20 times per second until it reaches the seventh image in the `image` array (switch6.gif); then it stops, and the browser is told that the switch is on. The opposite occurs when the mouse rolls over the area established by the image map's coordinates that corresponds to the off position.

Although we've gone a long way to describe how this animated effect works, notice that none of this would have been possible without the image map. The effect could not have been created by cutting the frames in half. But, with image maps, Balay was able to easily isolate the two halves of the images to generate the on/off switch effect. In fact, if he had wanted to, he could have drawn the image maps more tightly around the actual lever on the switch. In any event, this example shows that image maps can be handy tools for JavaScript animation effects.

Object-Oriented Animation with JavaScript

Throughout this chapter we mention that using JavaScript to create animations can have distinct advantages over using GIF animations. In fact, there is a term for this advantage. JavaScript animations are *object-oriented*. This means that JavaScript (as well as Shockwave, Flash, and Java) can treat each frame in an animation as an independent unit. To understand this concept more clearly, let's first look at the nature of a GIF animation. Figure 7-14 shows a simple GIF animation. The arrows point to frames in the animation that are duplicates. For example, frame 2 and frame 6 (on the top row) are exactly the same. The animation requires the duplicates so that the twisting animation can run smoothly. Effectively, there is redundant information—five sets of duplicate frames—in this GIF animation. Using letters to refer to frames in the animation, it works as follows:

A, B, C, D, E, F, G, H, I, J, K, L

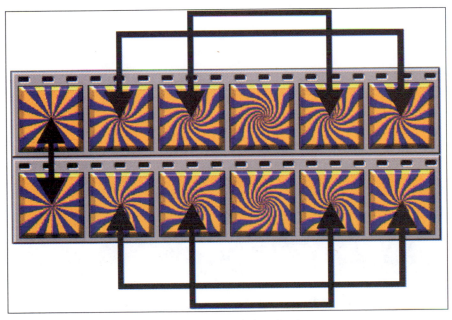

Figure 7-14   Arrows point to the duplicate frames in the animation.

Each letter represents a unique frame of animation. Even though there are five sets of duplicate images, the animation must contain each duplicate in order to run smoothly.

By contrast, JavaScript can treat each frame independently; that is, it can be employed to use the same independent graphic for frame B as it does for frame F. So the animation would work as follows:

A, B, C, D, C, B, A, E, F, G, F, E

In this scenario the duplicate images are being reused. There is no need to download another copy of the image for frame D; all you need to do is to use the image employed in frame C again. When an object-oriented animation mechanism is used for this animation, the image requirements are reduced from 12 to only 7.

You can take advantage of the object-oriented capabilities in JavaScript to achieve some bandwidth savings. Let's look at another example to drive this point home. Figure 7-15 shows an interface from Eyeland (www.eyeland.com/nav/face6/face6.html). The 3-D interface was created by Adrian Tübke-Davidson using 3D Studio Max. The JavaScript was written by Scott Balay. The interface features buttons on either side of a horizontal 3-D device: two buttons on the right and two on the left. When users roll over a button, a translucent bar emerges from the corresponding end of the device. When the animation is complete, the translucent bar displays the name of the link that corresponds to the button. When the mouse rolls off the button, the translucent bar returns into the device. The animation above the horizontal bar (not shown) is a non-interactive animated GIF (created by Scott Balay).

Two techniques were used to minimize the download requirements of this interface. First, because the two left and the two right animations moved into place in exactly the same manner, the images used to create the right animated effects are the same for both right animations, as are the images for both left animations; that is, the graphics required to generate the animation corresponding to the top left button (Figure 7-16) are also used to generate the animation corresponding to the bottom left button (Figure 7-17). The same is

Figure 7-15   When visitors roll over a button, a translucent bar animation emerges from the corresponding end of the interface.

Figure 7-16 These are the animation frames for both the phase out and phase in animations that correspond to the top left button in Figure 7-15.

Figure 7-17 Notice that the frames in each animation are the same except for the final frames.

true for the top and bottom right buttons. The only difference in each animation is the final state of mouseover animation, which is the animation that occurs when the user rolls over the buttons. This final frame is unique for each button and contains the name of the specific link associated with each button.

So for each set of right and left animations, the interface uses the same "in-between" frames both to open and to close the translucent bars associated with each top and bottom button. Because seven in-between frames were used to create the left and right frames, this approach kept the image requirements to only 14 in-between frames instead of a potential 56 in-between frames.

Another advantage of object-oriented animations is that the image quality does not have to be the same for each frame. In this example, the image quality of the in-between frames is different from that of the beginning and ending frames. In-between frame graphics were reduced to 16–32 colors instead of the 24-bit JPEGs used for the beginning and ending frames. Each in-between frame of the animation is displayed for only a fraction of a second, which is not enough time for the viewer to detect the difference in image quality. In fact, the lower quality of the images augments the "phasing" effect. As a result, each graphic for the in-between frames for the phasing animations was kept to 1K, adding a meager 14K to the overall download requirements.

Summary

Although implementing interactive animations requires a lot of extra thought and work, often the added depth they bring to the user experience makes the extra effort worthwhile. Whether they reinforce visual feedback or engage the viewer more fully, interactive animations can lead to a fuller sense of immersion, which can lead to a more compelling and satisfying user experience. The more that users can interact with your virtual creations, the more they will be able to suspend disbelief and enter into your virtual world.

CHAPTER **8**

Keeping Web Animations Fresh with JavaScript

Animations, like any other image, lose some impact every time they are seen. No matter how wonderful an image is, if you see it once it's great, twice it's neat, but by the third or fourth time it's "ho-hum." Netizens are spoiled by the dynamic nature of the Web, so if you want people to visit and revisit your site, it helps to keep your content fresh. Animations are no exception to the demand for novelty. In this chapter we look at techniques for keeping your animated Web pages fresh using randomization and customization. ▶

The basic approach to randomizing is to create a series of animations for a given Web page. Then you employ JavaScript to randomly serve one or more of these animations to the viewer at each visit. The prospect of continuously uploading new animations and updated HTML code for a series of Web pages is prohibitive, but if JavaScript or another technology is doing the work for you, you can concentrate on creating even more fresh content for your site's patrons.

> Although we do not cover these technologies, randomizing animations can be accomplished with almost any Web-oriented multimedia technology, including Perl, Java, Shockwave for Director, VBScript, and DHTML. ▶

Randomizing a Single Animation

Figure 8-1 shows an animation designed to display a customized message. This animated effect is achieved using three animations. The two rounded end caps are separate, two-frame animations that display a sort of barber-pole effect along with a random noise effect to simulate a "power field" on the inside tips of the end cap animations. At the center of these animations is a text field animation that displays a short message, fading it on and off.

The animation is fairly interesting, but it loses its luster after you read the message a time or two. Text animations are particularly susceptible to loss of interest because after viewers interpret the message, they tend to ignore the animation. To help avoid this problem, we will use JavaScript to randomly choose from a series of text animations for the center animation (see Figure 8-2).

Let's look at the script:

```
<script language="javascript">
<!--
function img (filename, width, height, link)
{
this.filename = filename;
this.width = width;
```

Figure 8-1   This image contains three animations, but the text animation in the center was designed to be randomized or customizable (or both).

Figure 8-2 These three animations contain stand-alone messages (each vertical strip is a separate animation).

```
this.height = height;
this.link = link;
}
function random(start, end)
{
var range = end-start+1;
var out = parseInt(parseFloat(Math.random()*range+start));
return (out);
}
var imgs = new Array();
imgs[0] = new img ("center.gif", 119, 40, "");
imgs[1] = new img ("center2.gif", 119, 40, "");
imgs[2] = new img ("center3.gif", 119, 40, "");
function link()
{
var r = random (0, imgs.length-1);
document.writeln ("<a href="+imgs[r].link+"><img width="+imgs[r].width+"
height="+imgs[r].height+" src="+imgs[r].filename+"></a>");
}
function nolink()
```

```
{
var r = random (0, imgs.length-1);
document.writeln ("<img width="+imgs[r].width+" height="+imgs[r].height+"
src="+imgs[r].filename+">");
}
// -->
</script>
```

This script randomly chooses among the three animations and then writes the HTML for the animation on-the-fly. Before we parse this code, note that even though this JavaScript handles images, it does not require a browser check. Because this code does not actually reference the image object, it is compatible with older browsers and a browser check is not required.

This script is written to be flexible, so let's look at how it works. We start with the first function:

```
function img (filename, width, height, link)
{
this.filename = filename;
this.width = width;
this.height = height;
this.link = link;
}
```

This function, called img, has four parameters: filename, width, height, and link. Each line within the function merely defines an object. Without the rest of the ensuing JavaScript, this function is worthless. However, each line serves to define and name an attribute of the animations. For example, this.filename is used to define the animation's file name as filename. As you will see, the order of the parameters is very important.

The next function is the random generator:

```
function random(start, end)
{
var range = end-start+1;
var out = parseInt(parseFloat(Math.random()*range+start));
return (out);
}
```

JavaScript has a built-in random function called Math.random(). Invoking the Math.random() is a simple matter of making a call to it. This function returns a floating-point number (not a whole number) between zero and 1. However, a floating-point number is of little use to us unless we convert it to a whole number. First, the result of `Math.random` is multiplied by the `range` (which, in this case, is 3 because we have three images in our image array, as discussed in a moment). The `+start` is an added level of flexibility. Although it is not used in this example, it allows for a range to exist that does not start at 1. For example, if we wanted the code to randomly choose from one set of images in the morning and another set of images in the evening, we could define a different set of `start` and `end` numbers for each part of the day. In this example, `start` is always 0, so `range+start` always equals whatever the `range` is (3 in this example). The code in parentheses says, "parse the floating-point number that the `Math.random()` function gives us and multiply it by 3."

JavaScript's `Math.Random()` generates a random number between 0 and 1. In other words, you get a number such as 0.65. When we multiply the number by 3, we obtain a number with a decimal point. For example, if `Math.Random()` came back with 0.65, it would be multiplied by 3 and we would get 1.95 (3×0.65). This number is still not useful, and that is why the `ParseInt` command is there. `ParseInt` lops off the decimal point, leaving a whole number. So out would equal 1.

Now that we have a random generator, we must define what will be randomly chosen; that is, we must define our animations. This is a job for an image array:

```
var imgs = new Array();
imgs[0] = new img ("center.gif", 119, 40, "");
imgs[1] = new img ("center2.gif", 119, 40, "");
imgs[2] = new img ("center3.gif", 119, 40, "");
```

We look at JavaScript arrays in Chapter 7, but this one is a little different. In this array, each parameter of the image object is listed in an order to coincide with the order of parameters defined in the `img` function. For example, the first parameter within the first object in the array is `center.gif`. This parameter is thrown into the `img` function whose first parameter is `filename`. Because the `img` function says that `this.filename = filename`, this code defines `center.gif` as the file name of the first object in the array. The `width`, `height`, and `link` attributes are defined in the same way.

Notice that there's nothing defined for the link within these image objects because the animations on this page aren't used as links. However, this script was written so that links could easily be added, and that explains the need for the next two functions:

```
function link()
{
var r = random (0, imgs.length-1);
document.write ("<a href="+imgs[r].link+"><img width="+imgs[r].width+"
height="+imgs[r].height+" src="+imgs[r].filename+"></a>");
```

```
}

function nolink()

{

var r = random (0, imgs.length-1);

document.write ("<img width="+imgs[r].width+" height="+imgs[r].height+"
src="+imgs[r].filename+">");

}
```

These two functions are very similar. The first one is for random images with links, and the second one is for random images without links. Because this example uses only the nolink() function, let's talk about it first. The nolink() function starts by defining a variable called r equal to the random generator function and passes the parameters 0 for start and imgs.length-1 for end. As discussed in previous chapters, JavaScript starts counting at 0 even though we nutty humans start counting at 1. For JavaScript, zero equals 1. So, imgs.length-1 counts how many images there are in the image array and then subtracts 1. Therefore, in this case the start parameter of the random function is set to 0, and the end parameter is set to 2. JavaScript starts counting at 0, so the random function will choose a random number from among three numbers: 1, 2, and 3.

Following this r variable is a JavaScript document.write command, which writes the HTML for the randomly chosen animation. Notice the first quotation mark after the opening parenthesis. Everything between this quotation mark and the closing quotation mark is taken or written literally. For example, the text "<img width=" will be written exactly as it reads when the document.write line is executed by the nolink() function. However, within the overall set of quotation marks is a set of embedded quotation marks that delineate JavaScript that is not to be written literally. In other words, "+imgs[r].width+" will not be written literally. Instead, the JavaScript will insert the result of this operation.

In this case, the results of the random function are fed into the brackets—"[r]". After the image object is determined (the results of the random function), it uses the img function to grab the width assigned to that image object. Then this number replaces the text "+imgs[r].width+". In other words, the result of the random function is a number between 1 and 3. When the number is fed into the brackets, the JavaScript then becomes a description for the width of one of the three images. For example, if the result of the random function were 1, the JavaScript would read "+imgs[1].width+". In this example, the

Avoid using document.writeln instead of document.write. Using document.writeln causes a problem in this example because JavaScript's document.writeln throws a break tag, or a hard return, at the end of the line it writes, whereas document.write does not. In this example, that would cause a problem, because the overall effect relies on keeping all the animations on the same line. If a break or hard return were inserted there, the final two animations would be centered below the first three.

Also, notice that this example doesn't require variation in the width and height attributes of the image objects. All the images are 119 pixels wide and 40 pixels high. However, this script allows for them to be variable. Nevertheless, this example would work exactly the same if the img function did not contain the width and height object definitions as long as the height and width attributes were defined within the document.write commands. ▶

"`imgs[1].width`" is defined early in the JavaScript as 119. So this translates to the text "`<img width=119`".

This process is repeated for the JavaScript code within each set of quotations, resulting in the HTML being written for each attribute of the IMG tag on-the-fly. The `link()` works almost exactly the same except that it also writes an anchor tag with an HREF attribute using the `link` parameter of the `img` function to write any link that is associated with the randomly chosen image object. (In the example, no URLs were associated with the image objects, so the `link` function wouldn't work properly.)

We now have flexible code, but we still need to put something within the HTML that will run the code. Here's the HTML used to display the overall animated effect (this code goes between the `<BODY>` and `</BODY>` tags in the HTML file):

```
<TABLE BORDER=0 CELLPADDING=0 CELLSPACING=0>
<TR>
<TD><IMG SRC=lnode.gif height=40 width=25 BORDER=0></TD>
<TD><IMG SRC=l_flash.gif height=40 width=6 BORDER=0></TD>
<TD><script language="javascript">nolink();</script></TD>
<TD><IMG SRC=r_flash.gif height=40 width=5 BORDER=0></TD>
<TD><IMG SRC=rnode.gif height=40 width=25 BORDER=0></TD>
</TR>
</TABLE>
```

Each animation has been placed within an HTML table cell to help guarantee that all the animations will be placed together seamlessly. The third cell contains a call to the `nolink` function. If links were defined within the image objects, you could simply replace `nolink()` with `link()` and the JavaScript would not only randomly write one of the animations but also write in any link that you specified for it.

Another flexible aspect of this code is that it is easy to add more animations to the total number of animations. To add another animation, you would simply add it to the array. For example, to add center4.gif so that the script would choose from four animations instead of three, you would add this line to the array:

```
imgs[e] = new img ("center4.gif", 119, 40, "");
```

Randomizing Multiple Animations

Randomizing animations can get even more interesting when there are multiple animations to randomize. In the preceding example, it's nice that there are a few different possibilities, but it would be even better if the range of possibilities were multiples of three (or more) instead of

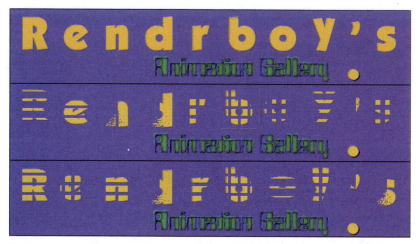

Figure 8-3   Each of these three shots of a series of animations that form the banner for "Rendrboy's Animation Gallery" was taken after a reload.

only three. Figure 8-3 shows a series of animations strung together to spell the word *Rendrboy's*. These animations serve as the first part of the title "Rendrboy's Animation Gallery."

The top version in Figure 8-3 shows each of the animations on its final frame; all the animations finish with the letter fully visible. The middle and bottom versions of the banner were taken after the Web page was reloaded. Note that some of the letters have different patterns. This is because there is one set of animations for each letter in the word *Rendrboy's* (including the apostrophe). For example, there are three different animations for the letter *R* (see Figure 8-4), three for the *e*, and so on.

The following script chooses an animation randomly from each letter's set and then writes the HTML for all 10 animations on-the-fly. The overall effect is that there are 90 potential variations of the animated text. Here's the code that makes it happen:

```
<script language="javascript">
<!--
var numsets = 3;

function random(start, end)
{
var range = end-start+1;
var out = parseInt(parseFloat(Math.random()*range+start));
return (out);
}
```

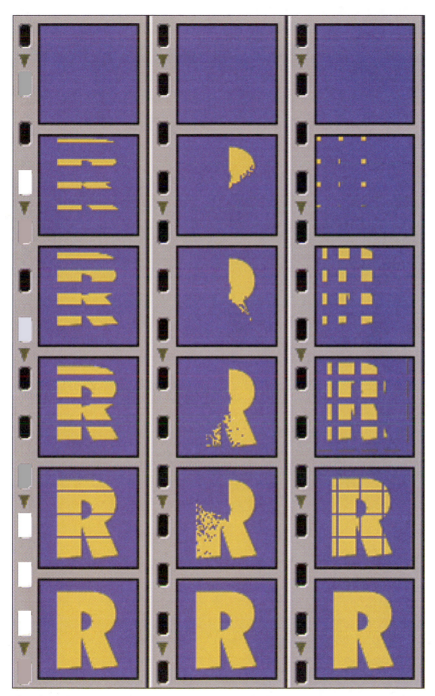

Figure 8-4   Each vertical stripe is a separate animation for the capital letter *R*. All the animations for the animated banner were created with SPG Web Tools and GIF Movie Gear.

```
function drawanims()
{
document.write ("<img width=60 height=60 src=r"+random(1,numsets)+".gif>");
document.write ("<img width=60 height=60 src=e"+random(1,numsets)+".gif>");
document.write ("<img width=60 height=60 src=n"+random(1,numsets)+".gif>");
document.write ("<img width=60 height=60 src=d"+random(1,numsets)+".gif>");
document.write ("<img width=60 height=60
src=sm_r_"+random(1,numsets)+".gif>");
document.write ("<img width=60 height=60 src=b"+random(1,numsets)+".gif>");
document.write ("<img width=60 height=60 src=o"+random(1,numsets)+".gif>");
document.write ("<img width=60 height=60 src=y"+random(1,numsets)+".gif>");
document.write ("<img width=30 height=60
src=apos"+random(1,numsets)+".gif>");
document.write ("<img width=60 height=60 src=s"+random(1,numsets)+".gif>");
}
// -->
</script>
```

If you made it through the explanation of the preceding example, this script should be easy to understand. First, notice that the `random` function is a duplicate of the `random` function in the earlier example, and it works in exactly the same way. In addition to the function that writes the HTML on-the-fly, the only other bit of code is this variable:

```
var numsets = 3;
```

This code states the number of sets for each animation. So if you created seven additional sets (seven different animations for each letter), you would change this number to 10.

Now let's look at the `drawanims()` function. Here is one of the `document.write` lines:

```
document.write ("<img width=60 height=60 src=r"+random(1,numsets)+".gif>");
```

Again we have a set of quotation marks just inside the opening and closing parentheses. Everything enclosed within these quotations is taken and written literally. The only thing not taken literally is the portion within the embedded quotations—namely, `"+random (1,numsets)+"`. This is a simple call to the `random` function. It feeds the number 1 as the `start` parameter for the `random` function and feeds the variable `numsets` (which is 3 for this example) for the `end`. So the `random` function picks a number between 1 and 3. When the `random` function returns the random number, it replaces the entire `"+random(1,numsets)+"` line. So, as an example, if the random function were to return the number 2, the `src` attribute would be written as `src=r2.gif`.

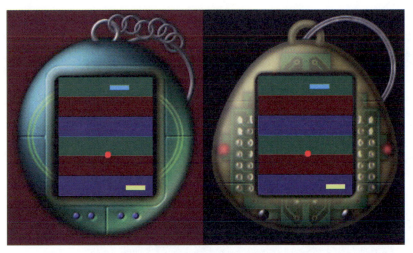

Figure 8-5   A randomizing JavaScript serves up a different interface for NavWorks'
Notagotchi Pong game every time the game loads.

Incidentally, there's no reason to limit random JavaScripts such as these to animations.
They can also come in handy with still images. For example, Figure 8-5 shows a Pong-like
game from NavWorks called Notagotchi Pong. The graphics that make up the interface are
JPEG images. These graphics surround, or frame, the actual Shockwave game. A random
JavaScript serves up a different set of interface graphics for the game every time the visitor
plays a different game. Each graphic for the interface amounts to less than 8K, and the
Shockwave is less than 25K, so the fresh interfaces help keep the diminutive game interesting without adding to the download hit.

🎞 Cycling Animations

Although randomized animations can help keep a Web page fresh, the fact that randomization is occurring at all can be easy to miss. A visitor who comes to the Web page only once
may never know that there are other variations of the page or animations waiting to be seen.
If you want your visitors to see the variations, you must cycle the animations into view.

Figure 8-6 shows an example of an interface that employs animation cycling using
JavaScript. The interface features four screens that display the animations. Each screen simultaneously displays the same animation. Each of the four screens is also associated with
a button on the interface. When the user rolls the mouse over one of the buttons, a still image replaces the animation on the screen that corresponds to the button.

After all the elements for the interface are loaded, three separate animations cycle onto the
screens, one every eight seconds (see Figure 8-7). After each animation has played through

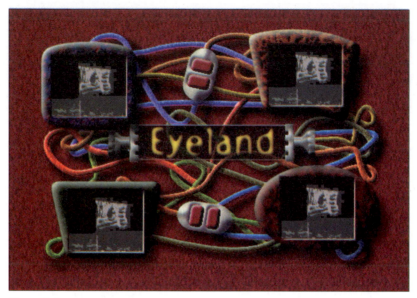

Figure 8-6   This interface features four screens in which video-like animations are displayed.

Figure 8-7   JavaScript cycles a series of animations on the individual screens.

its eight seconds, a short JavaScript animation plays on the screens. The JavaScript animation is a series of noisy images that simulate the effect of a television channel being changed.

Following is the entire JavaScript and HTML for this interface:

```
<HTML>
<script language="javascript">
<!--

function linkset (url, screen, screenimage, textimage)
{
this.url = url;
this.screen = screen;
this.screenimage = screenimage;
this.textimage = textimage;
}


var count;
var numlinks = 4;
var currentscreen = "";
var currentmovie = 0;
var screenlist = new Array ("ul", "ur", "ll", "lr");
var movielist = new Array ("nyny.gif", "astro.gif", "space.gif");
var imglist = new Array ("nyny.gif", "txt-biz.jpg", "txt-fun.jpg", "txt-
bli.jpg", "txt-stu.jpg", "tb1.gif", "tb2.gif", "bb3.gif", "bb4.gif", "txt-
eye1.jpg", "txt-eye2.jpg", "txt-eye3.jpg", "txt-eye4.jpg", "astro.gif",
"scn-biz.jpg", "scn-fun.jpg", "scn-bli.jpg", "scn-stu.jpg", "space.gif");
var img = new Array();
var links = new Array();


function loadimgs (list)
{
 if (!document.images) return;
 var imgcount;
 for (imgcount=0; imgcount<list.length; imgcount++)
 {
  img[imgcount] = new Image();
  img[imgcount].src = imglist[imgcount];
 }
```

```
}

loadimgs (imglist);

var staticimages = new Array();
if (document.images)
 for (count=0; count<3; count++)
 {
  staticimages[count] = new Image (100,80);
  staticimages[count].src = "static"+count+".jpg";
 }

links[0] = new linkset ("http://www.eyeland.com/biztrict/biztrict.html", 1,
"scn-biz.jpg", "txt-biz.jpg");
links[1] = new linkset ("http://www.eyeland.com/funzone/funzone.html", 2,
"scn-fun.jpg", "txt-fun.jpg");
links[2] = new linkset ("http://www.eyeland.com/blinks/blinks.html", 3,
"scn-bli.jpg", "txt-bli.jpg");
links[3] = new linkset ("http://www.eyeland.com/thestuff/thestuff.html", 4,
"scn-stu.jpg", "txt-stu.jpg");

function flickertext()
{
 if (!document.images) return;
 document.screen.src = "txt-eye1.jpg";
 setTimeout ("if(currentscreen=='')document.screen.src = 'txt-eye2.jpg';",
150);
 setTimeout ("if(currentscreen=='')document.screen.src = 'txt-eye3.jpg';",
300);
 setTimeout ("if(currentscreen=='')document.screen.src = 'txt-eye4.jpg';",
450);
 setTimeout ("if(currentscreen=='')document.screen.src = 'txt-eye.jpg';",
600);
}

function showstatic (frame)
{
 if (!document.images) return;

 var count;
```

```
if (frame<=9)
{
 for (count=0; count<screenlist.length; count++)
 {
  if (currentscreen != screenlist[count])
   document.images[screenlist[count]].src = "static"+(frame%3)+".jpg";
 }
 setTimeout('showstatic('+(frame+1)+');', 100);
}
else
 cycle();
}

function cycle()
{
if (!document.images) return;
var count;
for (count=0; count<screenlist.length; count++)
{
 if (currentscreen != screenlist[count])
  document.images[screenlist[count]].src = movielist[currentmovie];
}
setTimeout ("currentmovie = (currentmovie < (movielist.length-1) ?
currentmovie+1 : 0); showstatic(0);", 8000);
}

function on (imagename, screennum)
{
if (!document.images) return;
currentscreen = screenlist[screennum-1];
document.images[imagename].src = imagename+screennum+".gif";
document.images[screenlist[screennum-1]].src = links[screennum-1].
screenimage;
document.screen.src = links[screennum-1].textimage;
}

function off (imagename, screennum)
```

```
{
 if (!document.images) return;
 currentscreen = "";
 document.images[imagename].src = imagename+"0.gif";
 document.images[screenlist[screennum-1]].src = movielist[currentmovie];
 flickertext();
}

function click (screennum)
{
 window.location = links[screennum-1].url;
}

// -->
</script>
<title>Eyeland</title>
</head>
<body background=burgback.jpg bgcolor="#600000" text="#B0B000"
link="#B0B000" vlink="#B0B000" alink="#B0B000" onLoad="currentmovie =
(currentmovie < (movielist.length-1) ? currentmovie+1 : 0); showsta-
tic(0);">

<center>

<MAP NAME="tb">
<AREA SHAPE=POLY
COORDS="4,23,1,25,0,34,1,40,20,44,26,44,28,41,31,31,29,28,4,23"
HREF="javascript:click(1);" onMouseOver="on('tb', 1);"
onMouseOut="off('tb', 1);">

<AREA SHAPE=POLY COORDS="10,1,6,4,4,14,5,17,29,23,33,21,35,10,32,6,10,1"
HREF="javascript:click(2);" onMouseOver="on('tb', 2);"
onMouseOut="off('tb', 2);">

</MAP>

<MAP NAME="bb">
<AREA SHAPE=POLY COORDS="7,1,5,3,2,25,4,28,15,30,19,27,22,5,19,2,7,1"
HREF="javascript:click(3);" onMouseOver="on('bb', 3);"
onMouseOut="off('bb', 3);">

<AREA SHAPE=POLY COORDS="30,4,27,7,25,29,27,32,39,33,42,30,44,8,41,5,30,4"
HREF="javascript:click(4);" onMouseOver="on('bb', 4);"
onMouseOut="off('bb', 4);">
```

```
</MAP>

<table border=0 cellpadding=0 cellspacing=0>

<tr><td>

 <table border=0 cellpadding=0 cellspacing=0><tr>

 <td rowspan=3><img src=ulleft.jpg width=29 height=134></td>

 <td><img src=ultop.jpg width=100 height=42><br><img width=100 height=80
src=nyny.gif name=ul><br><img src=ulbottom.gif width=100 height=12></td>

 <td rowspan=3><img src=ulright.jpg width=83 height=134></td>

 <td><img src=tbtop.gif width=36 height=42><br><img src=tb0.gif
usemap="#tb" width=36 height=44 name=tb border=0><br><img src=tbbottom.gif
width=36 height=48></td>

 <td rowspan=3><img src=urleft.jpg width=73 height=134></td>

 <td><img src=urtop.gif width=99 height=26><br><img width=99 height=80
src=nyny.gif name=ur><br><img src=urbottom.gif width=99 height=28></td>

 <td rowspan=3><img src=urright.jpg width=70 height=134></td>

 </tr></table>

</td></tr>

<tr><td><img src=lwires.jpg width=152 height=44><img src=txt-eye.jpg
width=185 height=44 name=screen><img src=rwires.jpg width=153
height=44></td></tr>

<tr><td>

 <table border=0 cellpadding=0 cellspacing=0><tr>

 <td rowspan=3><img src=llleft.jpg width=51 height=154></td>

 <td><img src=lltop.jpg width=101 height=44><br><img width=101 height=80
src=nyny.gif name=ll><br><img src=llbottom.gif width=101 height=30></td>

 <td rowspan=3><img src=llright.jpg width=60 height=154></td>

 <td><img src=bbtop.gif width=45 height=61><br><img src=bb0.gif
usemap="#bb" width=45 height=34 name=bb border=0><br><img src=bbbottom.gif
width=45 height=59></td>

 <td rowspan=3><img src=lrleft.jpg width=80 height=154></td>

 <td><img src=lrtop.jpg width=100 height=26><br><img width=100 height=80
src=nyny.gif name=lr><br><img src=lrbottom.gif width=100 height=48></td>

 <td rowspan=3><img src=lrright.jpg width=53 height=154></td>

 </tr></table>

</td></tr>

</table>


 
<TABLE BORDER=0 WIDTH=490>
```

```
<TR>

<TD ALIGN=CENTER><B><FONT FACE="arial,helvetica" size=3><A
HREF="javascript:click(1);" onMouseOver="on('tb', 1);"
onMouseOut="off('tb', 1);">BIZTRICT</A></FONT></B></TD>

<TD ALIGN=CENTER><B><FONT FACE="arial,helvetica" size=3><A
HREF="javascript:click(2);" onMouseOver="on('tb', 2);"
onMouseOut="off('tb', 2);">FUNZONE</A></FONT></B></TD>

<TD ALIGN=CENTER><B><FONT FACE="arial,helvetica" size=3><A
HREF="javascript:click(3);" onMouseOver="on('bb', 3);"
onMouseOut="off('bb', 3);">BLINKS</A></FONT></B></TD>

<TD ALIGN=CENTER><B><FONT FACE="arial,helvetica" size=3><A
HREF="javascript:click(4);" onMouseOver="on('bb', 4);"
onMouseOut="off('bb', 4);">THE STUFF</A></FONT></B></TD>

</TR>

</TABLE>


</body>

</html>
```

Because the JavaScript that powers this entire interface is beyond the scope of this chapter, we look only at the part of the JavaScript that powers the cycling:

```
function cycle()

{

if (!document.images) return;

var count;

for (count=0; count<screenlist.length; count++)

{

if (currentscreen != screenlist[count])

document.images[screenlist[count]].src = movielist[currentmovie];

}

setTimeout ("currentmovie = (currentmovie < (movielist.length-1) ?
currentmovie+1 : 0); showstatic(0);", 8000);

}
```

Much of this cycle function contains JavaScript that keeps the animation from playing when the mouse is rolled over the screen's associated button. The important part of the code for our purposes is located in the setTimeout line. This line contains three sections. The first section determines which movie should be played, the second section runs a function called showstatic, and the third section sets the timing at every eight seconds. The first part of the setTimeout loop is a somewhat cryptic if statement.

The portion within the second set of parentheses reads (`currentmovie < (movielist.length-1`). This code says, "If the number of the current movie is less than the total number of movies minus 1. . . ." Again, the `-1` has to do with how JavaScript counts. There are three "movies" in `movielist.length`, but JavaScript counts them as 0, 1, and 2.

After the phrase within the second set of parentheses, there is a question mark followed by a parameter and then a colon followed by a parameter. These amount to "then" and "else." In other words, this code says, "If the number of the current movie is less than the total number of movies minus 1, then pass the parameter `currentmovie+1`; else, pass the parameter 0. So if the current movie is less than 3, then the number of the current movie is increased by 1. Otherwise, we start back at zero.

Even those who are familiar with JavaScript might be a little lost by now, so let's look at an example. If the second GIF animation has just finished playing, the script would work as follows. JavaScript would see the `currentmovie` as 1 (remember, that's how JavaScript counts). Because that is less than `movielist.length-1` (which is 2), `currentmovie` is increased by 1. Therefore, the third GIF animation would start to play after the `staticmovie` function plays the noisy JavaScript animation that separates the GIF animations. If you look in the code, you will see that the `staticmovie` function contains a call to the `cycle` function, which starts the process anew.

This effect results in a string of animations continually looping in the same spots instead of just one animation looping in the same spots. Although that is tantamount to having just one big animation looping, the difference is that animations can easily be added and rearranged. In this way, visitors can be served up a unique set of animations if they visit at another time.

Planning for Customization

JavaScript is not the only weapon Web designers have for keeping sites fresh. Sometimes a little old-fashioned forethought and planning are just as valuable as a bunch of lines of script. Figure 8-8 is a Web page from Gamani Productions' Web site. Gamani Productions is the maker of GIF Movie Gear, my preferred GIF animation utility. Because Gamani Productions makes a GIF animation utility, it wanted the interface to feature numerous GIF animations. Furthermore, to encourage repeat visits, the company wanted the design to accommodate a range of variable locations for the animations.

To accomplish these objectives, the interface designer used HTML tables to put together a large number of graphics. This technique allows for animations to be integrated seamlessly into the interface in a number of places. For example, Figure 8-9 shows an animation with GIF Movie Gear's slogan "Get The Gear" located below and to the right of the "gamani

Figure 8-8   The Web site of Gamani Productions, makers of GIF Movie Gear, features a large number of integrated GIF animations.

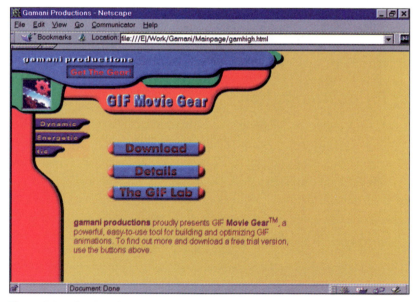

Figure 8-9   This interface was designed to "hide" a range of possible locations for animations such as the "Get The Gear" slogan animation shown here.

Figure 8-10 The "Get The Gear" animation's loop makes it appear to fall away to form a hole in the interface. Then the animation ends with the hole being plugged, making it briefly appear as though there is no animation in that spot.

productions" text. The animation starts so that the interface looks the way it does in Figure 8-8, as if there's nothing except solid blue in that location. As the animation plays, the rectangular area appears to drop, the slogan turns on and off, and the rectangular area appears to rise back into its original place (see Figure 8-10).

Several parts of the interface are designed to hide animations. For example, solid-color portions of the interface are actually table cells that contain single-pixel images. These single-pixel images are stretched to size using the Height and Width attributes of the <IMG> tag. When Gamani wants to use a GIF animation instead of the single-pixel image, it replaces the reference to the single-pixel image with a reference to the GIF animation within the HTML code and uploads the new HTML code for the Web page. JavaScript is employed on the page for basic rollover events, but Gamani prefers to update the page manually. Because all it has to do is to change references in a few SRC attributes of the specific image tags, it is easy for Gamani to add, replace, and remove animations to its interface to customize the appearance of the site.

▣ Summary

Whether you employ scripts or customize manually, efforts to keep your Web pages novel can encourage repeat visits and give your visitors an increased sense of the depth of your site. Building in a little randomness and customizability can help extend the life of many designs. Note that the techniques described in this chapter aren't limited to GIF animations. Many Shockwave and Flash animations are easily altered; if you use these technologies, consider making multiple versions of the Shockwave or Flash movies, each with variations, and then post the variations from time to time. Although there's something to be said for consistency of design and implementation, people are attracted to the original and atypical. Also, consider that many Web sites sport a design until they and everyone else is wholly sick of it. A little intelligently implemented change now and then never hurts.

PART III

Macro-media Flash

CHAPTER 9

Creating Animations with Macromedia Flash

Most of the latest innovations in Web animation are built into Macromedia Flash. Not only does Flash deliver highly compressible, resolution-independent vector-based imagery, but it also streams, it's object-oriented, it has automated animating features such as tweening (and tweening on a path), and it allows you to implement interactivity without programming. When Flash was introduced by FutureSplash, the technology was billed as a relatively low-end Web multimedia solution. It was touted primarily as a way to create easy interactive buttons that would download quickly. Then Macromedia acquired Flash and significantly bolstered the technology by adding features such as bitmap and audio support, the capability to apply color transitions to bitmaps and symbols, and, more recently, transparency and shape morphing. ▶

Symbols: The Key to Optimizing Flash Movies

Understanding How Flash Streams During Playback: The Preloading Trick

Step-by-Step Analysis of the "Bitzo in: The Big Splash" Flash Animation

Basic Animation Techniques in Flash

Combining Tweening and Key Frame Animation

n addition, Macromedia leveraged its considerable Web multimedia presence to gain broad acceptance for the Flash technology. Flash animations cannot play without a plug-in (there is a Java alternative to the Flash plug-in, but it is prohibitively slow). Nevertheless, people continue to download the Flash plug-in in record numbers. With deals to include Macromedia Flash in the latest browsers (Netscape 4.5 and later) and with operating systems (Windows 98), the Flash technology is second only to technologies such as GIF animation, JavaScript animation, and Java animation in terms of general viability.

As a development environment and as a general Web animation delivery technology, Flash has many unique characteristics. In this chapter we look at the basic methods for creating animations in Macromedia Flash and explain how to take advantage of Flash's unique characteristics to create compelling Web animations. For example, we look at how you can take advantage of Flash's object-oriented nature to generate animations that have much greater physical sizes and far longer run times than GIF animations while maintaining impressively small file sizes. We also look at how to take advantage of Flash's ability to easily generate interactive animations.

Symbols: The Key to Optimizing Flash Movies

Flash 3 has four kinds of *symbols*: graphic, button, movie clip, and audio. A graphic symbol is a static image, buttons are multistate symbols used for interactivity, and movie clips are animated symbols. Graphic, button, and movie clips are all image-oriented symbols that can include vector and bitmap imagery. Movie clips are essentially the same as any Flash animation. You create them with the same layered timeline as any other Flash movie, and they can contain tweens and even other symbols. Furthermore, you can place movie clips inside button symbols and thereby create animated buttons. We look at this capability later in the chapter.

A timeline shows an array of animation frames. A timeline lets you access individual frames of an animation, and it allows you to see how the frames play out over time. Macromedia Flash employs a layered timeline—that is, each layer has its own timeline.

Movie clips are symbols, and they enjoy the same object-oriented benefits described earlier. Their information is stored in the first key frame in which they are displayed. A useful aspect of this is that button symbols that contain movie clips also work in the same way. This is important because Flash 2 allowed you to create animated buttons, but these animated buttons lost their status as symbols. In other words, animated buttons in Flash 2 always add to the file size of the animation every time they are used.

There's no better way to understand the Flash advantage than to look at some examples. We begin the discussion using Figure 9-1 as an example. This example demonstrates one of Flash's key animation assets: symbols. Symbols are object-oriented elements in Flash. To review the benefits of object-oriented animation, refer to the section Object-Oriented Animation in Chapter 1.

Figure 9-1 shows a 40-frame animation created in Flash 3. It is the first few seconds of an online music video for a song called "Boy Blue." The first 30 frames are all key frames (each solid blue dot on the timeline represents a key frame). Key frames are frames whose contents have changed from the preceding frame. The final 10 frames repeatedly display the contents of frame 30. One shortcoming of Flash is that you cannot specify the length of time for a given frame to display, as you can with GIF animations. You can set the frame rate for the entire Flash animation, but each frame plays at the same rate. Later we talk about the circumstances that may lead to Flash animation frames not playing at the same rate. This first example demonstrates how much symbols affect Flash animation file sizes.

Although Flash's vector-based images allow for a high degree of compressibility, it is Flash's object-oriented symbols that provide some of its best compression advantages. Symbols are media (vector-based graphics, bitmaps, or sound) that can be used over and over again without adding appreciably to the file size of the animation. All Flash movies are converted to Flash Shockwave files when you export them. These

USING ANIMATED SYMBOLS IN FLASH 2

Sometimes Flash 2 does not repeatedly access symbol data stored in a previous frame. Flash 2 allows you to create essentially two types of symbols. You can create button symbols or what I refer to as "normal" symbols. Buttons cannot be animated, but they can be made interactive and you can assign actions to them, such as "Get URL" or "Goto" (as in "go to a frame"). Normal symbols can't have interactivity added to them nor have actions assigned to them, but they can be animated. When you edit a normal symbol, you get a separate set of layers and a timeline just as you have when you are editing the Flash movie as a whole.

Although this means that you can apply automated animation effects, such as tweening and animations on a path, to an animated symbol, there's a downside. Animated symbols are no longer object-oriented. Unlike non-animated symbols, animated symbols are not stored solely in the first frame in which they appear. All the data of an animated symbol is stored in each frame. Therefore, animated symbols should be used sparingly and with caution if you're using Flash 2.

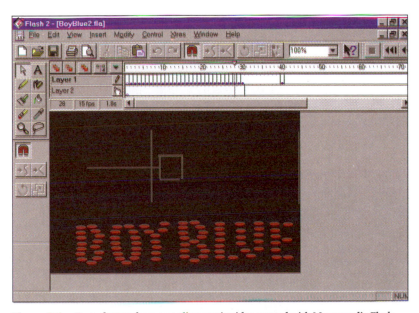

Figure 9-1 Forty frames from an online music video created with Macromedia Flash.

files have the .swf file extension. Macromedia Flash compresses the movie contents when you export to a Flash Shockwave. Note that whenever the file size of a Flash animation is referred to in this chapter, we are referring to the .swf file and not the native .fla Macromedia Flash file. In other words, we are referring only to Flash files that have been exported for use on the Web and not to the Flash files that you use for editing within the Macromedia Flash application.

The "Boy Blue" animation's stage size is 500 pixels wide by 320 pixels high. (The "stage" is the viewable area of the animation.) If you look closely at the frames of the animation shown in Figure 9-2, you see that the imagery in the entire animation in composed of two shapes: a burgundy oval and a thin gray rectangle. To demonstrate the value of symbols, I created two versions of the animation: one without symbols and one with symbols. The version of the "Boy Blue" Flash animation without symbols weighed in at 82.7K. Using symbols, the animation is only 18.4K. The version with symbols is more than four times smaller than the version without symbols.

Macromedia Flash allows you to export its animations as GIF animations (as well as AVI or as a sequence in many major graphics formats such as AI, EPS, WMF, and DXF). I saved this animation as a GIF animation and optimized it by reducing it to eight colors and by employing frame cropping and interframe transparency. Also, because GIF animations allow you to time each frame individually, I set the 30th frame of the GIF animation to approximately the same time as the duration of the final 10 frames in the Flash animations. With the optimizations, the GIF animation is 71.8K. That is more than 10K smaller than the version without symbols.

This demonstrates a very important point. The vector-based images are very compressible, but it's Flash's object-oriented symbols, and not the vector-based graphics, that bring home the real optimization results. It's not enough to rely on the compressibility of vector imagery. To truly realize the benefits of Flash, you must learn to take advantage of Flash's symbols.

Figure 9-2   The entire "Boy Blue" animation is composed of two shapes: a gray rectangle and a burgundy oval.

Macromedia Flash allows you to generate a size report when you export a movie, as shown in Figure 9-3. Because Flash's size reports give a frame-by-frame description of the size in bytes of each frame and a running tally of the total size in bytes from frame to frame, you can use a size report to analyze how each frame's contents affect the overall file size of the animation. Tables 9-1 and 9-2 show the first five frames of the size reports of each version of the "Boy Blue" animation.

By the fifth frame of the version without symbols, the animation is already 6,285 bytes, whereas in the symbol version it is only 1,346 bytes. No frame reaches more than 400 bytes in the version made with symbols, but no frame dips below 800 bytes in the version without symbols (except the first frame, which is 30 bytes in each version).

In the version without symbols, each use of the nonsymbol shapes adds to the file size, and it shows up clearly in the report. For example, frames 4 and 5 contain the most shapes and symbols in both versions. In the version without symbols, frame 4 amounts to 2,019 bytes' worth of data for the shapes, and frame 5 has 2,163. In the version with symbols, neither frame is more than 389 bytes.

Table 9-1 Size Report of "Boy Blue" Animation Without Symbols

Frame Number	Frame Bytes	Total Bytes
1	30	30
2	837	867
3	1,236	2,103
4	2,019	4,122
5	2,163	6,285

Table 9-2 Size Report of "Boy Blue" Animation With Symbols

Frame Number	Frame Bytes	Total Bytes
1	30	30
2	275	305
3	271	576
4	389	965
5	381	1,346

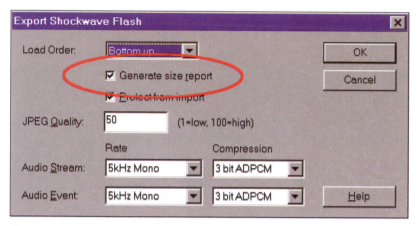

Figure 9-3   You can have Macromedia Flash generate a frame-by-frame report of your animations during export. (Circle added.)

Notice also that in the version without symbols frame 3 has roughly 400 bytes' worth of data more than frame 2 and that frame 5 has about 50 bytes of data more than frame 4. This indicates that frame 3 contains more shapes than frame 2 and that frame 5 contains more shapes than frame 4. However, this correlation is not reflected in the symbols version, where frame 3 has slightly fewer bytes of data than frame 2 and frame 5 has slightly less data than frame 4.

This observation may seem minor at first glance, but it is an indication of the way Flash uses symbols to generate its impressive compression. The first time a symbol appears in a Flash movie, the data for that symbol is stored in that frame. Every time that symbol appears subsequently within the movie, Flash refers to that data. For example, once the burgundy oval symbol appears in frame 2 of the version of the "Boy Blue" Flash animation with symbols, all subsequent frames refer to that data. So all the burgundy oval symbols in frame 3 use the symbol data from frame 2.

A small amount of symbol data must be stored on subsequent frames on which any symbol recurrently appears. When a symbol is reused on a subsequent frame, data about its size, position, orientation, color (tint), and transparency is stored on the subsequent frame. So each instance of the burgundy oval symbol on frame 3 adds only slightly to the file size of the overall Flash animation (usually no more than 2 bytes).

Notice, however, that most of these symbol characteristics do not change. The size, orientation, color, and transparency of the burgundy oval symbol instances always stay the same. Only the position of the symbols changes, and often a given instance of a symbol stays in the same position from frame to frame. This is why frames 3 and 5 are slightly smaller than frames 2 and 4, respectively, in the symbols version of the "Boy Blue" Flash animation. Even though frames 3 and 5 have more symbols than frames 2 and 4, respectively, many of the symbol instances in frames 3 and 5 are in the same positions as the same symbol instances in frames 2 and 4. Flash accounts for this during compression. So if the symbol instance doesn't change from frame to frame, Flash can achieve slightly better compression.

When you look at these numbers, it becomes clear that symbols are the key to creating high-impact Flash animations that have small file sizes. In other words, symbols are the key to optimizing Flash animations for the Web. All this might seem like splitting hairs (we're talking about 2 bytes per symbol instance, for heaven's sake). However, the point is that Flash's reports can be valuable when you are trying to optimize a Flash animation. They provide detailed information that you can use to analyze how to construct your Flash file to ensure that your animations are as small as possible and that they play back smoothly.

For example, if you are trying to keep a Flash animation below a certain size, you can export a test version and then look at the report. If your animation is too large, you can easily pick which frames are adding the most to the file size. Also, if you see a jump in the number of bytes for a given frame, you can check that frame to see why.

The fact that you can change the size, position, orientation, color (tint), and transparency of a symbol in Flash has huge implications. Specifically, you can resize (with the aspect ratio maintained either vertically or horizontally), reorient, rotate, skew, recolor, and adjust the transparency of a symbol without appreciably adding to the file size. Again, only the information necessary to apply these changes is stored in subsequent frames that use the symbol. In other words, the main data for a symbol is stored in the frame on which it is first placed; all subsequent frames store only the data necessary to make changes to its size, orientation, and so on. This means that you can generate a wide range of file-size-efficient animation effects using symbols. Animation effects such as making a symbol spin, increase and decrease in size, change color over time, blink, and fade in and out can all be done efficiently with Flash's symbols.

In Flash 3, animated symbols, called *movie clips*, act just like other symbols; their information is stored on the first frame in which they are used and then subsequent frames refer to the first instance. However, this arrangement can increase the load requirements for any frame containing an animated symbol. For example, if your animated symbol has a lot of imagery, audio, or bitmaps, the symbol can become disproportionately large. For this reason, animated symbols from Flash 3 are prime candidates for preloading, a trick we look at next.

▦ Understanding How Flash Streams During Playback: The Preloading Trick

Before we move to specific animation examples, you need to understand how Flash streaming works. As discussed in Chapter 1, streaming playback allows for an animation to begin playing before it has been fully loaded. The problem is that Flash provides no way to control *buffering*; there is no direct way to control how much of the animation must be loaded before it starts playing. This poses a bit of a problem because it means that Flash animations can easily end up playing in spurts. The animation might start playing and then stop as it waits for more of the Flash file to download, continuing this stop-and-start routine throughout the animation. If the animation loops, it will play back smoothly on the subsequent passes—but you know what they say about first impressions.

The solution is to use a popular trick for *preloading* symbols that are used in the animation. This trick takes advantage of the way Flash playback works and the fact that symbols are stored in the first frame in which they appear. The key is the fact that Flash does not display a frame until all the contents of the preceding frame have loaded. In other words, Flash continues to the next frame only after everything on the current frame has downloaded over the Internet.

So the idea behind preloading is to load symbols early in the animation so that subsequent frames that use those symbols will play back smoothly. For example, if you have a bunch of symbols used to play a complex animation on frames 2–10 in a Flash animation, the animation will play back smoothly if all the symbols have already been loaded on frame 1.

Let's look at an example. Figure 9-4 shows a sequence of selected frames from a little Flash animation "toon" from ToyLab (toylab.com). The animation starts with a title screen that says, "Bitzo in: The Big Splash." After a few moments, the scene opens to reveal a fire hydrant at the left side of the stage. Next, "Bitzo" peeks out from the right edge of the stage and then bounds over to the fire hydrant. He looks at you and then back at the fire hydrant. Then he gives the fire hydrant a few good whacks and looks at you again. Finally, Bitzo looks back at the fire hydrant and gives it one final whack. The fire hydrant has had enough, so it lets Bitzo have it with a big splash of water, dismantling poor Bitzo as he flies off the stage in pieces.

Many of the symbols used to generate this animation were used over and over to minimize the animation's file size. For example, each time Bitzo looks at you (including when he peeks out from the right edge of the stage), the same series of symbols is used. Also, the same series of symbols is used over and over for the bounding motion. Even most of the audio symbols were used repeatedly. Consequently, there are only 21 symbols (including the four audio symbols) for the entire animation.

Figure 9-4   Select frames from "Bitzo in: The Big Splash" Flash animation (frame numbers added).

The animation plays back smoothly over the Internet (no matter how slow the viewer's connection) because all the symbols are preloaded on the first couple of frames. Here's how it's done. The title screen displayed during the first few frames is hiding the fact that all the symbols are loading below it. Figure 9-5 shows the frames 2 through 5 with the title screen layers turned off. Each frame preloads a few of the symbols that are used later in the animation. During playback, you can't see these symbols preloading because the title screen covers them.

Notice that no preloading is done in the first frame. This allows the title screen to show up first; because it's the only thing in the first frame, it loads faster. If some of the preloading symbols appeared in the first frame, there would be a chance that they would load before the title screen, destroying the illusion. Flash allows you to specify a loading order for layers. For example, if you specify **Top Down,** the layers on top load first. However, in practice this does not always seem to work, so placing only the title screen within the first frame ensures that no preloading symbols will be seen. After the title screen is loaded, it covers all the preloaded symbols in subsequent frames.

This sample Flash movie also contains four pieces of audio, and the audio files are much larger than the graphic symbols in terms of file size. Fortunately, you can also preload audio symbols. The trick is to make sure that they don't play out of sequence; you load the audio in the frame but turn down the volume so that it can't be heard. In the example, each

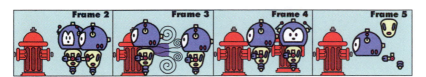

Figure 9-5   All of the symbols used for the entire movie are placed on the stage behind the title screen layer in frames 2 through 5.

of the audio events was dragged onto a key frame along with some of the other graphic symbols that were being preloaded.

Adjusting a sound's volume in Flash is poorly documented. In fact, the technique discussed here to turn off a sound is not documented at all. Here is how it is done. First, open the Properties dialog box for the key frame that contains the audio. To open the Properties dialog box, right-click (PC) or click and hold (Mac) on the key frame (on the timeline) that contains the audio; then select **Properties** from the Frame pop-up menu, as shown in Figure 9-6.

Assuming that the key frame contains an audio file, there should be a **Sound** tab on the Properties dialog box. Click on the **Sound** tab. Now there are at least two ways to adjust the sound. First, you can drag the Envelope handles (circled in red in Figure 9-7) all the way down. This has the effect of turning down the volume. However, a slightly more efficient way is to simply stop the sound from playing at all. You can do this by selecting the **Stop** option from the Sync drop-down menu, as shown in Figure 9-7. Any number of things can go wrong if you use the method of merely turning down the volume. For example, you might inadvertently forget to turn down both channels. It's a little easier just to stop the sound. In that way, you can be sure that it will load but won't play.

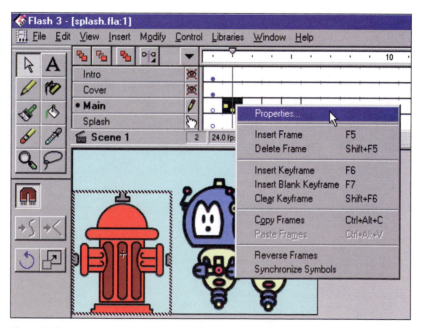

Figure 9-6 To access the Properties dialog box, right-click (PC) or click and hold (Mac) on a key frame. This brings up the Frame pop-up menu, which has an option for opening the Properties dialog box.

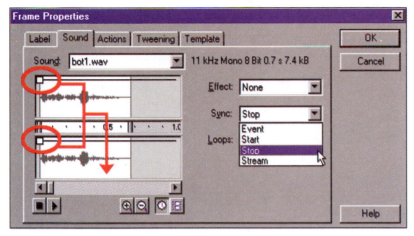

Figure 9-7 You can turn down the volume of a sound in a key frame by dragging the Envelope handles (circled here in red) down for the right and left stereo channels. The safer way to make sure that no audio is heard during preloading is to stop the sound from playing at all by selecting **Stop** from the Sync drop-down menu.

Step-by-Step Analysis of the "Bitzo in: The Big Splash" Flash Animation

Now that we have everything preloaded, let's walk through what happens during playback. Table 9-3 shows the movie report for the first 10 frames of the "Bitzo in: The Big Splash" Flash animation. First, the viewer accesses the Web page and the Flash animation begins to

Table 9-3 Movie Report for the First 10 Frames

Frame Number	Frame Bytes	Total Bytes
1	2,077	2,077
2	6,855	8,932
3	4,112	13,044
4	5,353	18,397
5	5,237	23,634
6	18	23,652
7	2	23,654
8	2	23,656
9	2	23,658
10	2	23,660

download over the Internet. The first frame is only 2,077 bytes, so it loads very quickly. It's a blue rectangle, some spiral lines, and the text "Bitzo in: The Big Splash." These elements cover the preloading symbols in the ensuing four frames.

Frame 2 contains one audio symbol and three graphic symbols (see the frame marked "Frame 2" in Figure 9-5). Most of the 6,855 bytes in frame 2 come from the audio file, which is 4,006 bytes. Although frame 2 has the largest file size in the entire 183-frame animation, it takes only about two seconds to download with a 28.8Kbps modem. Again, you cannot see the three graphic symbols loading on frame 2 because they are covered by the elements that loaded on frame 1, and you cannot hear the audio file that is loading on frame 2 because it has been stopped from playing. As far as the viewer is concerned, nothing has changed from frame 1.

Frames 3 and 4 continue the preloading process. Both frames preload three new graphics as well as an audio event. Frame 3 is only 4,112 bytes, requiring only about a second and a half to download, and frame 4 is only 5,353 bytes, requiring slightly less than two seconds to download. As with frame 2, most of the bytes in frames 3 and 4 come from the audio files that are preloaded in each frame.

Flash's movie reports also provide an itemized breakdown of the file size of each of the elements in a Flash movie. The movie report tells you how many bytes each symbol and audio file requires. It even tells you how many bytes each font adds to the Flash movie. This information can be valuable for optimizing your Flash animation. For example, if you see that an audio file is adding a substantial amount to the Flash movie's overall file size, you could look into using an audio file that has a smaller file size. ▶

Frame 5 finishes the preloading process with four graphics symbols and one final audio symbol. As with all the other frames that contain preloaded symbols, most of the 5,237 bytes in frame 5 come from the audio file. The grand total of bytes up to frame 5 is 23,634 (23K). On a 28.8-Kbps modem, that takes about 6.5 seconds to load.

The total file size of the entire Flash movie is 26,612 bytes, which means that more than 88% of the media required for the entire 183-frame animation loads within the first five frames. Again, when a Flash animation plays, each frame must be fully loaded before Flash proceeds to the next frame, so this technique effectively creates a buffer of 88% of the animations, allowing the remainder of the animation to run smoothly. It takes only about six seconds for the preloading. Because most title screens for cartoons and movies pause briefly to give the viewer time to read, the pause is hardly noticed.

▦ Basic Animation Techniques in Flash

Now that we have talked about the benefits of using symbols, let's look at the basic animation techniques in Flash. Essentially there are two ways to create an animation in Flash: using key frames and tweening. Generating animation using key frames is somewhat similar to generating GIF animations. Like frames in a GIF animation, key frames contain imagery that changes from frame to frame. So you animate with key frames simply by placing new artwork in each key frame.

Before we go any further, let's establish a common frame of reference. Figure 9-8 is a screenshot of Flash 3's layered timeline window. Each layer is clearly marked Layer 1, Layer 2, and Layer 3. Layers can be renamed. The red line on Layer 1 indicates that the animation on Layer 1 is generated using tweening. The blue dots on Layer 2 indicate that each frame contains a key frame, so any motion generated from the contents of Layer 2 is generated with key frames. Layer 3 contains 10 blank frames. The hollow blue circle in frame 1 indicates that frame 1 is a key frame, but there is nothing in it. In other words, the key frame on Layer 3 is empty. Finally, notice the downward-pointing marker. Called the *current frame pointer*, this arrow is used to scroll through the frames in a Flash animation. The current frame pointer is over frame 5.

Animating with Key Frames

Now that we have a little basic Flash terminology down, let's take another look at the earlier example to clarify how key frame animation works. Figure 9-9 shows a numbered series of key frames inside Flash 3 from "The Big Splash." The screenshots show images from the sequence in which Bitzo hits the fire hydrant and then the fire hydrant unleashes on Bitzo, blowing him apart. The first screenshot, numbered 137 in the lower right (137 indicates that it's frame 137 in the overall animation), shows Bitzo hitting the fire hydrant. All of the imagery for this frame is located on one key frame, which is on the layer named Main. The first key frame in this sequence has only two symbols: the fire hydrant symbol and the symbol of Bitzo reaching out to hit the fire hydrant.

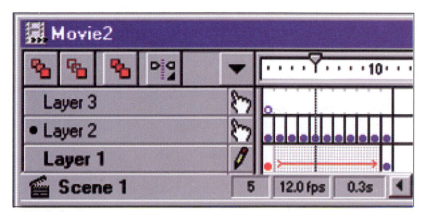

Figure 9-8   The layered timeline in Macromedia Flash.

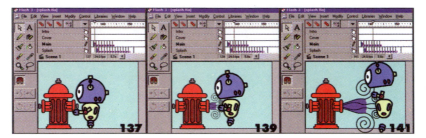

Figure 9-9   Bitzo hits the fire hydrant and then gets blown apart by the resulting spray (numbers added).

The screenshot from frame 139 in Figure 9-9 shows the water as it starts to spew from the fire hydrant. The contents of frame 139 are composed of imagery located in two key frames located on two layers. The imagery on the Main layer contains five symbols: the head, arm, body, and legs of Bitzo as well as a new version of the fire hydrant. These symbols are all different from those used on frame 137. The imagery that makes up frame 139 also includes a symbol that is located on the Splash layer. This symbol is also on a key frame.

The screenshot from frame 141 in Figure 9-9 shows the water at full power and poor Bitzo's various body parts now scattered all over the stage. Again, the contents of frame 141 are composed of imagery located in two key frames located on two layers. The imagery on the Main layer contains the same five symbols that were in frame 139 except that most of the symbols are in different positions. Similarly, the symbol on the Splash layer is the same symbol that was used on frame 139 except that it has been repositioned and resized.

This example shows that generating animation with key frames is a matter of creating a key frame and repositioning or otherwise manipulating symbols or nonsymbols within each key frame. In other words, a key frame defines a frame in which something has changed from the preceding frame.

Animating with Tweening

In Flash, creating animation using tweening is much simpler than using a series of key frames. You define two key frames, position the elements you want to tween, and then apply tweening between the frames. Again, it's easier to cover the details by looking at an example. Figure 9-10 shows a Flash-based interface whose animated components are generated primarily with tweening. The Flash file was created by Larry Larson for NavWorks (navworks.i-us.com).

Tweening was employed in the example to generate the animated effect of a button panel sliding out. In this example, tweening actually occurs on four separate layers because Flash allows you to animate only one shape or symbol per layer. However, you can group multiple

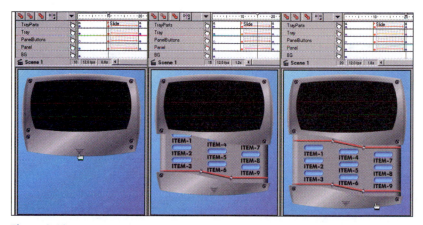

Figure 9-10 The panel slides up and down in this Flash animation using tweening.

shapes or symbols and tween them together. All the elements that make up this Flash-based interface must be on separate layers because some of them are buttons. The buttons would not work if all the elements were grouped.

Generating the tweening animation for each layer was simple. First, Larson created a key frame on frame 10 of the animation. He then positioned all the artwork for all the layers in the starting or closed position of the interface. Next, he added 10 frames to each layer and then placed a key frame on frame 20 for each layer. Then he repositioned all the sliding panel elements for each layer on frame 20. Finally, he added tweening between each layer.

To add tweening to a layer, you simply right-click (PC) or click and hold (Mac) a frame on a given layer anywhere between two key frames. This action opens the Frame pop-up menu. Select **Properties** and then select the **Tweening** tab, as shown in Figure 9-11. As Figure 9-11 shows, there are two basic types of tweening in Flash 3: motion and shape tweening. Motion tweening was used in this example.

With *motion* tweening, Flash interpolates the contents of each key frame. In this example, Flash takes the contents of each layer and moves them in even increments between frames 10 and 20. *Shape* tweening is slightly different. With shape tweening, Flash morphs between ungrouped nonsymbols located in different key frames. So, for example, you can shape-tween between a circle and a square or between a shape of a dove and text that says "DOVE."

Most tweened animation effects in Flash 3 should be done with symbols. As mentioned, the exception to this rule is shape tweening or morphing. Morphs in Flash must be applied to ungrouped nonsymbol imagery. Although this requirement is unfortunate for optimization, it's not a total loss because Flash 3 interpolates all morphing effects on-the-fly-during

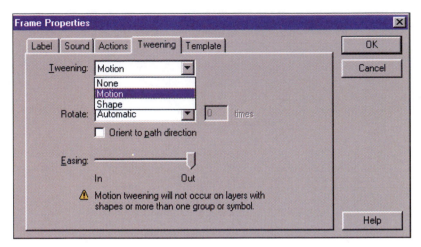

Figure 9-11   Use the **Tweening** tab in the Frame Properties dialog box to generate tweened animation in Flash.

playback. This means that while morphing generates a bunch of different shapes, these in-between shapes do not actually have to be downloaded, because the in-between shapes are generated on-the-fly during playback after the animation has been downloaded over the Internet.

It's commonly held that it is better, in terms of optimizing Flash animations, to use tweening, rather than key frames, for generating animations. However, that is not always true. For example, when tweening was employed to create the animation of Bitzo flying apart in "The Big Splash," the file size of the overall animation went up slightly. Using tweening, however, is usually much faster than generating similar animation effects using key frames. ▸

Fortunately, all other tweened animation effects can take advantage of symbols, and this means that most tweened effects can be file-size-efficient. For file-size optimization, it's usually better to create an animation using tweened symbols whenever possible rather than create the motion in a series of key frames. Even if you use symbols in key frames, tweening is always at least slightly more efficient (not to mention that it's easier and faster to let the computer create the animation for you).

▣ Combining Tweening and Key Frame Animation

Not all animation effects can be achieved using tweening. Figure 9-12 shows an animation from NavWorks. This Flash animation serves as an expandable/collapsible unit for navigating the key sections of a site. The animation plays when the buttons expand or collapse. Figure 9-13 shows the layers that are employed to create the animations. The small red pointing lines in the layers labeled Small Ball and Pipe correspond to the gray pipe and the

Figure 9-12   This expandable/collapsible navigational bar from NavWorks was created largely with frame-by-frame animation in Flash.

small orange ball. Both layers contain symbols that have been animated with tweening; the small ball merely moves in a linear path from the top of the stage to the bottom of the stage (or vice-versa), and the pipe merely stretches or shortens.

Animations for the expanding and contracting buttons could not be created with tweening, and instead key frames were used. To keep the file size down, all the key frames use only two symbols in addition to the four individual button symbols. For example, as the navigational unit expands, the pipe and the ball travel downward. As they move downward, a blue circular

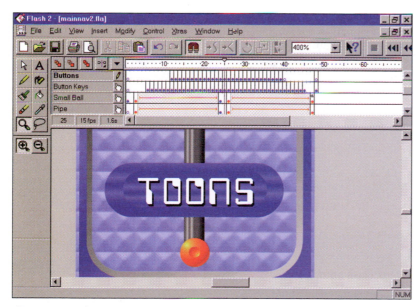

Figure 9-13   The Small Ball and Pipe layers move on linear paths, so it was feasible to animate them with tweening.

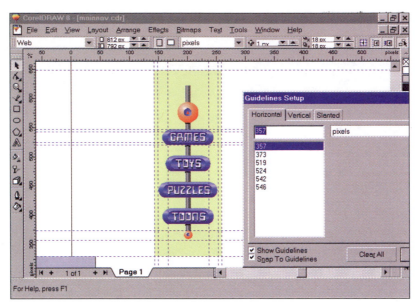

Figure 9-14   The precision placement requirements for this animation were achieved by importing the artwork created in CorelDRAW into Flash.

symbol moves down the pipe. When the blue circular symbol reaches the location where one of the buttons will be, it stops, and the second symbol, a blue ovoid, replaces it in the next key frame; in turn, the button symbol replaces the blue ovoid symbol. This progression is effectively repeated for each button until the navigational unit is fully expanded.

Although this animation may seem complex, Flash makes it easy to create such integrated animation sequences. To tween two copies of a symbol, you need only create two key frames on the same layer (generally at least a few frames apart from each other), select the frames, choose tweening, and adjust the tweening options (such as whether the tweening will apply to the size or rotation of the objects). When the tweening is applied, Flash calculates the in-between frames, automatically generating the animation for you.

Creating the key frame layers is only slightly more involved. When you create a key frame on a layer and add an object to it, all frames added to the layer subsequent to that key frame will contain the object in exactly the same position as in the key frame. To change the position, size, and the like of the object in

---

POSITIONING ART AND IMPORTING VECTOR ART IN FLASH

Precise positioning is not one of Flash's strong points. Flash has guide layers, an alignment feature, and nudging, but all these features are hampered by debilitating deficiencies. For example, Flash's alignment tools suffer from poor implementation. When you align the right, left, top, or bottom edges of objects, you make alignments to the bounding box of the selected objects. In other words, if you draw two squares and align one to the top of the other, the alignment always occurs to the object that is higher on the stage. If you were to align the objects to the right edge, the alignment would occur to the right edge of the object that's farther to the right. Center alignment is worse. When you center objects, their positions are averaged, and this means that both elements move.

Flash's lack of absolute alignment is superseded by its unfortunate approach to nudging. Essentially, the distance an object is nudged is

(cont.)

a different frame you must add a key frame to that frame. For example, if you have an object on one key frame on the first frame of a 10-frame layer and you want to change the position of the object in the second frame, you must add a key frame to the second frame. If a key frame is not added to the second frame, any edits of the object in the second frame will apply not only to the first frame but also to all the other frames.

After you get used to this characteristic of Flash, it can become a valuable asset for creating animations. For example, I created the key frames on the Buttons layer in Figure 9-13 by first position-ing all four buttons within a key frame at frame 12 (see the note on importing vector artwork for tips on positioning graphics in Flash). Then I selected frames 12–25 and selected the **Insert Key frames** option, making key frames for frames 12–25. Each frame contained all four buttons in the correct position. Then all I had to do was to go back frame by frame and delete the buttons that weren't supposed to be visible on each given frame.

One of the key challenges of this animation was the position-ing of the art. Figure 9-14 shows the button artwork for the animation. The artwork has been positioned precisely over a yellow rectangle. This yellow rectangle is exactly the same size as the stage size of the Flash animation. I selected and exported this artwork to the Adobe Illustrator (AI) format from Corel-DRAW! using **Selected Only**.

related to the zoom level. The farther zoomed-out you are, the farther an object will move when nudged. Because Flash's guide layers are merely layers on which you can draw lines and shapes as guides, they suffer from the lack of control offered by the alignment and nudging tools. With no numerical moving op-tions, precision is a tedious prospect at best in Flash 2. Flash 3 contains an Inspector tool that allows you to position and size things with pixel coordinates, but you have to know what the target coordinates are.

The solution is often to import art from a vector-based application that contains better precision tools, such as CorelDRAW!, Adobe Il-lustrator, and Macromedia Freehand. Corel-DRAW! is the front-runner in this regard. Contrary to popular rumor, CorelDRAW! sports the best alignment features since Illustrator, and both of Freehand's alignment features work like Flash's. However, importing Corel-DRAW! files can be problematic. The problem is that CorelDRAW! assumes high-resolution output and defaults to a 300-dpi page. Illustra-tor, Freehand, and Flash default to 72 ppi. So if you export artwork from CorelDRAW! for use in Flash, the 300-dpi page setup will result in the artwork importing to the wrong size. To fix this problem, you must change the default page settings in CorelDRAW! To do this, go into CorelDRAW!'s Page Setup (located in the Layout menu in CorelDRAW! 8) and change the **Resolution** setting to **72** and the units of measurements to **Pixels**. This will make Corel-DRAW!'s resolution match Flash's, resulting in the artwork created and exported from Corel-DRAW! importing at the correct size in Flash.

When artwork is imported into Flash, the artwork is centered into the work area if **Work Area** is selected in the View menu. If **Work Area** is not selected, the artwork is centered on the stage if Flash is at 100% view. To ensure precise positioning of the imported art, I made sure that the **Work Area** option was unselected and set the zoom level to 100%. Because the imported art-work's size was defined by the yellow rectangle, which was the same size as the Flash movie's stage, the artwork centered perfectly on the stage. Thus, the precise position of the buttons as established in CorelDRAW! was maintained. The final step was to ungroup the imported art-work and delete the yellow rectangle.

You can facilitate precise positioning in Flash by creating and exporting artwork over an object that is sized exactly the same as the Flash movie's stage size.

After I created the key framed layers and tweened layers for the expanding animation se-quence, it was simple to create the collapsing sequence. I merely copied the frames on all layers of the animation, pasted them into frames 26–48, and then chose **Reverse Frames.** This command reversed the sequence of the selected frames, automatically creating the collapsing sequence of the animation.

Summary

Although Macromedia Flash represents one of the better combinations of advanced Web-based animation technology, paying close attention to optimization is still a prerequisite for effective delivery. With a firm understanding of how symbols work and how Flash streams its content, you can arrive at strategies for making small Flash animations even smaller. Flash not only offers a fast Web animation delivery vehicle but also makes it easy to create many kinds of animation effects. With careful implementation, Flash can be used to serve up some of the richest possible interactive Web animations.

CHAPTER **10**

Interactive Animation in Flash

One way to add intrigue to a Web animation is to make parts of it interactive and/or conditional. Adding interactivity essentially adds new elements, such as discovery and user control. In this chapter we look at techniques for making Flash animations interactive, conditional, and even random. ▶

Using Movie Clips

Interactivity Without Movie Clips

Using Tell Target

Simple If/Then Logic with Tell Target

▦ Using Movie Clips

One of the most valuable features for creating interactive animations in Flash is the movie clip. Movie clips are essentially animated symbols and can contain everything that a normal Flash animation can contain. For example, a movie clip can have layered animation, button symbols, graphic symbols, audio, and frame actions (that is, actions applied to a specific frame). Basically, movie clips are Flash animations that can be embedded within Flash animations. Probably the most basic application of movie clips is to create animated rollovers. Let's look at an example.

Figure 10-1 shows a Flash-based interface from NavWorks (navworks.i-us.com). The interface features eight yellow buttons that initially are static. When a visitor rolls the mouse over a button (as shown in Figure 10-2), it changes to blue and a short nonlooping animation plays (see Figure 10-3).

To create this effect, first the blue nonlooping animation was made into a movie clip named Blue Button Over. As you can see in Figure 10-4, the Blue Button Over movie clip contains only one layer and five key frames. Each key frame contains artwork for the various stages of transition of the blue ball (shown in Figure 10-3). The final key frame contains a stop action so that it stops on frame 5 when the movie clip plays.

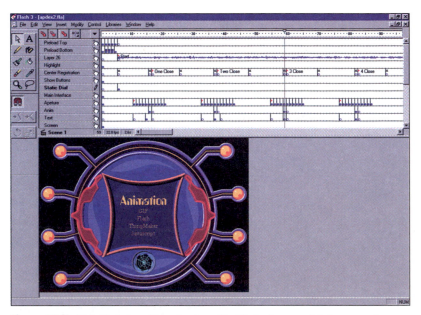

Figure 10-1   This Flash-based interface from NavWorks features eight buttons, a large screen for text, and a small blue aperture.

Figure 10-2 When a visitor rolls the mouse over a button, the button changes color and briefly moves. The corresponding text appears on the screen, and the aperture opens to reveal another animation.

Next, the imagery for the yellow default state of the button was made into a button symbol called Small Yellow Button (shown in Figure 10-5). Button symbols in Flash have four states: Up, Over, Down, and Hit. The Up state is the default state. In other words, the Up state of a button symbol is what you see when no event is taking place. The Over state of the button symbol is what the viewer sees when the mouse cursor is placed over the button. The Down state determines the visible state of the button when the viewer clicks on the button with the mouse. Finally, the Hit state determines the area of the button that responds to the mouse. For example, you can have imagery for the Up, Over, and Down states of a button symbol that takes up the entire viewable area of the Flash movie, but the button area itself can be a tiny dot. In that case, the viewer would see the Over and Down

Figure 10-3 The rollover animation, generated by a movie clip nested within the Over state of the button, contains only five frames.

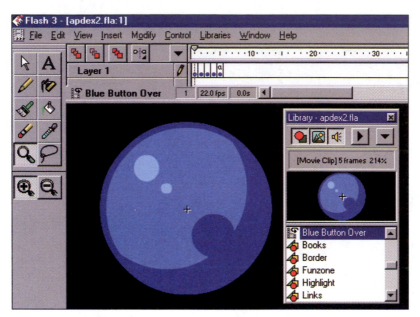

Figure 10-4 The Blue Button Over movie clip has only five frames, all of them on one layer.

states of the button symbol only if the mouse were over the small area defined by the tiny dot in the Hit state. However, in this example, the Up, Over, Down, and Hit states of the button are all the same size.

After the Small Yellow Button symbol was created, the Blue Button Over movie clip was placed in the Over state. In essence, the Blue Button Over movie clip becomes an embedded movie within the button. The result is that when the viewer rolls the mouse over any copy of the Small Yellow Button symbol, the short animation plays.

One of the benefits of this approach to generating the rollover animation is that it is file-size-efficient and also time-efficient. The yellow button is still a symbol even with the movie clip embedded in it. This means that even though there are eight copies of the button, it as if there is only one copy because Flash's buttons are object-oriented, as discussed in Chapter 9, Creating Animations with Macromedia Flash. In addition, the animated rollover button had to be created only once; all eight buttons are copies of the same button symbol.

Movie clips can also be used to help manage the production of an interactive animation in Flash. To understand this point, refer to Figure 10-1. Notice that the animation has numerous layers and that there are many key frames on the various layers. When the mouse rolls over the yellow buttons, not only does the blue movie clip play, but also several other things

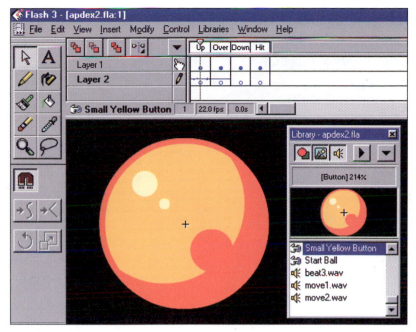

Figure 10-5 The Blue Button Over movie clip was placed in the Over state of the Small Yellow Button symbol. This symbol is used eight times in the sample interface.

happen at the same time. The small blue aperture opens (see Figure 10-6) to reveal an animation (another movie clip), and text comes into view on the large screen in the center.

All this animation takes place in the main Flash movie; none of this animation is embedded in the yellow button. Instead, each of the buttons has a set of actions applied to it. For example, when the mouse rolls over the button at the upper left, a rollover action tells the animation to jump to the frame labeled 1 Open (see Figure 10-7). This starts the screen and aperture animation associated with the upper-left yellow button. Although this approach works fine, it is a little difficult to manage all the layers with all the various key frames. For example, all the key frames for the aperture animations must match all the key

Figure 10-6 The frames for the aperture animation are located on individual key frames on the main timeline.

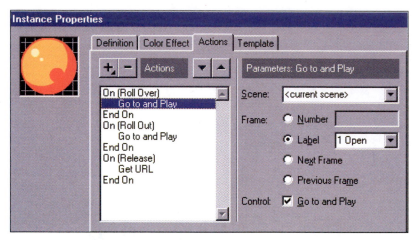

Figure 10-7   A rollover action tells the main timeline to jump to the frame labeled
1 Open.

frames for the screen animations. Fortunately, movie clips and another Flash feature called Tell Target provide a solution to this problem, as you will see later in this chapter. Before we look at Tell Target, let's talk about a few other simple tricks that you can use to add interactivity to your animations.

▦ Interactivity Without Movie Clips

Movie clips are new to Flash 3. Before movie clips, Flash animators had to resort to a little trickery to implement interactivity. Although movie clips free Flash animators from having to use these tricks in all cases, these techniques are still useful for adding depth to Flash animations. For the most part, these techniques use the most fundamental characteristics of Flash, such as the basics of how a Flash button works and the basics of layers. If you understand how to implement the following tricks, you can easily use them in tandem with the techniques discussed earlier.

Animating on Rollover Without Movie Clips

Figure 10-8 shows a Flash movie from NavWorks (navworks.i-us.com) that is composed of a series of buttons. These buttons are designed to serve as basic navigational controls that replace the browser's own button. When the mouse is not over one of the buttons, they appear to be static. However, when you roll over one of the buttons with the mouse, the button turns blue and a little triangle moves over and under the name of the button, subtly reinforcing the visual feedback of the Over state.

Figure 10-8 These buttons move only when the cursor rolls over them.

To achieve this effect in Flash, you set the buttons one layer above the animations. In Figure 10-9 you can see that the Buttons layer is on the top and there are three layers below it. Two of these layers—the Bottom Text layer and the Back Buttons layer—contain static elements. The other layer, the Animated Triangles layer, contains a bunch of tiny blue animated triangles that are constantly moving back and forth. The visitor can't see the little blue triangles moving because the buttons on the Button layer are covering them.

The little animated triangles become visible only when the mouse rolls over one of the buttons. This functionality is made possible by the fact that the buttons on the top layer have no imagery in their Over and Down states. For example, Figure 10-10 shows the states of the button labeled **Back**. The frame marker is over the Up, or default state, which is the state that the viewer sees when the mouse is not over the button. Notice that the Over and Down states contain tiny hollow blue circles rather than solid blue circles on the timeline. This indicates that there is no content within these states of the button. Figure 10-11 shows the contents of the Over state. As you can see, there is no imagery in

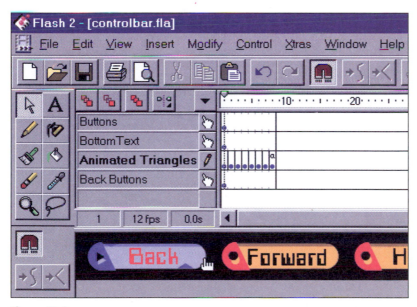

Figure 10-9 The layer containing the buttons is above the layer containing the animations.

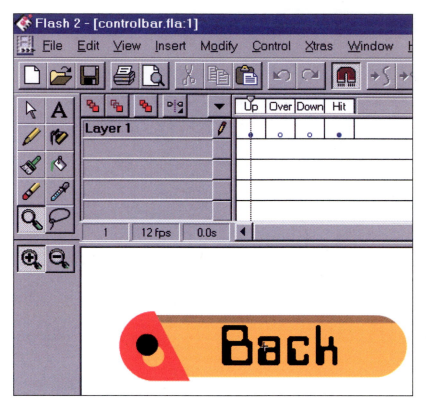

Figure 10-10   The Up state of the **Back** button contains the imagery that viewers see when the mouse is not over the button.

the Over state. This means that when the mouse is over the **Back** button, the button shows through to the layers below.

Note that the Hit state contains a copy of the button. When you create buttons that move with rollover using this technique, it's easy to forget that the Hit state must have an image to define the "hot" region for the rollover. If you forget to put an image in the Hit state of the button, the button won't work. Incidentally, you may wonder why the contents of the Bottom Text and Back Buttons layers are separated on different layers. This is so that the graphics on the Back Buttons layer could be made into symbols. I saved a slight amount of file size by creating a symbol from one of the blue buttons and then using the symbol multiple times.

This example demonstrates that you need not use movie clips to generate the effect of having a button move when you roll over it. The drawback to this approach is that the animation must be playing at all times, and that can slow down playback. However, the value of this technique is that it can be combined with interactive animations using movie clips.

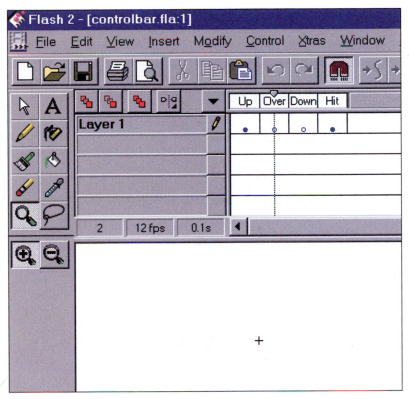

Figure 10-11   The Over state of the **Back** button contains no imagery. When the mouse is over the button, the button disappears, revealing the animation below.

For example, you could have a button with a movie clip in the Over state that is partially transparent. The movie clip in the Over state could stop moving after a while but still show through to a looping animation on a layer below the button. Now let's look at a variation of this trick.

Stopping an Animation on Rollover Without Movie Clips

You can achieve the effect of stopping an animation when a mouse rolls over a button in Flash using a simple variation of the technique described in the preceding section. Figure 10-12 shows a Flash animation from ToyLab (toylab.com) that features several small animations. At the bottom of the screen to the left of the yellow robot is an **on/off** button that allows visitors to turn off the animations if they wish. When the animations are on, electrical charges appear to emanate from the button. However, when the mouse rolls over the **Off** button, the electrical charges disappear, visually cueing visitors that if they click the **Off** button all the animations will stop playing.

Figure 10-12   Electrical charges emanate from the **Off** button as an indication that the animations are currently on and to help call attention to the button, which can be used to turn the animations off.

This effect is achieved with a combination of layers and button states. First, notice that the OFF Button layer is above the ON/OFF Animation layer. The OFF Button layer contains only the **Off** button, whereas the ON/OFF Animation layer contains the animated electrical charges. The animation appears to stop when the mouse rolls over the **Off** button because the Over state of the **Off** button contains an image that covers the animation that is taking place on the ON/OFF Animation layer. Figure 10-13 shows the Up state of the **Off** button, and Figure 10-14 shows the Over state of the **Off** button. As you can see, the Over state contains a green rectangle behind the imagery for the depressed (shadowless) **Off** button, whereas the Up state contains only imagery for the button itself. Because the **Off** button is on a layer above the animation, its Over state covers the animation below, making it appear as if the animation has stopped.

Using Button States to Create Interactive Rollover Animations

Another fun interactive animation trick involves using button states to create interactive animations. This trick creates animation that is even more dependent on the actual movement and position of the mouse cursor. The Flash movie shown in Figure 10-15 has another simple interactive animation. As the viewer rolls the mouse over the blue and green buttons below the small blue screen (located in the lower-left corner), an animation of a rocket

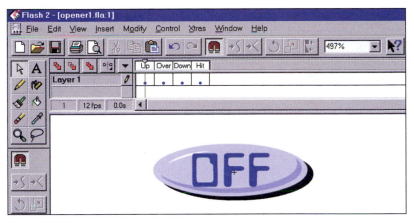

Figure 10-13   The Up state of the **Off** button contains only the **Off** button.

colliding with an asteroid plays. The user controls the pace and direction of the animation. This interface is displayed every time users visit the site. Although the interface is updated regularly with information on new games and online cartoons, this interactive animation was designed to be customizable to help keep the interface fresh.

The interactive animation effect was created simply by assigning each frame of the animation to the Over states of a series of adjacent buttons. Each blue and green shape is a button. Figure 10-16 and Figure 10-17 show the Up and Over states, respectively, of the center button. The Up state contains only the button, but the Over state contains the images for a

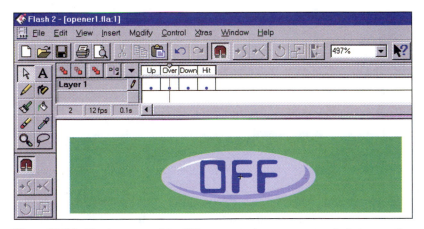

Figure 10-14   The Over state of the **Off** button contains a green rectangle that covers the underlying electrical charge animation.

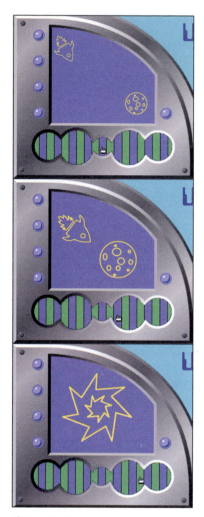

Figure 10-15 An interactive animation of a rocket colliding with a meteor plays as the mouse rolls over the blue and green buttons below the small screen.

single frame of the animation. Each of the other adjacent buttons has a different frame for the animation in its Over state. As the mouse rolls over the buttons in sequence, the Over states of the buttons are displayed to form the interactive animation.

All of these tricks are fun, but now let's look at one of the new features in Flash 3 that provides probably the most powerful possibilities of all for interactive animations in Flash. Everything we've looked at so far is essentially limited to the button. What if you want interactivity to initiate motion that is not directly attached to a button? That sounds like a job for Tell Target.

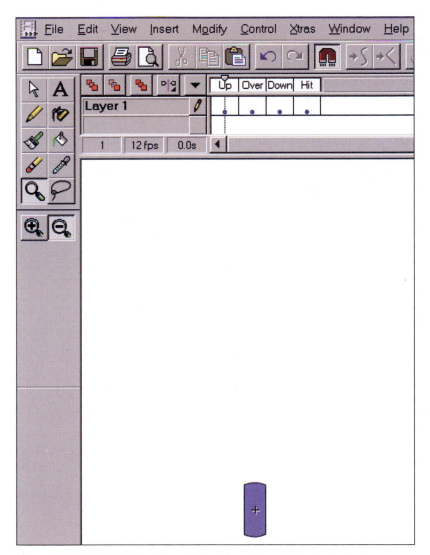

Figure 10-16   The Up state of the center button contains only the button itself.

Using Tell Target

Figure 10-18 shows a Flash-based interface for eyeland.com, my personal Web site. I'll use this interface as an example to talk about Tell Target, but first I want to point out something about the movie clips that are used in this example. This interface essentially works like the first example interface that we looked at in this chapter. When you roll the mouse over a button, the button moves and some text moves into view within a small text screen

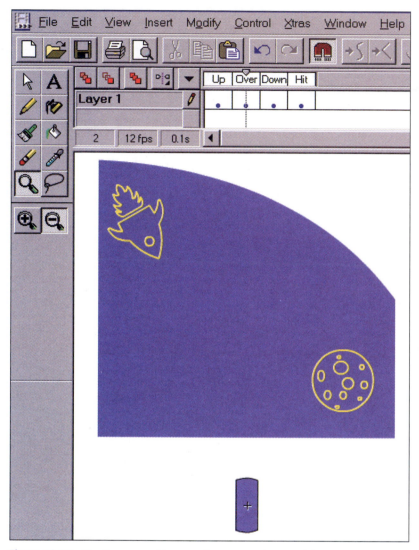

Figure 10-17   The Over state of the center button contains one of the frames of the interactive animation.

area, as shown in Figure 10-19. However, not all the buttons in this example are the same. Each button has its own unique embedded movie clip.

Figure 10-20 shows one of the movie clips for one of the buttons. Notice that this movie clip is very different from the one we looked at in the first example. That first movie clip had only one layer and five key frames, but this movie clip has seven layers and 20 key frames. Also notice that tweening was used heavily on many different layers. The resulting 20 frames

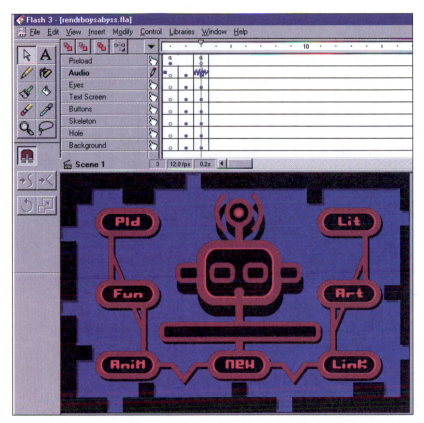

Figure 10-18   All the motion on this Flash-based interface from Eyeland takes place on movie clips, leaving the main timeline with only a few frames.

of animation are shown in Figure 10-21. This example shows that movie clips can contain complex animation if you want them to. Even this example is relatively simple. Movie clips can contain animation that is far more complex than the examples shown here.

Refer to Figure 10-8 and notice that unlike the first example, this Flash-based interface has only three frames. In fact, the first two frames are used for preloading, so all the action that the user sees happens on a single frame. This is because everything is done with movie clips, which are embedded in all the buttons, and the text screen is a button. When the mouse rolls over a button, the button sends a message to the text screen movie clip to play a short text animation that corresponds with the button. The messenger that gets the message from the button to the text screen movie clip is the Tell Target feature.

Tell Target allows you to send commands to movie clips, have movie clips send commands to other movie clips, or have movie clips send commands to the main movie itself. First,

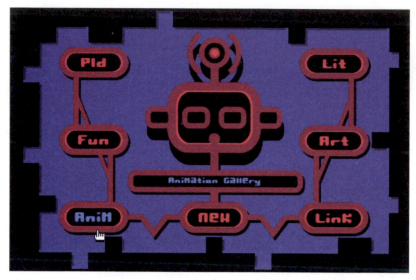

Figure 10-19 The button and corresponding text screen move when the mouse rolls over a button.

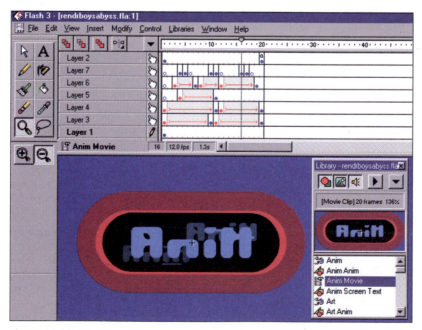

Figure 10-20 The button movie clips contain numerous layers of tweened and key frame animation.

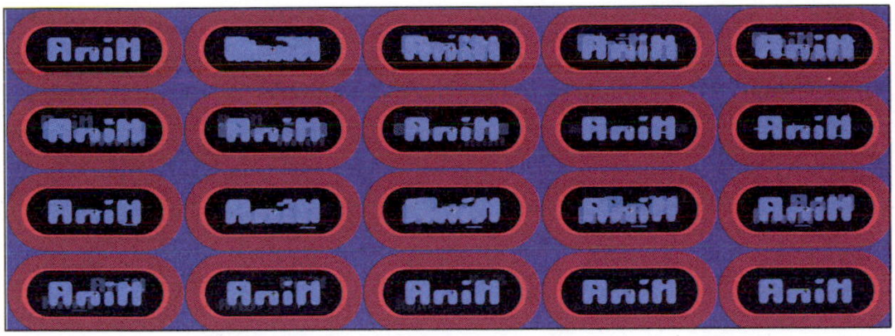

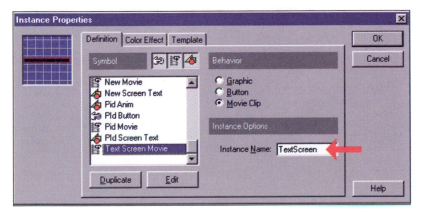

Figure 10-21 Each button's movie clip animation is unique.

let's talk about using Tell Target to send a message to a movie clip. The real trick to understanding how to use the Tell Target feature to send a message or command to a movie clip is to understand that Tell Target needs an *address* in order to deliver a message. This means that you must name your movie clips. Movie clips are symbols that can be used over and over again. Each time you use a symbol, it becomes an *instance*, or a copy of a symbol. For Tell Target to send a message to a movie clip, Tell Target must be able to determine which instance of the movie clip to send the message to.

Flash doesn't automatically name an instance of a movie clip when you place it on the stage. You must assign a name to an instance of a movie clip manually in the Instance Properties dialog box. You can open the Instance Properties dialog box by selecting **Instance** from the Modify menu or by double-clicking on the instance (of the movie clip) on the stage. Figure 10-22 shows the Instance Properties dialog box. Here, the instance of the Text Screen movie clip has been named Text Screen.

Figure 10-22 You must assign a name to an instance in order to control it with the Tell Target command.

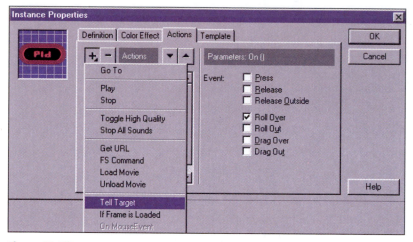

Figure 10-23   Click on the + sign on the **Actions** tab of the Instance Properties dialog box to select **Tell Target.**

After you've named an instance of a movie clip, you can use Tell Target to control it. The Tell Target action is assigned to a button in the same way that any other action is—via the **Actions** tab of the Instance Properties dialog box. To assign a Tell Target action to a button, click on the + button on the **Actions** tab and select **Tell Target**, as shown in Figure 10-23. Next, click on the **Begin Tell Target** line. The Parameters section of the **Actions** tab displays the named instance of the movie clip (see Figure 10-24). If an instance of a movie clip is not named, it will not show up in the Parameters section. Double-click on the in-

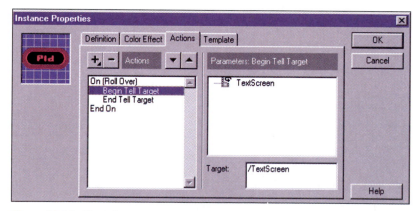

Figure 10-24   The Tell Target command needs an instance name in the Target field. In essence, this is the "target" that the command will "tell" to perform a specified action.

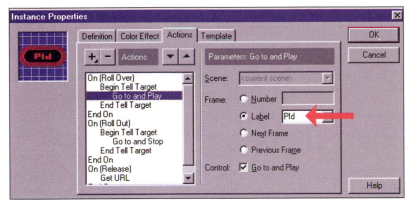

Figure 10-25 Referencing frame labels (see arrow) rather than frame numbers is a more reliable way to send "Go to" commands.

stance you wish to send the Tell Target command to, and it will show up in the Target window. (Alternatively, you can type the instance name into the Target field.)

After you assign a named instance to a Tell Target command, you must tell it what command to send. To do this, you must have the **Begin Tell Target** action selected; then click on the + button again. In this example, the Tell Target command was used to tell the movie clip to go to a frame. Rather than direct the movie clip to go to a specific frame number, this example employs frame labels, as shown in Figure 10-25.

Refer to Figure 10-26 to see how the Text Screen movie clip is constructed. Each button has corresponding text. For example, the text that goes with the PId button is "Pure Imagination design." Each string of text comes into view in a short animated sequence. A Stop

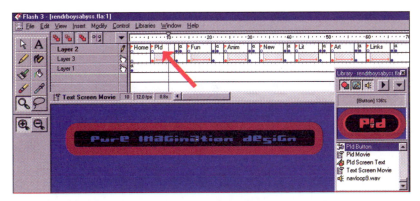

Figure 10-26 The Text Screen movie clip is sectioned off with frame labels.

action is placed at the end of each text animation sequence. The beginning of each of these text animation sequences is marked with a label. You can assign a label to a frame using the Frame Properties dialog box.

Using labels instead of frame numbers is more reliable. It allows you to freely edit the movie clip without worrying about whether a given sequence starts on a given frame number. For example, when I was finished adding all the text animation sequences for the Text Screen movie clip, I decided that each animated sequence was too short. I added a few frames to each sequence. I didn't have to worry about the fact that this editing redistributed the beginning frame of most of the text animation sequences because I had directed the Tell Target command to look for a frame label, and not a frame number.

To recap, this sample Flash-based interface is more organized and navigable on the production end because there aren't a bunch of frames on the main timeline. Instead, each key element either is a movie clip, which has its own timeline, or has an embedded movie clip. This arrangement made it easier to construct and edit the file because everything had a logical hierarchy. For example, when I wanted to edit the text animations, I didn't have to find them on the main timeline; instead, I only had to edit the Text Screen movie clip. The key to making all this work was the Tell Target command.

Simple If/Then Logic with Tell Target

One of the more interesting things about the Tell Target command is that it can be used to implement simple if/then logic in Flash animations. With Tell Target, you can make something happen after a certain number of key events take place; if conditions A, B, and C are met, then D will occur. Normally, this sort of functionality is found only in Web animation technologies such as Shockwave or Java, but Tell Target opens the door to basic if/then logic in Flash.

Figure 10-27 shows a Flash-based puzzle and greeting card from ToyLab (toylab.com). It's a classic puzzle in which pencils are arrayed in a seemingly random pattern. As the instructions state, you must click to remove six pencils to reveal ten. The solution is to remove six pencils so that the remaining pencils spell the word *ten*. First, let's talk about how it works for the user. Then we'll talk about how the effect was generated in Flash.

When players first start the puzzle, they are presented with the array of pencils shown in Figure 10-27. If they click on a pencil that should remain (to spell the word *ten*), they are presented with a screen that says "Whoops," as shown in Figure 10-28. If they click on a pencil that must be removed to spell the word *ten*, the pencil falls away from view. If they click on all the pencils that must be removed to spell the word *ten* without clicking on any

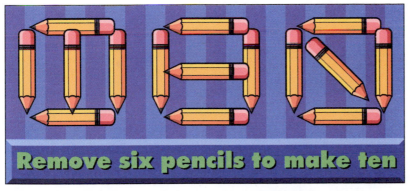

Figure 10-27   This example is a simple puzzle that employs simple if/then logic: If you select the right pencils, Then you win; and if you select the wrong pencils, then you lose.

Figure 10-28   Players see this screen when they click on any of the wrong pencils.

of the pencils that need to remain, they see the pencils spell the word *ten* (Figure 10-29); a few seconds later they are presented with a message (Figure 10-30) along with an opportunity to play again if they like.

Now let's look at how all this was accomplished in Flash. Figure 10-31 shows the overall Flash movie. As with the preceding example, there are only a few frames in the animation because all the motion takes place within movie clips. Notice the layer named Pencil Buttons. This layer, shown in Figure 10-32 with all the layers turned off, contains two kinds of buttons made from the same pencil symbol.

The light blue buttons in Figure 10-32 indicate buttons that are transparent (the transparent light blue is how Flash displays transparent buttons). The Up, Over, and Down states of

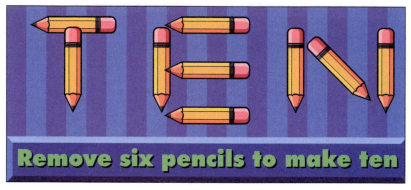

Figure 10-29   Click on all the right pencils to reveal the solution to the puzzle.

these buttons are empty, as shown in Figure 10-33. Only the Hit state contains the pencil artwork, which defines the clickable portion of the transparent button. As you will see in a moment, these invisible buttons show through to movie clips that contain the same pencil artwork on a layer below the Pencil Buttons layer.

All the rest of the buttons on the Pencil Buttons layer are copies of buttons with the same pencil artwork in all four states of the button. These buttons look the same when the cursor is off and over the buttons as well as when you click on the buttons. When the user clicks on one of the visible buttons, the second frame in the main movie appears. It contains the "Whoops" message and the **Try Again** button shown in Figure 10-28.

The layer directly below the Pencil Buttons layer is the Pencil Movies layer (shown in Figure 10-34 with all other layers turned off). This layer contains movie clips for all of the pencils that must be removed to solve the puzzle. Each pencil shown in Figure 10-34 is a copy of the same movie clip (shown in Figure 10-35). Each pencil movie clip has an instance name.

Figure 10-30   A few moments after "winning," players see this greeting card.

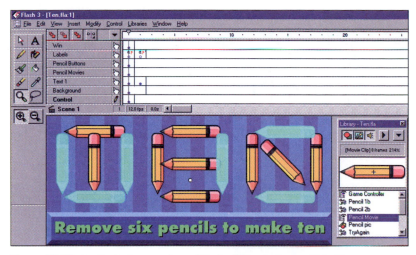

Figure 10-31   To display buttons that will be invisible, Flash uses a light blue transparent screen.

The pencil movie clips on the Pencil Movies layer start with Stop action in frame 1. The second frame is labeled "bye." When the player clicks one of the invisible buttons on the Pencil Buttons layer, it sends a command (using Tell Target) to the corresponding pencil movie clip on the Pencil Movies layer to go the frame labeled "bye." This initiates a short animated sequence within the pencil movie clip that shows the pencil falling away or shrinking out of view. The final frame in the pencil movie clip is blank and contains a Stop action. The result is that pencils disappear (after a brief animation) when the user clicks on the invisible buttons.

To this point we've talked about nothing very complicated. The invisible buttons use Tell Target to initiate movie clip animations when you click on the right pencils, and the visible buttons use the standard "Go To" action to go to the next frame when you click on the wrong pencils. The trick is getting the Flash movie to recognize that the player has won the

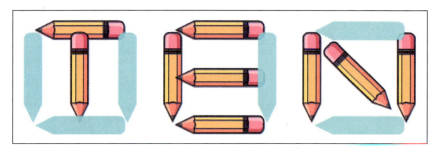

Figure 10-32   The Pencil Buttons layer has two kinds of buttons: visible pencil buttons and invisible buttons.

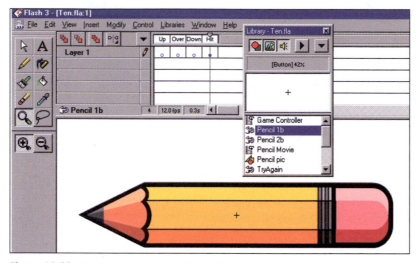

Figure 10-33   The button has nothing in the Up, Over, and Down states. Only the Hit
state of the button defines the button.

game. In other words, when the player clicks on all six of the correct pencils, the Flash
movie must recognize that the player has won.

This was accomplished with two additional hidden movie clips. First, notice the top
layer, called Win, in Figure 10-31. This layer contains a movie clip, called Winner, that
has an instance name Win. The Winner movie clip, shown in Figure 10-36, is blank in
the first frame. Notice the small white dot in the middle of the stage or movie area in
Figure 10-31; that is how Flash displays invisible movie clips. The first frame of the
Winner movie clip has a Stop action applied to it. The second frame is labeled End. All
the remaining frames in the Winner movie clip are blank except the final frame, which
contains artwork that covers all the frames below. The final frame of the Winner movie

Figure 10-34   The Pencil Movies layer contains movie clips for all the pencils that must
be removed to solve the puzzle. The invisible pencil buttons show through
to these pencil movie clips.

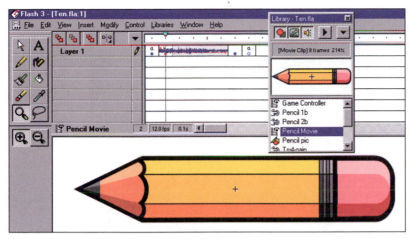

Figure 10-35   The Pencil Movie clip (which is used repeatedly) has a Stop action in the first frame. Then the remaining frames show the pencil fading away and play a swoosh sound effect.

clip also contains the greeting card message "You're a Perfect Ten" and a button to try again.

The second hidden movie clip is on the layer called Control. It contains a movie clip called Game Controller, which has an instance name of "controller." The contents of the Control

Figure 10-36   The Winner movie clip is blank in the first frame. Winning starts the movie clip playing from the second frame to the 25th frame. All frames are blank except the 25th frame.

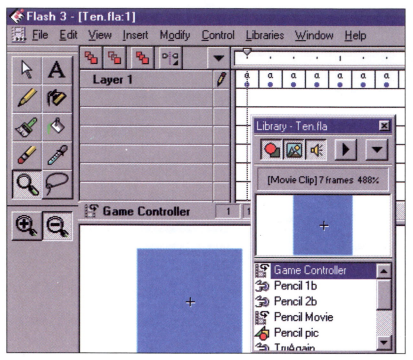

Figure 10-37   The Game Controller movie clip manages the if/then logic of the game. If the sixth frame of the Game Controller movie clip is reached, then the Winner movie clip is initiated.

layer are covered by the Background layer, so the Game Controller movie clip is essentially invisible. Figure 10-37 shows the Game Controller movie clip, which contains seven frames. The first six frames contain a Stop action, and the final frame has a Tell Target frame action.

Each time the user clicks one of the invisible buttons, another Tell Target command is sent. The Tell Target command is the same for the first six buttons. It simply tells the "controller" instance of the Game Controller movie clip to go to the next frame. So each invisible button sends two Tell Target commands: one to a corresponding pencil movie clip to make the pencil disappear, and another one to the Game Controller movie clip to make it advance one frame. When the sixth correct pencil is clicked, it sends the Game Controller movie clip to the seventh frame.

The seventh frame in the Game Controller movie clip has a Tell Target frame action assigned to it (see Figure 10-38). This Tell Target is slightly different because this movie clip sends a message to another movie clip: the Win instance of the Winner movie clip. Notice that the Target parameter is a little different from those shown in the earlier example. The Target parameter in this example reads _level0/Win.

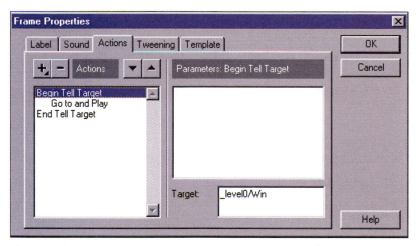

Figure 10-38 The undocumented _level0 path statement sends the message back to
the main timeline of the overall Flash movie.

The _level0 is needed because the Tell Target command must
be sent along a certain path in order for the message to get from
the Game Controller movie clip to the Winner movie clip. Figure 10-39 shows the basic hierarchy of the overall Flash movie.
In terms of hierarchy, the Game Controller movie clip is under
the main movie. The same is true for the Winner movie clip. To
send a command from the Game Controller movie to the Winner movie, the message must be sent up from the Game Controller movie clip to the main movie and then down to the
Winner movie clip.

The _level0/ sends the command back up to the main movie.
The main movie, as far as Flash is concerned, is Level 0. The
/Win refers to the Win instance of the Winner movie clip.

> This example was created to be a stand-
> alone executable. In other words, the puzzle
> can be played just as a standard program
> can be run. To create an executable from
> any .swf (Shockwave Flash) file, locate the
> .swf file using a file manager such as Win-
> dows Explorer. Double-click on the .swf file
> to launch it in the player and then choose
> **Create Projector** from the File menu. Give
> the file a name, and the Shockwave Flash
> player will save the file as an EXE file. The
> EXE file will have the Shockwave Flash
> player built-in, so you can freely distribute
> the EXE. People will be able to view it apart
> from the browser, whether or not they have
> the Shockwave Flash player loaded on their
> system. ▸

Figure 10-39 Flash movies that employ movie clips have a distinct hierarchy. You must
observe this hierarchy when attempting to send messages back and forth
to nested movie clips.

Without the _level0, Flash would assume that the /Win target was located within the Game Controller movie clip. In other words, Flash would try to send the Tell Target command to a movie clip nested within the Game Controller movie clip instead of trying to send a command to a movie clip nested within the main movie.

With the correct address or target path, the Tell Target command in the seventh frame of the Game Controller movie clip sends a `Go to "End" label` command to the Winner movie clip. As a result, the greeting card message is displayed after a few moments (time enough for the layer to see that the pencils spell the word *ten*), and that indicates that the puzzle has been solved.

This example shows how you can create a basic if/then mechanism in Flash using Tell Target. Tell Target is used to send commands to a hidden movie clip, which keeps track of whether a certain number of events has taken place. After the events occur (in other words, after all the `if` conditions have been met), the hidden movie clip sends a command with Tell Target (in other words, `then` something happens) to yet another movie clip to indicate that the puzzle has been solved or the game has been won.

Summary

Flash provides a lot of options for adding interactivity to your animations. Although implementing some of the options may seem a bit complex and time-consuming, it is certainly no more complex and time-consuming than scripting or programming with the likes of JavaScript, Java, and Lingo (for Shockwave). On the other hand, Flash's interactivity and if/then "programming" capabilities are limited. If you want more of that kind of thing, you'll have to look into another Web animation technology such as Java or Shockwave.

Case Studies

🎞 Precision Design
http://www.precisiondesign.org
GIF Animation

Tiny (88×31) Web banner buttons are an increasingly popular way to get people to link to a Web site. In fact, there are so many Web banner buttons on the Web that numerous buttons often compete with one another on the same Web page. The more your buttons stand out the more likely it is that they will be noticed and clicked on.

Web designer Bill Jackson created highly animated Web buttons for his site (precision design.org) using Photoshop and GIF Movie Gear. The example shown in Figure A-1 contains 57 frames, and when fully compressed it is only 9,620 bytes. The example shown in Figure A-2 contains 59 frames and weighs in at only 9,601 bytes when fully compressed. Although 9,000+ bytes for a Web banner button is a bit large, the file sizes are remarkably small when you consider how many frames of animation they contain.

The small file sizes reflect two main factors. First, there are very few colors in each of the animations. The first example uses only a 32-color palette, and the second only a 16-color palette. In addition, the motion from frame to frame tends to be very small. This means that a significant savings in file size can be realized with frame cropping and interframe transparency optimization.

Figure A-3 shows the animation from Figure A-2 fully optimized. All the medium gray areas are portions of the frames that have been optimized with frame cropping, and all the orange

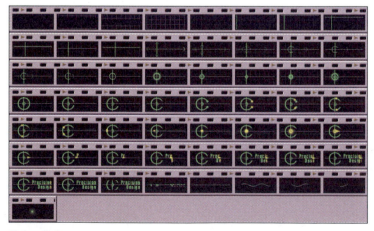

Figure A-1   Courtesy of Bill Jackson, Director, Precision Design.
http://www.precisiondesign.com

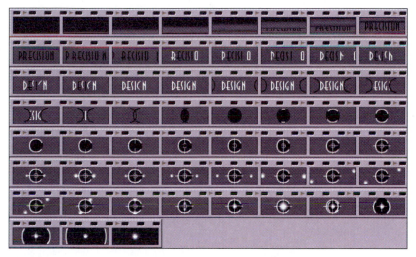

Figure A-2   Courtesy of Bill Jackson, Director, Precision Design.
http://www.precisiondesign.com

areas are portions of the frames that have been optimized with interframe transparency. The medium gray and orange areas dominate the optimized view, indicating that a significant savings in file size was realized with this optimization. For more information on GIF animation palettes, see Chapter 3, Mastering the Palette. For more information on frame cropping and interframe transparency, see Chapter 4, Frame Cropping and Interframe Transparency Optimization.

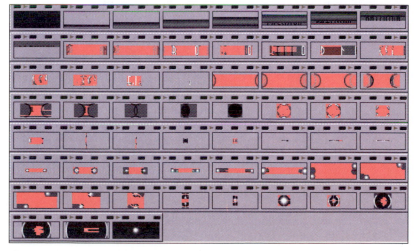

Figure A-3   Courtesy of Bill Jackson, Director, Precision Design.
http://www.precisiondesign.com

▣ Muffin-Head Productions, Inc.
http://www.muffinhead.com
GIF Animation

One way to increase the impact of small GIF animations is to stretch them using the HEIGHT and WIDTH attributes of their image tags (<IMG>). Muffin-Head Productions uses this technique on the main page of its site (which won the prestigious 1998 One Show Interactive Gold Pencil Award for best self-promotion Web site), shown in Figure A-4. Muffin-Head's home page is covered with large multicolored blocks. Many of them are animations that have been tiled seamlessly with simple HTML.

Most of the images and animations are only a single pixel square. Figure A-5 shows one of the animations magnified 1,000%. The animation is one pixel square. Each frame is a solid color. Muffin-Head uses several of these single-pixel animations throughout the overall main page design. In fact, many of them are used repeatedly. For example, the animation shown in Figure A-5 is used twice. In the first instance it is stretched to a size of 71 pixels high and 76 pixels wide using the HEIGHT and WIDTH attributes of the image tag. The second instance is stretched to 71 pixels square.

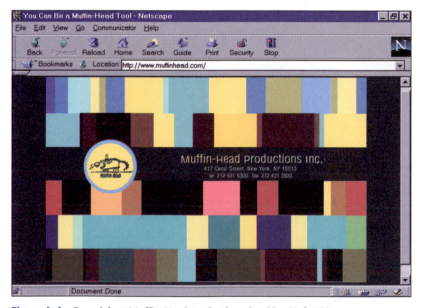

Figure A-4   Copyright © Muffin-Head Productions, Inc. New York, NY.

Figure A-5   Copyright © Muffin-Head Productions, Inc. New York, NY.

Although the two copies of the animation are similarly sized, it is difficult to see that they are the same animation because it takes the browser a small amount of time to stretch images into place. So the first instance of the animation starts playing slightly before the second one. Thus, they tend not to display the same colors at the same time. Muffin-Head stretches several single-pixel animations into place, creating a sort of animated wall that fills an 800×600 screen with animations that total less than 7K.

Muffin-Head employs a similar trick on the pages within the site. Figure A-6 shows a page that has a multicolored animated bar running along the top. The animation, shown in Figure A-7, is actually only 1 pixel high and 640 pixels wide. Muffin-Head stretched the animation to 50 pixels high using the HEIGHT attribute of the image tag. In addition, two copies of the animation play side-by-side. The animations play within a nonscrolling frame, so even though the two 640-pixel-wide animations play side-by-side, they do not

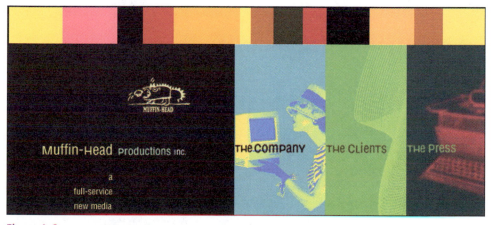

Figure A-6   Copyright © Muffin-Head Productions, Inc. New York, NY.

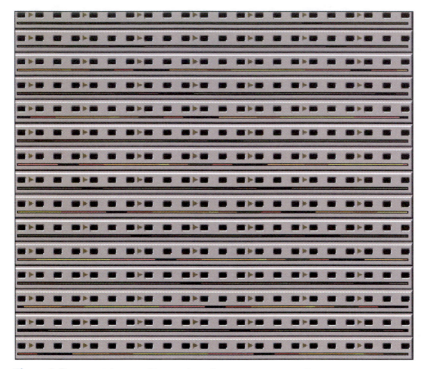

Figure A-7   Copyright © Muffin-Head Productions, Inc. New York, NY.

force the browser to scroll. The result is an animated bar along the top of the page that fits the window size of any browser.

▣ **NavWorks**

http://navworks.i-us.com
GIF Animation

The Solar interface (shown in Figure A-8), from NavWorks, employs GIF animations that play directly on top of a static JPEG image without using DHTML. Furthermore, this interface is unique because it has only one table cell. In most interfaces, each part of the image that changes has a table with a table cell; the rest of the interface is cut up just to maintain rectangular cells (see Chapter 6, Seamless Integration).

Having only one table cell in the table takes advantage of the fact that Internet Explorer 4 and Netscape 4 allow you to place background images inside table cells. Most Web designers know that you can designate a GIF or JPEG for the Web page's background. Then you can overlay images on top of this background using standard HTML. This is exactly what is happening with the Solar interface at NavWorks except that the "background" image is within a table cell.

Transparent images overlay the background interface image in the table cell. These transparent images have JavaScript rollover events assigned to them. When the viewer rolls the mouse over the transparent images, partially transparent GIF images replace the transparent images. These partially transparent images play on top of the JPEG image in the table cell below, as shown in Figure A-9.

Figure A-8

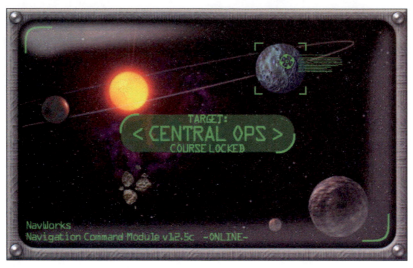

Figure A-9

▦ Organic Online, Inc.
http://www.organic.com
http://journals.riven.com/
GIF Animation

Why use three animations when you can use only one? Figure A-10 shows a page from the Riven Journals created by Jean-Paul Leonard of Organic Online for Cyan's and Red Orb Entertainment's Riven: The Sequel To Myst. The yellow "microscopic organisms" that appear among the hand-drawn seaweed are three copies of the same animation, taking advantage of the fact that browsers allow you to display multiple copies of a single animation or image.

The animations have been seamlessly integrated with the surrounding GIF still images. If you look closely, you see that the seaweed imagery interacts with each animation uniquely, giving the appearance that each microorganism is a separate entity.

To create this effect, Leonard first drew the seaweed background texture on a light table, as shown in Figure A-11. He then duplicated this drawing three times, spread out the copies and drew the seaweed texture around each copy, as shown in Figure A-12. The sketch was

Figure A-10   Copyright © Cyan, Inc.

then integrated with the background texture in Photoshop. Then the seaweed texture was cut into pieces, exported as GIFs, and integrated with the animation using HTML tables.

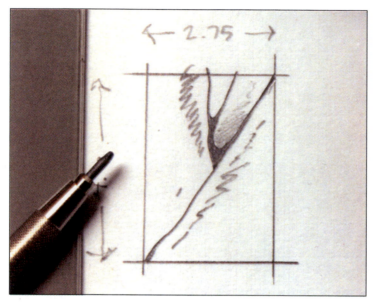

Figure A-11   Copyright © Cyan, Inc.

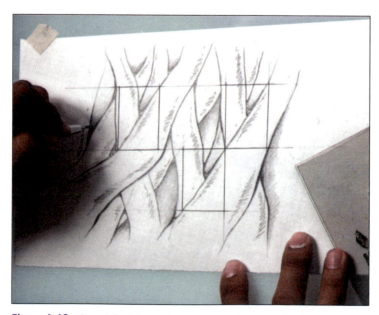

Figure A-12   Copyright © Cyan, Inc.

▦ ToyLab
http://www.toylab.com
JavaScript

Who said JavaScript can't be fun? Figures A-13, A-14, and A-15 show a series of screens from an interactive animation called Find Sticks, from ToyLab, a family entertainment site. Small, 40-pixel-square animations are tiled in a checkerboard pattern. JavaScript randomly selects from an array of 12 animations and tiles them within a small browser window. JavaScript is also used to randomly set one of the animations as a link each time the browser window is filled with a new set of animations. Viewers must roll the mouse over the animations to find the link and then click it to see a new animated pattern.

All the animations are preloaded to make the Find Sticks toy run as smoothly as possible. Preloading takes place on the page that is used to launch the Find Sticks toy. This page, shown in Figure A-16, provides simple directions for the interactive GIF animation/JavaScript toy. While visitors are reading the instructions, the animations are being preloaded, using basic HTML, at the bottom of the page (directly below the Let's Play! link).

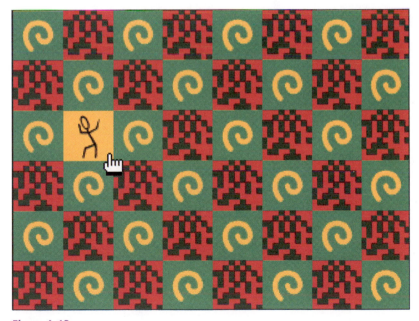

Figure A-13

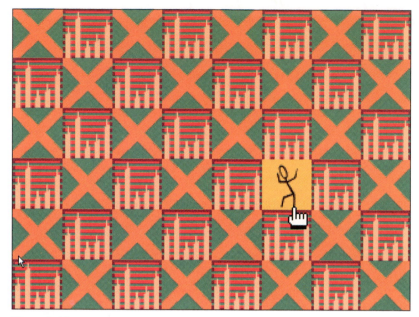

Figure A-14

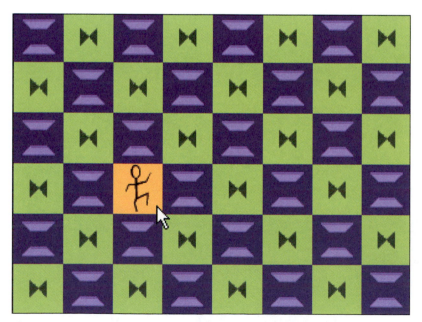

Figure A-15

Figure A-16

For example, the first of 12 animations is loaded with the following HTML:

```
<IMG SRC="bit1.gif" WIDTH="5" HEIGHT="5">
```

Note that the 40-pixel-square animation has been resized to 5 pixels square with the WIDTH and HEIGHT attributes of the image tag. All 12 animations are preloaded in this manner to form a small animated line at the bottom of the page. After the animations are downloaded, they are stored in the browser cache on the visitor's computer. When the visitor moves to the Pop Kaleidoscope interactive toy, the browser gets the animations from the cache rather than download them again via the Internet.

▣ InfiniteFish Productions
http://infinitefish.com/js/eyeball/eyeball.html
JavaScript

D id you know that JavaScript can be used to create a universe? Figure A-17 shows a whimsical JavaScript shooting gallery game created by Scott Balay; it is called Killer Mutant Eyeballs from Beta Centauri III. The starfield is one big JavaScript animation that serves as the background for the game's playing field. The entire starfield animation was created with only fourteen 20-pixel-square GIF files that total a mere 947 bytes. JavaScript is used to create a table that is then randomly filled with these GIF files. Then JavaScript replaces random cells of the table with randomly selected copies of one of the 14 images. The overall effect is a starfield animation that appears to be unique every time it is displayed and changes randomly as you play the game.

Figure A-18 shows 16 of the 17 total images, magnified at 400%, for the starfield animation and the game pieces (the "mutant" eyeballs, the shot, and the spaceship). The other

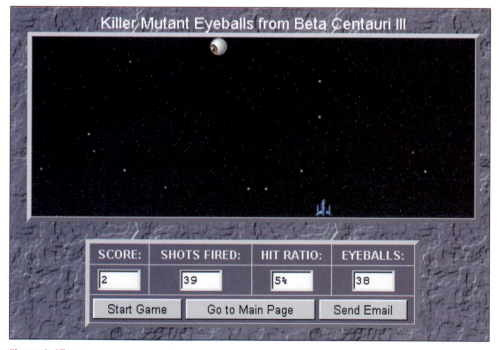

Figure A-17

Figure A-18

image is single-pixel black image. The entire game area is 500 pixels wide by 200 pixels high. These 16 tiny images (plus a single-pixel black GIF image) are used to populate the entire 500×200 pixel area. The total graphic for the game is only 2.43K. JavaScript also animates the eyeball and the laser shot as shown in Figure A-19.

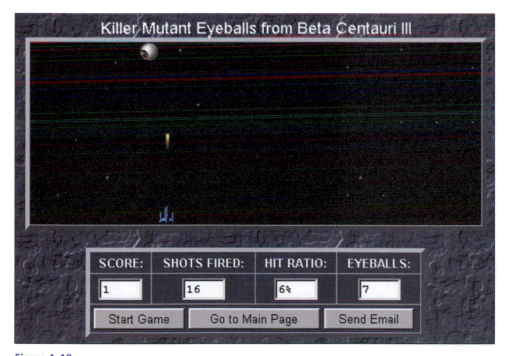

Figure A-19

▣ JumpList
http://www.jumplist.com
JavaScript

Sometimes animations can provide subtle yet valuable feedback to users that tell them that everything is working fine. Figure A-20 shows an interface from JumpList, an online links management program created by Jim Shaw and I/US Corporation. Most of the interface is static, but it expands and contracts depending on how many links the program is managing. The larger the interface gets, the longer it takes for it to redraw in the browser window.

JumpList's designers use subtle animations to let viewers know that everything is working properly. For example, Figure A-21 shows a row of orange lights that animate every 20

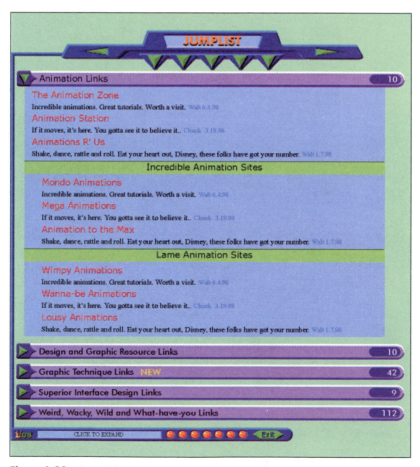

Figure A-20   Copyright © i/us Corp. http://www.i-us.com

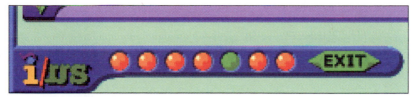

Figure A-21   Copyright © i/us Corp. http://www.i-us.com

seconds using JavaScript. Although the frames for the animation total slightly more than 8K, the animation doesn't go through its first run until 20 seconds after the page has loaded, allowing plenty of time for all the frames to load. The animation also serves as a mild attention-getter in case users get distracted from using the links management application.

A similar technique is employed for the buttons shown in Figure A-22. These buttons are used to expand and contract links categories. When the user clicks on the button, the little diamond button animates. The JumpList application is an online application, so the page must reload in order to show the category. There is normally a brief pause before the page is reloaded, so the animation helps reassure the user that something is indeed happening as a result of the mouse click.

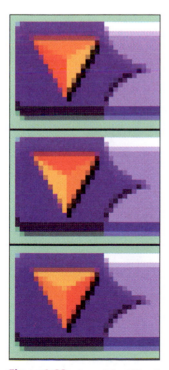

Figure A-22   Copyright © i/us Corp. http://www.i-us.com

▦ Blue Hypermedia
http://www.bluehypermedia.com
Macromedia Flash

Blue Hypermedia uses Flash's ability to apply tweening to bitmap images to create a range of common broadcast television effects, including panning, zooming, and fades. The company was given the task to convert television advertising spots for Sally Hansen products into Web-based commercials.

Figure A-23

Flash is not adept at delivering 24 frames per second of digital bitmap images over the Web, so Blue Hypermedia didn't try to convert the actual television commercials. Instead, it captured selected images from the television spots and re-created the common television effects using various tweens. Figure A-23 shows a series of frames from the Flash-based Sally Hansen Web commercial. A close-up shot of Sally Hansen products pans from right to left as a series of text strings is displayed over the image. This entire sequence was created using a single bitmap symbol.

This sequence shows two types of tweening. First, a single image is moved right to left in a series of tweened frames, creating the panning effect. Second, the image fades from black to full color and then to white. Because Flash tweens only between one color at a time, this effect requires two tweens. First, the bitmap image was tweened from a key frame that contained a copy that was sent from a 100% blank tint to a key frame that contained a 0% black tint. This accomplishes the fade from black to full color. Then another tween was added from a copy of the image in a key frame set to 0% white tint to a key frame with the image set to 100% white tint.

Figure A-24

This entire sequence lasts about 10 seconds at 15 frames per second. With digital video or a GIF animation, this sequence would require 150 frames of bitmap images. With Flash, it takes only a single low-quality JPEG image. One of the benefits of using fading is that it hides the flaws in the image that result from JPEG compression. The flaws become apparent only briefly when the bitmap images are at 0% tint in both tweens. Figure A-24 shows that Blue Hypermedia also employs these techniques in standard 468×60 Flash-based banner ads. This one advertises Blue Hypermedia's services.

Speared Peanut
http://www.spearedpeanut.com/
Macromedia Flash

Preloading in Flash provides for a seamless visual experience by loading graphic and audio elements, or symbols, before they are used. If symbols in Flash are not preloaded, viewers might have to watch a given frame's elements display piece by piece. However, preloading in Flash means that viewers must wait while the various elements load so that all the elements can be displayed at once.

In Flash, all the elements contained in a given frame must be loaded before the Flash movie can proceed to the next frame. After a symbol is loaded in a given frame, it can be used on subsequent frames without any additional download requirements. If a given frame requires a large number of symbols, you can preload them and thereby avoid having them display piece by piece. If all the symbols are preloaded, the frame's content will display all at once.

Although preloading symbols avoids a problem, it also causes one: viewers must wait until the symbols are preloaded. Speared Peanut devised a way to make the preloading time more entertaining. Typically, symbols that are preloaded in a Flash movie are loaded

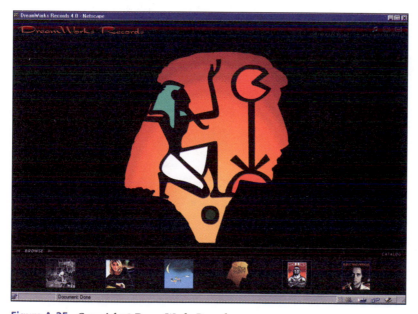

Figure A-25   Copyright © DreamWorks Records.

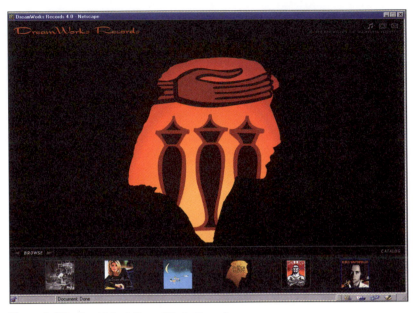

Figure A-26   Copyright © DreamWorks Records.

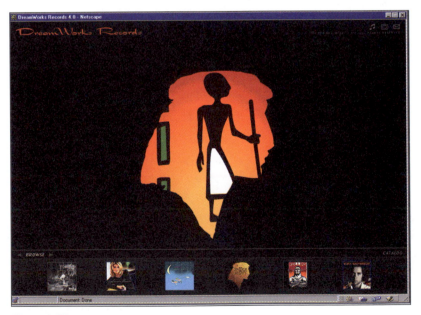

Figure A-27   Copyright © DreamWorks Records.

behind a large filled rectangle image or symbol so that the viewer can't see the symbols as they load. However, Speared Peanut used a mask layer (a layer in Flash that acts as a mask) for the preloading sequence in a Flash-based navigation element created for the soundtracks of "Prince of Egypt" by DreamWorks Records.

The mask, in the shape of the Prince's head, shows through to a series of symbols. The mask becomes progressively smaller as the symbols load and display, creating a cinematic effect (see Figures A-25 through A-27). When the symbols are finished loading, they are displayed on the main page, shown in Figure A-28.

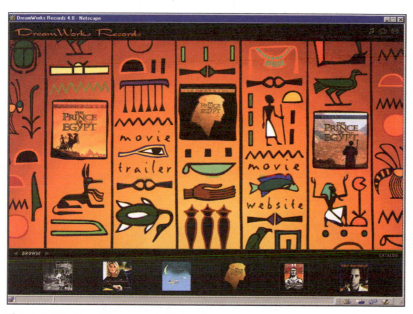

Figure A-28   **Copyright © DreamWorks Records.**

🎞 Second Story
http://www.secondstory.com/
Macromedia Flash

One of the most unheralded benefits of Flash movies is that they are resolution-independent. This means that Flash movies can be resized on-the-fly without visibly degrading the image quality of the movie. (If the Flash movie contains bitmaps, the bitmap images might suffer some deterioration.)

When Second Story designed the site for DreamWorks Records, the designers took advantage of this aspect of Flash movies by using DHTML to automatically size its Flash movies to the viewable area in the browser according each visitor's monitor size. For example, when a visitor logs on to the DreamWorks Web site and goes to any of the Web pages that contain Flash movies, the height and width of the movie is adjusted on-the-fly according to the size of the visitor's monitor and screen resolution (see Figures A-29 and A-30).

There are several key benefits to this approach. First, the interface and Flash animation always fills the entire screen, providing a more immersive experience that is free from any other distractions that might exist on the visitor's desktop. In addition, the designer need only design one Flash file. With other Web technologies you must design multiple versions

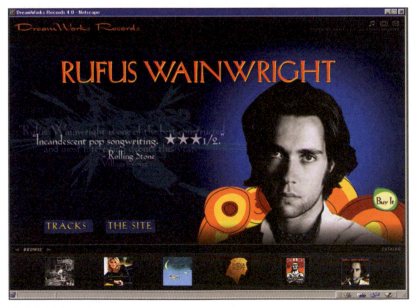

Figure A-29   **Copyright © DreamWorks Records.**

of a Web page and its graphics if you want to accommodate multiple screen sizes. The combination of Flash and DTHML allows you to design one Flash animation that is resized as needed, saving you a lot of time and effort.

See the following URL for more information on how this was accomplished with DHTML: http://developer.netscape.com/docs/manuals/communicator/jsref/wina3.htm#1090

Figure A-30 **Copyright © DreamWorks Records.**

▦ Blue Hypermedia
http://www.bluehypermedia.com
Macromedia Flash

Macromedia Flash features streaming audio, but its streaming rates and quality leave much to be desired. Fortunately, Macromedia has teamed up with RealNetworks to offer RealFlash, a much better streaming audio option for Flash. RealFlash reflects the

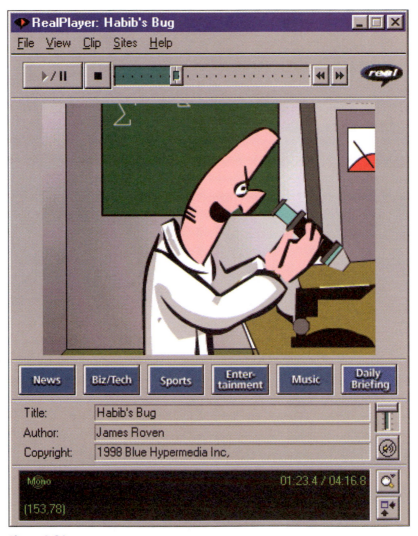

Figure A-31   Copyright © 1998 Blue Hypermedia.

recognition that Flash's real strength is streaming vector-based animation delivery and not streaming audio delivery. RealFlash combines Flash's streaming graphics with RealNetworks' streaming audio: better quality audio, more control.

One of the key benefits of RealFlash is the ability it gives you to synchronize the audio with the animation. For example, Figure A-31 shows a shot from a sequence in "Habib's Bug," created by Blue Hypermedia for the RealFlash Animation Festival. The Flash-based animation plays along with a soundtrack that contains background audio and sound effects. The sound effects play in sync with the audio. For example, during a portion of the animation you hear Habib laugh maniacally at the same time that you see him laugh (see Figure A-31). Even though the audio and animation are separate files, RealFlash ensures that they play in unison.

The basic setup for a RealFlash animation is straightforward. First, you manually export your Flash .fla file as two files: one for the Flash animation (animation only without audio) and a second one for the Real Audio track. You export to a basic Shockwave Flash (swf) file for the Flash animation file, being careful to turn off the audio during export. For the Real Audio file, you need something that you can import into RealPublisher or RealEncoder to convert to Real Audio (see Figure A-32). If you are using Flash 2, you can export as an AVI file.

Figure A-32 Copyright © 1998 Blue Hypermedia.

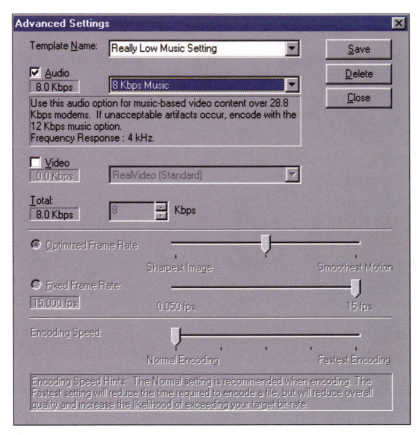

Figure A-33   Copyright © 1998 Blue Hypermedia.

RealPublisher can import the AVI file, strip off the video, and compress the audio. If you have Flash 3, you can export directly to WAV format, saving RealPublisher the added burden of stripping the video (and saving your hard drive the added burden of storing it).

When you have converted the audio to Real Audio, you will have an .rm file that matches the .swf file. The next step is to create a .ram metafile. This is the file that the Real Audio plug-in needs to play the RealFlash animation. You can create a .ram file manually with any text editor such as Windows Notepad. The .ram file must contain one text line using the following structure:

http://www.domainname.com/subdirectory/x.rm+y.swf

The *www.domainname.com* is the domain name of the server where the RealFlash is located, and *subdirectory* would be any subdirectory(s) where the RealFlash is located. In other words, the path should correspond to the location of the swf and rm files. The *x* equals the Flash file name, and the *y* equals the real Real Audio file name. To play the RealFlash presentation from a local drive, it would be *file: c:\subdirectory\x.swf + y.rm*. This line assumes that the file is located on your local C drive, including any subdirectories. As before, the *x* equals the Flash file name and *y* equals the Real Audio file name.

After you have the ram file, you link it from your Web page and send the .ram plus the .swf and .rm files via FTP to your server. This is all that is required for the .swf and .rm file to play in the RealAudio player, a separate player/plug-in that you must download. You must have a Real Server to play Real Audio. In other words, no object tags are required to play the RealFlash files in the Real Audio player. You can set up a RealFlash animation to be viewed within a browser, but then you must include object tags for the Flash and Real Audio files on the Web page where the RealFlash animation will play.

Although RealFlash can play stereo music tracks, audio is generally reduced to mono for the sake of compression. The soundtrack for "Habib's Bug" is mono, but it was originally created and edited in stereo. Blue Hypermedia typically processes the audio for RealFlash presentations using a two-track audio editor such as Cool Edit (see Figure A-33). The advantage of using a program such as Cool Edit is that you can place the sound effects in one channel and the music in another channel so that they can be edited independently. For example, if you decide that a certain sound effect isn't right or is too loud, you can easily replace or edit it without affecting the music.

RealFlash is a combined streaming technology; a Flash presentation is streamed along with a Real Audio file. Because both files are streamed to the viewer, the file size of the Flash animation and Real Audio file isn't as important as how effectively the two files can be delivered in a timely manner. Because the files are streaming, it is only important that both files play without any halting or "hiccups." To achieve this, you must determine the appropriate bit rate for Flash animation.

The term *bit rate* is used to describe the upper limit on the amount of data that can pass through network connections per second. Bit rate is another way of referring to bandwidth. Bit rates, or bandwidth, on the Internet are commonly calculated in kilobits per second—Kbps for short (note that's kilo*bits* and not kilo*bytes*). Modems use this standard of measurement. For example, a 28.8-Kbps modem can transfer data at as many as to 28.8 Kbps a second.

When you set up a RealFlash animation so that it will play back acceptably at a given network connection speed, you are targeting that network connection's bit rate. For example, if you decide that most of your visitors will be connected on a modem whose bit rate is at least 28.8 Kbps, you would target the bit rate of the RealFlash animation for a 28.8-Kbps modem. In fact, Web developers typically target RealFlash animations for 28.8-Kbps modems.

However, modems don't always transfer data at the rate that they are capable of. Much like a highway, the Internet is subject to traffic. The speed limit might be 70 miles per hour, but congestion can often result in much lower speeds. This problem is so prevalent on the Internet that the term *bandwidth* has come to be nearly synonymous with the word *traffic*.

For this reason, Macromedia and Real Networks recommend that you use a bit rate of 20 Kbps if you are targeting a 28.8-Kbps connection. This means that if you want the RealFlash animation and audio to play without stutters or halts for a visitor connected on a 28.8-Kbps modem, you need to make sure that both the .swf file and the .rm file stream over the Internet at no more than a 20-Kbps bit rate. Notice that this is the total bit rate for both files. For example, if the bit rate for the Flash file is 12 Kbps, there's room only for 8 Kbps for the Real Audio file.

One other factor that affects the effective ability of a given RealFlash animation to play at a certain bit rate is buffer time. *Buffer time* refers to how much time elapses between the time the streaming files load into the cache and the time the RealFlash animation starts playing. (See Chapter 1 for more information on how streaming content works.) Buffer time has a direct effect on bit rate. The longer the buffer time, the lower the bit rate can be. The shorter the buffer time, the faster the bit rate must be. This is because the more data there is buffered in the cache, the less data you must download in a given time to maintain a smooth playback.

However, the object is to make the playback as close to real time as possible. When you turn on the TV you see the images and hear the audio as they are being broadcast. The goal is to emulate this as closely as possible. Typically, developers try to minimize the amount of buffer time, assuming that the longer that visitors must wait, the more likely they will be to leave the site.

Developers commonly refer to bit rate as *stream* and buffer time as *preroll*. For example, if the bit rate for the Real Audio portion of a RealFlash animation is 12 Kbps, you would refer to it as a 12-Kbps stream; if the buffer time for the overall RealFlash animation is 5 seconds, you would say that the preroll for the RealFlash animation is 5 seconds. Buffer time can also be referred to in terms of *latency*. The longer the buffer time, the greater the latency.

Blue Hypermedia used a free utility called RealFlash Bandwidth Tuner along with RealPublisher to balance the bit rates of the .swf file and the .rm file for "Habib's Bug" with the amount of buffer time for the overall RealFlash animation. Part of the process of generating an .rm file with RealPublisher is to select the desired bit rate. Although the templates that come with RealPublisher have prescribed bit rates assigned to them, you can create your own templates and assign your own bit rates in the Advanced Settings dialog box. You determine the bit rate for your .rm file when you generate it with RealPublisher.

When Real Audio plays by itself, it automatically adjusts the buffer time according to the user's connection speed for each file it plays. For example, the Real Audio player might automatically come up with a buffer time of 20 seconds if a given visitor connected to the Internet with a 28.8-Kbps modem, whereas it might use only 5 seconds of buffer time for a visitor connected with an ISDN. However, when you create your .swf file from Flash, Flash does not allow you to target the bit rate.

That's where the RealFlash Bandwidth Tuner utility comes in. This tool allows you to adjust the bit rate and buffer time of the .swf file. After you import the .swf file, you select the target bit rate from the Options menu. Then you refer to the RealFlash Bandwidth Consumption graph and adjust the graph using the slider. Dragging the slider up increases the bit rate, and dragging it down decreases the bit rate. You can adjust only the bit rate. The buffer time is automatically adjusted according to the bit rate.

The settings that you arrive at in RealFlash Bandwidth Tuner depend on the settings that you used for the Real Audio file. For example, Blue Hypermedia initially set the .rm file for "Habib's Bug" to 12-Kbps. This meant that there was only 8 Kbps left for the .swf file. (The company was targeting 28.8-Kbps modem connections, for which a 20-Kbps maximum is suggested.) So Blue Hypermedia opened the .swf file for "Habib's Bug" in RealFlash Bandwidth Tuner and found that the buffer time for the Flash file would have to be slightly more than 52 seconds, which is unacceptably long (Real Networks discourages buffer times of more than 30 seconds). The solution was to reduce the bit rate of the audio file to 8 Kbps. Although this reduced the quality of the audio, it meant that Blue Hypermedia could set the .swf file to a bit rate of 12 Kbps, which requires only a 5-second buffer time.

Although the ability to synchronize Real Audio with Flash animations provides for a television-like delivery, there are some drawbacks to RealFlash. For example, RealFlash animations must be non-interactive and unscripted. In other words, RealFlash animations cannot take advantage of frame actions or external scripting with JavaScript. Also, there is no way to go from RealFlash to RealVideo or to play RealVideo in a RealFlash animation. Although Flash animations can have bitmaps, RealNetworks' RealVideo is far better at delivering continuous feeds of bitmap-based video.

The RealFlash Bandwidth Tuner is part of the RealFlash Content Creation Kit, a free download from Real Networks. It can be found at

http://www.real.com/devzone/library/stream/flash/

Index

◱ Effective Web Animation CD-ROM Contents

AniPack 1 (full version)

AniPack 1 from NavWorks (http://navworks.i-us.com) features twenty unique customizable animations. Each animation comes with either an animation tutorial or notes on how to generate the animation from the supplied Photoshop file, as well as suggestions for variations, looping techniques, and more. All animations are designed to be integrated easily into any Web page, no matter what background color or seamless texture is used.

In addition, AniPack 1 comes with 10 tutorials that cover animation techniques using Adobe Photoshop. The animation tutorials include versatile techniques such as how to make a scrolling animation from any seamless texture, how to generate controlled distortion animations, and how to generate an animated dissolve effect. The 20 fully customizable animations combined with 10 animation tutorials add up to virtually unlimited potential for professional-looking animations.

Demos

Animation Factory (Eclipse Digital Imaging)
    GIF animation collection
Animation Stand (Linker Systems) *Mac, PC*
Extensis PhotoAnimator *Mac, PC*
GIF Movie Gear (Gamani Productions) *PC*
HVS Animator (Digital Frontiers) *Mac, PC*
Macromedia Flash 3 *Mac, PC*
Macromedia Fireworks *Mac, PC*
Macromedia Dreamweaver 1.2 *Mac, PC*

NavWorks FlashPack 1 *Mac, PC*
NavWorks NavPack 1 *Mac, PC*
NavWorks NavPack 2 *Mac, PC*
SPG Web Tools Pro 4 for Photoshop (SPG Inc.) *PC*
SPG Web Tools Essentials 4 for Paintshop Pro (SPG Inc.) *PC*
Universal Animator (Auto F/X Corporation) *Mac, PC*
WebSpice Animations (Demorgan Industries)
    GIF animation collection

Example Animations

The CD-ROM contains most of the animations featured in this book as well as various tutorial files. Many of the files used to create the animations also are included on the CD-ROM, so you can see how the example animations were constructed.

More information and updates are available at http://www.awl.com/cseng/titles/0-201-60600-3/